SRA
LANGUAGE
for
LEARNING

Siegfried Engelmann
Jean Osborn

Teacher's
Guide

A Direct Instruction Program

McGraw Hill **SRA**

Columbus, OH

SRAonline.com

 SRA

Copyright © 2008 by SRA/McGraw-Hill.

All rights reserved. No part of this publication may be
reproduced or distributed in any form or by any means, or
stored in a database or retrieval system, without the prior
written consent of The McGraw-Hill Companies, Inc.,
including, but not limited to, network storage or
transmission, or broadcast for distance learning.

Permission is granted to reproduce the printed material
contained on pages with a permission-to-reproduce copyright
line on the condition that such material be reproduced only
for classroom use; be provided to students, teachers, or
families without charge; and be used solely in conjunction
with *Language for Learning*.

Printed in the United States of America.

Send all inquiries to this address:
SRA/McGraw-Hill
4400 Easton Commons
Columbus, OH 43219

ISBN: 978-0-07-609430-1
MHID: 0-07-609430-8

10 11 12 QVS 16 15 14

The *McGraw-Hill* Companies

Table of Contents

Introduction

Why Language Instruction? 1
What Are the Special Features of *Language for Learning*? 2
What Is New in the 2008 Edition of *Language for Learning*? 3
Who Benefits from *Language for Learning* Instruction? 3

Program Information

What Are the Program Materials?. 5
Teacher's Presentation Books. 5
Teacher's Guide 5
Children's Workbooks 6
Additional Materials 6
What Is the Content of the Program? 6
How Is the Program Organized?. 6
Program Scope and Sequence Chart 7

Implementing the Program

How to Use the Materials 9
Directions for Daily Use 9
Forming Groups 10
The Fast Cycle 11
Adjusting the Program for Preschool Children . . 12
Teaching Children Whose First Language Is Not English. 12
Coordinating Language and Reading Instruction 16

Teaching Effectively

How to Set Up a Group 17
Getting into the Lesson 17
What Is Good Performance?. 18
Handling Responses Different from Those in the Book. 19
Individual Turns 19
Group Progress. 19
How to Make the Program Succeed 20

Teaching Techniques

How the Exercises Are Organized 21
Signaling the Children's Responses 22
Differentiated Instruction 24
Corrections 24

The Program 27

Actions 27

Beginning Actions 28
Actions—Parts of the Body 32
Actions—Pictures 32
Actions—Pronouns 34
Tense 35
Tense—Pictures 37
Actions—Review 38

Descriptions of Objects 39

Object Identification 40
Identity Statements. 41
Common Objects. 45
Missing Objects 46
Opposites 47
Plurals 50
Comparatives. 54

Information and Background Knowledge 56

Basic Information 56
Names 57
School Information 57
Days of the Week. 58
Months of the Year 59
Seasons 60
Part/Whole 61
Materials 64
Common Information 67
Locations 69
Signs 71

Instructional Words and Problem-Solving Concepts 73

Spatial and Temporal Relations 73
Prepositions 75
And—Actions 79
Same/Different 80
Some, All, None 88
Actions—Or 91
First/Next and Before/After 92

If-Then Rules. 95
Where, Who, When, What 101

Classification. 103

Problem-Solving Strategies and Applications 109
Review 110
Concept Applications 111
Absurdities 118

Workbook Activities. 122

Workbook Scope and Sequence Chart. 123

Stories and Poems 144

Expanded Language Activities 145
Appendices 147
Appendix A—The Placement Test 149
Placement Test Scoring Sheet. 153
Appendix B—The Transition Lesson 154
Appendix C—The 15 Program Assessments . . . 160
Individual Score Sheets 162
Percent Correct Tables 165
Appendix D—The Management System 168
Individual Profile Charts 171
Group Summary Chart 173
Appendix E—Home Connection 174
Family Letters. 175
Appendix F—The Practice Lesson 179

Introduction

Why Language Instruction?

Language for Learning teaches children the words, concepts, and statements important to both oral and written language. The program emphasizes language as a means of describing the world and as a tool for thinking and solving problems. This language can be described as the language of learning and instruction. *Language for Learning* provides for the direct teaching of this language.

The Foundation for School Success

The language of learning and instruction is the underpinning of school success. For many children, this instruction occurs informally in their homes and preschools before they reach kindergarten. But for other children, basic language instruction must occur in school. *Language for Learning* offers these children this kind of instruction through carefully sequenced exercises that teach the concepts and skills they need to succeed in school.

The content of *Language for Learning* is based on analyses of the words, concepts, and sentence structures that teachers use as they teach, as well as an analysis of the directions and the content of school textbooks and other instructional materials. *Language for Learning* provides a basis for reading comprehension. The program's vocabulary, background- and world knowledge-building exercises, as well as its statement analysis, questioning, and concept-application exercises, prepare children for the literal and inferential comprehension of the books and other materials they will read both in and out of school.

Precise Communication

Most important, knowledge of the language of learning and instruction permits more precise communication between children and adults. It is the basis for the kind of communication that uses precise words to describe such diverse concepts as how objects are the same and different, their position, as well as the order of events in a story and the details of what happened in the story. This kind of communication is not necessarily social communication but is communication that is used to transmit and receive important information, solve problems, and engage in higher-order thinking.

Oral Language and Reading Comprehension

If children do not understand something that is presented in oral language, it is highly unlikely they will understand the same information presented in written language. In other words, children must have a solid language understanding of what is to be read before they read it. Certainly, children learn new words, new information, and new ideas from reading; however, for this to happen, a language foundation that permits such learning must be in place.

Children in the elementary grades who have typical reading comprehension understand commonly used vocabulary, sentence forms, and instructions used in textbooks, workbooks, and library books. These children have precise knowledge of the "little words" used in instructions and descriptions and in the questions their teachers ask—words such as next, between, in front of, who, what, when, and where. They make inferences easily because they are practiced in describing the world, following and giving directions, and asking and answering questions. They are good at connecting the content of what they are reading to knowledge they already possess. These children are also good at logical thinking—they understand how logical "rules" work and when and how to apply these rules in different situations.

Following Directions and "Figuring Out"

Kindergarten and first-grade children who don't have a solid language foundation frequently don't understand the meaning of many of the words their teachers use as they explain things. They often have trouble following the directions that appear in their textbooks and workbooks. They typically have other problems related to language as well: they are not able to repeat sentences accurately; they lack much of the general information other children possess; and they have trouble with the logical "figuring out" aspects of language—for example, the classification of objects and "if-then" reasoning.

The Difference between Success and Failure

In time, some of these children will pick up these important language concepts—through the informal and formal instruction that they experience in their classrooms and at home. Some children, however, will not pick up a sufficient number of essential language concepts in their experiences at home and school. It is these children who, when they get to third and fourth grade, have trouble comprehending what they read—even though they may have the ability to read the words. These are the children who urgently need careful language instruction.

For such children, the teaching of the language of learning and instruction can mean the difference between success and failure in learning to read, as well as in the other academic subjects they will encounter in school.

What Are the Special Features of *Language for Learning*?

Language for Learning is a comprehensive oral language program. Its special features include

- a Direct-Instruction approach to the teaching of a wide range of important language concepts and skills.
- carefully organized sequences of exercises that make up the daily lessons.
- teacher directions for the clear presentation of the concepts and skills taught in the program.
- the opportunity for both group and individual practice of the content of the exercises.
- statement-repetition exercises that help children become practiced with both the concepts and statements of the language of learning and instruction.
- the application of newly-learned language concepts and thinking skills to problem-solving situations.
- a continuous integration and review of all the concepts and skills that appear in the program.
- directions for extending language instruction to games and other classroom activities.
- original stories and poems to be read to the children.
- workbook activities that teach new concepts and skills that apply what children are learning to new contexts.
- a fast cycle for those children who can progress more quickly through the program.
- a placement test and fifteen program assessments to ensure that children are working on concepts appropriate for their abilities and are progressing through the program at a reasonable rate.

What Is New in the 2008 Edition of *Language for Learning*?

In addition to a number of minor changes, there are some major improvements in this new edition.

1. All of the illustrations that appeared in earlier editions of *Language for Learning* have been replaced.
   - ■ Each of the new illustrations presents a clear example of the concept being taught.
   - ■ The new illustrations are more attractive and up-to-date.
2. The program assessments appear in the Teacher Presentation Books after every tenth lesson. Each assessment evaluates whether individual children perform at mastery on the content presented in the preceding ten lessons.

3. Instructional remedies are specified for children who do not perform at mastery on each part of the program assessments. The teacher provides differentiated instruction by presenting the specified Extra Help exercises.
4. Planning pages appear in the presentation books at the beginning of every five lessons.
5. Procedures for adjusting the program for preschool children appear in this guide.
6. Procedures for coordinating language and reading instruction are available.
7. Procedures for further accelerating the program for children whose scores on the Placement Test indicate they should start the program at lesson 40 are included.
8. The workbook exercises for each of the 150 lessons in *Language for Learning* are contained in two workbooks rather than four. Home-connection direction lines have been added for each exercise.
9. An Answer Key is now available for Workbooks A/B and C/D.
10. Language for Learning Practice and Review Activities CD-ROM is now available.

Who Benefits from Language for Learning Instruction?

- ■ Kindergarten and primary age school children who have less than adequate language knowledge and skill for their age.
- ■ Four-year-old children in preschool programs
- ■ Primary age school children in bilingual and ELL programs

Program Information

What Are the Program Materials?

Teacher's Presentation Books

The teacher's presentation books contain the daily lessons you will present to the children. These books also contain directions for the workbook activities, as well as the stories and poems that were written especially for the program. The teacher presentation books also include the program assessments, directions for differentiated instruction, and the planning pages. In addition, suggestions for expanded language activities appear at the beginning of each presentation book.

The daily lessons are divided into four presentation books.

Book A	Lessons 1–50
Book B	Lessons 51–85
Book C	Lessons 86–120
Book D	Lessons 121–150

Teacher's Guide

You are reading the Teacher's Guide. The guide provides directions on how to use the program materials and how to implement the program in your classroom. In addition, the Teacher's Guide summarizes the content of the program and describes useful teaching techniques and specific correction procedures for a number of the exercises in the daily lessons.

Appendix A includes the Placement Test and directions for giving and scoring that test. Also included is the blackline master for the Placement Test Scoring Sheet. You will need to have a copy of the Placement Test Scoring Sheet for each child in your class. The children's scores on the Placement Test determine the lesson at which they will begin instruction. Appendix B contains the Transition Lesson. You will teach this introductory lesson to children who will start the program beyond lesson 1. Appendix C contains directions for giving and scoring the 15 program assessments. It also contains blackline masters for the Individual Score Sheets that you will use to record the responses of each child .You will need a set of score sheets for each child in your class. The Percent Correct Tables will enable you to quickly calculate the percentage of items each child answers correctly. Appendix D provides information about how to use the program's management system, the extra help activities, and the black line masters for the Individual Profile Charts and Group Summary Charts that will enable you to summarize the progress of the children throughout the program. Appendix E provides two blackline masters for parent letters to be sent home at the beginning and end of the school year. Appendix F contains a complete *Language for Learning* lesson to be used as a practice lesson during staff development sessions.

Children's Workbooks

The two workbooks contain activities the children do as part of each daily lesson. Each child in the class will need a set of workbooks. Some of the workbook activities are done under your direction, and some are done as independent seat work.

Additional Materials

Behavioral Objectives Booklet This booklet lists the concepts and skills of the program and behavioral goals to be achieved by individual students.
Behavioral Skills Folder This folder provides a convenient way for you to record dates individual students complete specific skills lessons.
Answer Key This key provides answers to the workbook activities.

What Is the Content of the Program?

The Scope and Sequence Chart that appears on page 7 presents a summary of the content of *Language for Learning*. The concepts and skills of the program are organized into six groups:

- **Basic Actions**
- **Descriptions of Objects**
- **Information and Background Knowledge**
- **Instructional Words and Problem-Solving Concepts**
- **Classification**
- **Problem-Solving Strategies and Applications**

Program Organized?

With the exception of Classification, the content of each of the six groups is divided into strands, or tracks. For example, the Information and Background Knowledge group contains nine tracks: Names, School Information, Days of the Week, Part/Whole Relationships, Months of the Year, Materials, Common Information, Seasons, and Locations.

Tracks and Lessons

Each track continues across a number of lessons and contains a variety of exercises that focus on a set of related concepts. For example, in the Classification track, which begins in lesson 51 and continues through lesson 136, the children learn a number of different classification terms (vehicles, containers, food, and so on), the names of many members of these classes (cars, trucks, ships, and so on; cups, boxes, suitcases, and so on; bananas, lettuce, ice cream, and so on), and definitions or "rules" about each class ("A vehicle is made to take you places"; "If you can put things in it, it's a container"; "If you can eat it, it is food"; and so on). By the end of the program the children have learned ten classification terms, a number of classification rules, and many new vocabulary words.

As the children progress through the program, they encounter new concepts and skills in new tracks. What they have learned in the exercises of earlier tracks is applied to the exercises of the later tracks.

The Daily Lesson

Each day's lesson contains exercises from several tracks. For example, lesson 32 contains eight exercises from seven different tracks: Actions—Prepositions; Information—School; Missing Objects; Part/Whole; Picture Prepositions; Action Statements—Pictures; and Opposites.

The workbook activities for the lesson include Colors, Cross–Out/Circle, and Matching.

Language for Learning
Scope and Sequence

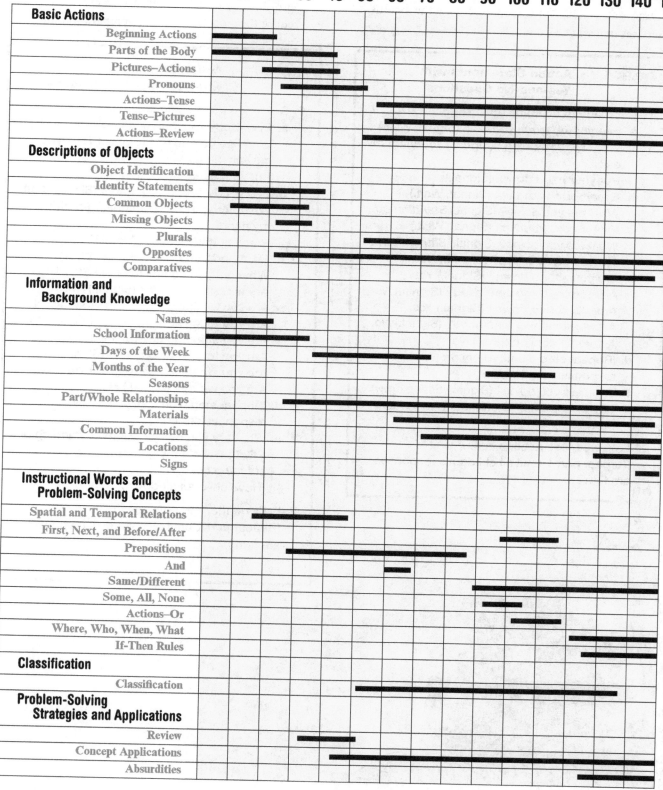

Lessons	0	10	20	30	40	50	60	70	80	90	100	110	120	130	140	150

Basic Actions
- Beginning Actions
- Parts of the Body
- Pictures–Actions
- Pronouns
- Actions–Tense
- Tense–Pictures
- Actions–Review

Descriptions of Objects
- Object Identification
- Identity Statements
- Common Objects
- Missing Objects
- Plurals
- Opposites
- Comparatives

Information and Background Knowledge
- Names
- School Information
- Days of the Week
- Months of the Year
- Seasons
- Part/Whole Relationships
- Materials
- Common Information
- Locations
- Signs

Instructional Words and Problem-Solving Concepts
- Spatial and Temporal Relations
- First, Next, and Before/After
- Prepositions
- And
- Same/Different
- Some, All, None
- Actions–Or
- Where, Who, When, What
- If-Then Rules

Classification
- Classification

Problem-Solving Strategies and Applications
- Review
- Concept Applications
- Absurdities

Patterned Exercises

Exercises of a particular type are formatted, or "patterned." Patterned exercises are easier for you to teach and easier for the children to follow. By learning how to present one exercise of a particular type, you know how to present similar exercises that appear in subsequent lessons. For example, here are the actions exercises in lessons 17 and 19.

Note that the actions the children perform in these two exercises are different but that the steps for presenting each exercise are the same. Exercises that follow the same pattern

1. allow children to learn a concept by practicing it with different examples.
2. show the similarity among various exercises.
3. reduce the amount of teacher preparation time.

EXERCISE 1 Action Statements with Yes-and-No Questions

1. Get ready to do some actions.
    a. Everybody, touch your ear. (Signal. Wait.)
        What are you doing? (Signal.) *Touching my ear.*
        Put your hand down. (Signal.)
    b. Everybody, stand up. (Signal. Wait.)
        What are you doing? (Signal.) *Standing up.*
    c. Everybody, sit down. (Signal. Wait.)
        What are you doing? (Signal.) *Sitting down.*
        Are you standing up? (Signal.) *No.*
        Are you sitting down? (Signal.) *Yes.*
        Are you touching your head? (Signal.) *No.*
        Are you sitting down? (Signal.) *Yes.*
        Are you touching your shoe? (Signal.) *No.*
        Are you eating? (Signal.) *No.*
    d. (Repeat step c until all children's responses are firm.)
    e. What are you doing? (Signal.) *Sitting down.*
        Say the whole thing. (Signal.) *I am sitting down.*

2. Let's do those actions again.
    (Repeat part 1 until all children's responses are firm.)

EXERCISE 1 Action Statements with Yes-and-No Questions

1. Get ready to do some actions.
    a. Everybody, touch your ear. (Signal. Wait.)
        What are you doing? (Signal.) *Touching my ear.*
        Put your hand down. (Signal.)
    b. Everybody, touch your hand. (Signal. Wait.)
        What are you doing? (Signal.) *Touching my hand.*
        Put your hand down. (Signal.)
    c. Everybody, stand up. (Signal. Wait.)
        What are you doing? (Signal.) *Standing up.*
        Are you sitting down? (Signal.) *No.*
        Are you touching your nose? (Signal.) *No.*
        Are you touching your hand? (Signal.) *No.*
        Are you standing up? (Signal.) *Yes.*
        Are you touching your leg? (Signal.) *No.*
        Are you standing up? (Signal.) *Yes.*
        Are you eating? (Signal.) *No.*
    d. (Repeat step c until all children's responses are firm.)
    e. What are you doing? (Signal.) *Standing up.*
        Say the whole thing. (Signal.) *I am standing up.*
        (Have children sit down.)

2. Let's do those actions again.
    (Repeat part 1 until all children's responses are firm.)

Implementing the Program

How to Use the Materials

A lesson should be scheduled for each instructional group on every available school day. Allow twenty-five to thirty minutes each day for each group's lesson. Allow five to ten minutes for independent workbook activities.

Directions for Daily Lessons

The Teacher's Presentation Books The presentation books provide you with directions for teaching each of the 150 lessons in the program.

- The presentation books are divided into lessons. The number of the lesson appears in the upper left corner of the first page of the lesson.
- The lessons are divided into exercises.
- The exercise heading indicates the track name, that is, the concept the exercise focuses on.
- What you are to say is in blue type.
- What you and the children are to do is in black type enclosed in parentheses.
- The oral response expected from the children is in italics.
- Fast cycle exercises are indicated with a star (⭐).

Teacher's Workbook Directions Workbook activity directions appear at the end of each lesson in the presentation books, starting with lesson 1. These activities are to be completed in class as part of the daily language lesson and then taken home.

Stories and Poems Stories and poems written especially for the program are located at the end of each presentation book in the storybook section. These stories and poems support the language concepts taught in the daily lessons. Directions for stories and poems to read appear at the end of each lesson, beginning with lesson 21.

Expanded Language Activities The lists of expanded language activities appear at the beginning of each teacher's presentation book. These lists suggest a variety of games, art projects, and other activities that are coordinated with the content of the daily lessons.

Teacher's Presentation Books

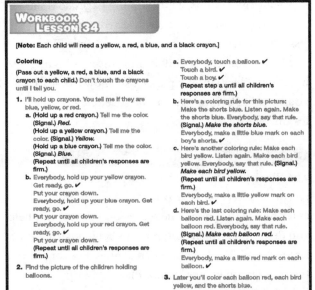

Teacher's Workbook Directions

Children's Workbook Page

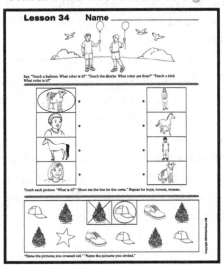

Program Assessments The fifteen program assessments appear after each tenth lesson. They are to be given at ten-lesson intervals, beginning when the children complete lesson 10 and ending when they complete lesson 150. These assessments, to be administered individually, will provide you with information that will help you monitor the progress of the children as they move through the program. The assessments will also help you identify the children who need extra help. (See Appendix C for information on administering and scoring the assessments.)

Planning Pages Each five-lesson span in the presentation books begins with a planning page—a brief summary of the concepts and skills taught in the following five lessons. The planning pages summarize what is taught in the teacher-directed part of the lessons and what appears in the workbooks. The lesson in which a concept or skill is introduced is highlighted in yellow. The planning pages also show the stories and additional activities that can be scheduled for the five-lesson spans.

Forming Groups

The Placement Test The placement test measures the receptive and expressive oral language of children entering the program. The scores on this test will help you determine which children will begin instruction at lesson 1 and which children are candidates for starting the program in a later lesson. Placement options include beginning the program at lesson 1, lesson 11, lesson 21, lesson 31, or lesson 41. The test will also help you identify any children who should not be in the program, and children who are candidates for the fast cycle. (See pages 11–12 for more information about the fast cycle.)

The placement test is an individual test, to be given to each of the children at the beginning of the school year. The test, directions for giving and scoring the test, and the reproducible Placement Test Scoring Sheet are found in Appendix A.

The Transition Lesson The transition lesson is the first lesson for children who will start the program at a lesson other than lesson 1. The transition lesson appears in Appendix B of this guide.

A classroom of twenty-five or more children is normally divided into three groups for language instruction. Although the placement test provides for five possible starting lessons, it is difficult to manage more than three groups. Therefore, some compromises must be made. Follow these guidelines for grouping the children:

1. Place the children with the most nearly similar scores in the same group. There may be only three children who score six points or more and therefore place at lesson 1. These three children should probably be grouped with children who score four or five points. It would be safest to begin this group at lesson 1.

   Another example: There may be three children whose scores indicate that they should start the program at lesson 41, while the scores of eight other children place them at lesson 31. These two groups of children should probably be combined and started at lesson 31.

2. Try to make the highest-performing group the largest—as many as twelve children.

   Try to make the lowest-performing group the smallest—no more than six children if possible.

   The middle group should have eight to ten children.

   An alternative procedure is to divide the children into two groups—one composed of two-thirds of the class or more and a smaller group composed of the lowest-performing children.

3. Regroup the children on the basis of their performance in the daily lessons. Children should be moved from group to group when it becomes apparent that their placement is no longer appropriate. How children perform on the individual turns at the end of most exercises provides you with daily information about the performance of individual children. If some children tend to perform poorly on individual turns, they are probably out of phase with the group and, if possible, should be placed in a lower group.

Transfer Children and Frequent Absences If a child transfers into your classroom very early in the year, administer the placement test to determine the group most suitable for the child. Observe the child closely after this initial placement to be sure it is appropriate.

Children transferring into the program later in the year are often more difficult to place. Some may require special tutoring before they can enter the lowest-performing group. Begin by placing such children in the lowest group and, if possible, work with them at other times during the day.

After about a week, if the children are performing well, move them to the next group. Observe their performance closely for about a week, and then evaluate them again. If their performance is a little weak at this point, don't be too quick to move them back to the lower group. Give them another week before making your final judgment.

Children who are absent a great deal should be treated like children who transfer in.

The Fast Cycle

The fast cycle is for children who are able to progress through the program at an accelerated rate. Beginning at lesson 31, some exercises are marked with a star ( ). These are the fast-cycle exercises. Children in the fast cycle are taught only the starred exercises. Fast-cycle children will cover the same content as the other children, but because they need less practice, they will skip some of the practice exercises. (Children going through the program at the regular rate are taught every exercise—both starred and un-starred—in each lesson.)

Identifying Fast-Cycle Children To determine which, if any, of your groups should be taught from the fast cycle, use the results of the placement test. Children whose scores indicate that they should start at lesson 31 or lesson 41 are candidates for the fast-cycle program. Put these children in one or more groups (depending upon how many children in your classroom fall into this category).

Teaching Fast-Cycle Children Another way to determine which, if any, of your groups should enter the fast cycle is by observing the children as you teach them. You may decide to start teaching all of your groups—no matter where they are first placed in the program—at the regular rate, and then make decisions about the fast cycle as you evaluate the children's progress. Some children learn more easily and

remember more readily; such children are candidates for a fast-cycle group.

On the first day of instruction, children beginning the fast cycle should be taught the transition lesson found in Appendix B of this teacher's guide. The next day they are taught from either lesson 31 or 41. Teach only the starred fast-cycle exercises to these children.

Accelerating Children Who Place at Lesson 41 According to the placement test, lesson 41 is the highest entry point for *Language for Learning*. Some children who place at lesson 41 already know many of the language concepts that are presented after lesson 41. Here is a schedule for accelerating these children:

■ Teach the transition lesson.

■ Teach lessons 41 and 42, and then give the children the lesson 50 program assessment (Assessment 5).

■ If children do not pass Assessment 5, teach the fast-cycle (starred) exercises in lesson 51, and continue through the program, presenting only the starred exercises.

■ If children pass Assessment 5, teach lessons 51 and 52, and then give the children the lesson 60 program assessment (Assessment 6).

■ If children do not pass Assessment 6, teach the fast-cycle exercises in lesson 61, and continue through the program, presenting only the starred exercises.

■ If children pass Assessment 6, teach lessons 61 and 62 and then give them the lesson 70 program assessment (Assessment 7).

■ Whether or not the children pass Assessment 7, begin teaching the exercises from lesson 71. Teach only the fast-cycle exercises marked with a star.

This schedule provides you with an accelerated plan of instruction that will enable you to teach more than one lesson a period. You may teach two or more fast-cycle lessons in one period. If, as you progress through the program, this accelerated schedule proves to be too fast for the children, return to teaching every exercise in every lesson.

Adjusting the Fast-Cycle Program Because the number of exercises fast-cycle children skip varies from lesson to lesson, you should consider the period of time you teach them as the unit of instruction rather than a single lesson. On some days, you will be able to teach the starred exercises in two lessons, whereas on other days you may teach only a little more than one lesson. As a result, you may end the language period in the middle of a lesson. If so, simply mark the next starred exercise. You will begin with that exercise the next day. Fast-cycle children should complete almost all of the workbook pages (including pages from lessons you have skipped). You will find they can do most of them independently with a minimum of direction.

Children in the fast cycle should be taught with the same standards in mind as children going through the program at the regular rate: their responses to every exercise should be firm and assured.

You may decide that a group that has spent several weeks or months in the fast cycle needs to be taken out of it and reentered into the regular program. If fast-cycle children start making a lot of mistakes or give evidence of not remembering what they are learning, they are being moved through the program at too fast a rate and should be slowed down. This is easy to do. You simply start teaching every exercise in a lesson instead of only the starred exercises. However, before switching a group from the fast cycle to the regular program, you may want to teach some of the un-starred exercises from several previous lessons.

Children who spend all or part of the year in the fast cycle will finish the program before the end of the school year. They should be put directly into Language for Thinking and begin that program at lesson 15.

Adjusting the Program for Preschool Children

Most preschool children have less understanding of language than children in kindergarten or first grade. *Language for Learning* is designed to accommodate these children. However, the expectations for progress are different for preschool children than for older children. The basic adjustments for preschool children are as follows:

1. Begin all children at lesson 1.
2. Initially, schedule short periods of instruction, possibly five minutes for each period.
3. Schedule more than one period a day—possibly three, but not one right after the other.
4. Change the schedule after about two weeks so that children have one or two periods of twenty minutes each day.

5. Progress through the lessons as fast as the children achieve mastery of the exercises.
6. If children have serious problems achieving mastery, present the first five lessons in sequence, and then repeat those lessons, starting with lesson 1.
7. If children complete half a lesson in one period, review any exercises they had trouble with during the next period, and then present the exercise that follows the last one the children had completed.
8. A good plan is to start each lesson with an exercise from the Actions track.
9. For children for whom English is a second language, an effective initial procedure is not to teach entire lessons, but rather to teach only the Actions exercises. (See the next section of this guide for more information.)

Teaching Children Whose First Language Is Not English

Language for Learning is effective with children whose first language is not English. It has been used with ELL children who are in preschool, kindergarten, the primary grades, and with older children who know little or no English. The program is well-designed for teaching English to children who do not know the language.

Language for Learning provides both the instruction and the practice to accelerate the children's ability to construct new sentences that describe (a) what they want to do or have, (b) what they are doing, (c) what they were doing, and (d) what and where things are. Within one school year, children who have never spoken English speak English so well that it is hard to believe they learned so much in less than a calendar year. The teaching requires no knowledge of the children's first language. It does, however, require some adaptation of the program. Here are the general guidelines for using *Language for Learning* with children whose first language is not English.

Actions Exercises First (See Actions in the Program section of this guide.) Make the actions exercises the primary teaching vehicle. These exercises are labeled *Actions* or have the word Actions in the exercise title (for example, *Actions—Prepositions, Actions—Pronouns*).

Start with the actions exercises in lessons 1 through 10. Teach these exercises until the children's responses are firm. Do this by repeating them, but make the exercises a game, not a drill. Do the actions exercises in more than one lesson during each period.

In the first actions exercises, the children learn the instructions "stand up" and "sit down." Most of the directions in the actions exercises also include the word *everybody*; for example, Everybody, stand up and Everybody, sit down.

In teaching the actions exercises, model each action by demonstrating how to do it. For example, point to yourself and say, My turn. Stand up. Then stand up. You can help the children learn the word *everybody* by saying, Everybody several times as you motion to or tap each child. Then say, Stand up. If the children do not stand up, motion or physically help them stand up. Then point to the children and say, Stand up as they are standing. Show your approval by smiling or clapping your hands.

Repeat the same procedure for Everybody, sit down.

The exercises in the actions track are effective because you give the children a simple direction, and the children are able to do what you say immediately—on the first day. No translation is required; no readiness activities are necessary. The children experience success on the first day of instruction.

By lesson 3, the children are not only following directions for performing simple actions, but they also are telling you what they are doing. Here is the exercise from lesson 3 of the Actions track.

EXERCISE 1 Actions—Following Directions

1. Get ready to do some actions. Watch my hand. Remember to wait for the signal.
   a. Everybody, stand up. (Signal. Children are to stand up.)
   Everybody, sit down. (Signal. Children are to sit down.)
   b. (Repeat step a until all children respond to your signal.)

2. Let's do those actions again.
   a. Everybody, stand up. (Signal.) What are you doing? (Signal.) *Standing up.*
   b. Everybody, sit down. (Signal.) What are you doing? (Signal.) *Sitting down.*

3. Let's do those actions some more.
(Repeat part 2 until all children can perform the actions and say what they are doing.)

Note that what the children tell you is a simple transformation of what you tell them. You say, Stand up. After they stand up, you ask, What are you doing? The answer is not *Stand up*, but *Standing up*. You help the children produce the response and repeat the exercise until all of the children are able to follow the routine:

   Everybody, stand up. (Children respond.)
   What are you doing? *Standing up.*
   Everybody, sit down. (Children respond.)
   What are you doing? *Sitting down.*

If the children make mistakes, stress the word *doing*. They will soon catch on that the ending they add is the same as the ending on *doing*. The children's responses must be firm. Present a lot of repetition, but make it fun, and be positive.

Information Exercises (See Information and Background Knowledge in the Program section of this guide.) You may also want to teach the exercises in the Information track as part of your initial lessons with the children. Here is one of these exercises.

EXERCISE 4 Information—School

1. Here are some things you should know.
   a. Listen. I'm your teacher. My name is _____. Everybody, what's your teacher's name? (Pause. Signal. Children say the teacher's name.)
   b. (Repeat step a until all children's responses are firm.)
   c. Listen. You go to _____ School. Everybody, what's the name of the school you go to? (Pause. Signal. Children say the name of their school.)
   d. (Repeat step c until all children's responses are firm.)

2. Let's try those questions again.
   a. Everybody, what's your teacher's name? (Pause. Signal.)
   b. What's the name of the school you go to? (Pause. Signal.)

3. (Repeat part 2 until all children's responses are firm.)

Individual Turns
(Repeat the exercise, calling on different children for each step.)

If the children have trouble answering the questions in part 2, shorten the questions: Teacher's name? Name of the school? After the children respond correctly to these abbreviated questions, return to the questions that appear in the exercise.

When the children are firm on the actions and information exercises in the first ten lessons, return to lesson 1, and present complete lessons (including the actions and information exercises). The new tracks they will work on are Object Identification and Identity Statements.

Developing Speech and Understanding (See Descriptions of Objects material in the Program section of this guide.) After completing lesson 10, continue through the program, trying to complete a lesson a day. You will discover that the program develops speech and understanding together in a systematic way. For example, after the children learn to identify objects with a two-word phrase, they learn to make complete statements. Here is a part of an identity statement exercise:

> What is this? *A ball*.
> Say the whole thing. *This is a ball*.

If children have trouble with this exercise, change your directions to Say the whole thing about what **this is**. Now the last two words you say are the first two words the children say. Use these directions for a few days, and then return to Say the whole thing.

Children also learn to "Say the whole thing" about actions. They go through three steps:

1. Touch the floor.
2. What are you doing? *Touching the floor*.
3. Say the whole thing about what you are doing.
   I am touching the floor.

Note that the children construct the entire statement by simply saying the words *I am* before saying the words that tell what they are doing.

Therefore, for both the identity statements and actions exercises, the children learn a variation of the same pattern. They answer the question that asks what something is or what they are doing with a word or two. Then they "Say the whole thing" by saying *I am* or *this is* before the familiar words. With this knowledge, children can speak in the present tense. They know how to identify things and how to explain what they are doing.

Pronouns and Tense (See Actions in the Program section of this guide.) The program adds to the children's knowledge by showing them how to construct sentences that tell what (a) *he* is doing, (b) *she* is doing, (c) *we* are doing, and (d) *they* are doing. Then the children learn how to tell about past events. The children first learn to use statements that tell what they were doing (not what they did). The statements are the same as those that tell what the person is doing, except for the verb.

I am walking. I was walking.

I am touching my head. I was touching my head.

The pairing is obvious. The reason this approach is so effective is that it permits the children to describe events that have taken place without having to learn a host of irregular verbs to tell what happened. Some examples are listed below.

say—said	stand—stood
take—took	go—went
eat—ate	ride—rode
ran—run	drink—drank
sit—sat	feel—felt

The ability to generalize is very important for the emergent language learner. In *Language for Learning*, the children first learn to express meanings in the present tense (*I am riding a bike*) but soon are able to construct past-tense statements (*I was riding a bike*).

More Objects and More Words (See Descriptions of Objects in the Program section of this guide.) Because ELL children have more to learn than children whose first language is English, they may not be able to complete a lesson a day during the first fifty lessons of the program. Furthermore, they will probably need additional demonstrations of some of the objects named in the Common Objects track. After lesson 20, a good practice is to begin lessons with a routine in which you point to different objects in the room. For each object, you ask a series of yes/no questions: Is this a table? Is this a window? Is this a chair? If the answer is *yes*, give the children the instruction Say the whole thing. If the answer is *no*, present another, or go to another object.

The value of this kind of "yes/no routine" early in the program is that although the children may not be able to produce the names of the various objects, they will recognize the name when you say it in your questions. But after about lesson 50, you should change the routine so that the children answer the question What is this?

Note that the program does not teach all the common objects the children need to know. You can provide additional practice with other common objects in the classroom and that you and the children bring from home or from outside the school. A good plan is to make a list of all the common-object words the children have learned. These are words that should be reviewed. You can post the list with the words written and pictures next to the words. The list provides you with a measure of what the children have learned and provides the children with a way of reviewing what they are learning. Make sure that once you introduce a new object, you give children practice in identifying it on at least five different occasions before assuming that they have learned it. Then add the word to the list of words that should be reviewed.

After lesson 50, the children should begin to progress faster through the program. By lesson 100, they should be able to complete most lessons during a single period.

Language Games The children really like to play language games. As the children progress through the program, you can develop a number of language games based on what they are learning. For example, after the children learn new class names and opposites, you can play games that give children practice in applying this knowledge. Here are some ideas to start with:

Classification Games Announce a class that the children have learned, and then point to different children. The children are to name something in that class. For example, Listen. You are going to name vehicles. Point to each child in turn. Each child names one vehicle. When the group runs out of vehicle names, challenge them with another classification term (animals, for example.).

Materials Games A similar game can be played with materials. For example, I am thinking of wood. Name some things that can be made of wood.

Opposites Games As children are learning opposites, you can play a variety of opposites games. You can present pairs of things or pictures of pairs of things (for example, a tall building and a short building). Touch one member of the pair. Ask, Is this building tall or the opposite of tall? Or say, Tell me about this building. Tell me about the other building. You can collect sets of objects and pictures to use to play this game and add to your collection as the children learn more opposites.

For some opposites, you can play a kind of guessing game. For example, walk slowly. The children are to guess that you are *slow*. Ask, What is the opposite of slow? For another example, make a sad face. Children are to guess the word *sad*. Ask, What is the opposite of sad? You can use a variation of this game for quiet/noisy, old/young, awake/asleep, and other opposites.

Combination Games Another activity is a combination game in which children make statements about the color and name of an article of clothing that one child is wearing. As you point to an article of clothing that one child is wearing, the other children are to name the article of clothing and name its color. The statements should start with *He is wearing . . .* or *She is wearing . . .* and are completed with the color and name of the article. For example, *She is wearing orange socks* or *He is wearing a brown shirt*.

This game provides a lot of opportunities for the children to construct descriptive statements. Expect the children to have problems constructing statements that use plurals such as *She is wearing brown shoes*. Sometimes they leave out the verb or add an unwanted article—for example, *She is wearing a brown shoes*. Correct any mistakes by first letting the child know that the observations are correct. Then model a correct statement, and have all the children in the group repeat it. For example, say, You are right. But listen: She is wearing brown shoes. Let's all say that.

If-Then Games An if-then game can be played when the children are learning about if-then reasoning. For example, say, If you are wearing some blue clothing, stand up. Ask each child who stands, Why are you standing up? *I am wearing some blue clothing*. What are you wearing that is blue? *Jeans*.

Have fun with the directions: If you have two legs, clap your hands. If you like dogs, jump up and down.

Real-Life Routines As a rule, use real-life routines for all the new concepts the children are learning. For instance, when the preposition *over* is introduced, go through this type of routine several times a day: Watch my hand. Is it over the desk? Is it on the desk? Where is my hand? Say the whole thing. When prepositions are introduced, play a variation of the same real-life routine.

Go through similar routines with other language concepts. For example, when children learn the classification term *containers*, you can point to different things in the classroom and ask about the classes the children are learning. Point to a wastebasket, and ask, Is this a vehicle? Is this a container? What kind of container is it? Say the whole thing about this container. (Note that these routines are the same routines that children practice during the language lesson.)

Use the same approach for the materials the children are learning to identify. Display objects made of the different materials they are learning about, such as cloth, paper, metal, wood, glass, and plastic. Review these objects regularly by asking, What is this? and What is it made of?

With the addition of each new language concept, the children learn new statement patterns. Throughout the program, follow this general rule: Once children learn a new concept and a new statement pattern in the program, make sure that they use them to communicate with others in real-life situations. This will show you if the children have any problems understanding what they are learning and if they are having trouble applying the new concepts and statements in real-life situations.

The games and demonstrations described in this section are appropriate for all children. For children who do not speak English, however, the demonstrations are very important. They will help bridge the gap between simply understanding English and being able to use it as a means of communication.

Coordinating Language and Reading Instruction

Language for Learning may be introduced as a support program for any Direct Instruction reading program. There are two important rules for effectively coordinating reading and language instruction in kindergarten and first grade:

1. Children are never to read something they would be unable to understand if it were presented orally. Children should not read words, sentences, or stories they wouldn't understand if somebody said those words, sentences, or stories.

2. Language instruction must stay ahead of reading instruction at the beginning levels. You should never have to stop and explain the meaning of a word while students are engaged in beginning reading instruction. Later, when children have advanced to reading second-grade level material, they will learn new ideas and the meanings of unfamiliar words as they read. During instruction in kindergarten and first grade, however, the children's language skills must stay ahead of what they are decoding in print so that they always understand what they read.

What follows are some procedures for scheduling *Language for Learning* and Direct Instruction reading in kindergarten and first-grade classrooms:

1. Do not begin teaching reading until students have completed lesson 40 in *Language for Learning* and have passed the lesson 40 program assessment (Assessment 4). Use the period designated for reading instruction as a second language period until children complete lesson 40. Then continue with one language period and one reading period each day.

2. The amount of language instruction that you cover each day will depend on where the children place in the language program and on how much practice they need to achieve mastery. If children do not completely master an entire lesson during the first language period, review that lesson during the second language period, and then start on the next language lesson. Expect children who place at lesson 1 to go the most slowly through the language program and children who place at lesson 31 or lesson 41 to go faster.

    If you follow this plan of teaching each group two language periods a day, most groups should be able to average about two lessons a day. This means that even the children who start the program at lesson 1 and don't always complete a lesson in a period will require about thirty school days to complete their preparation for reading.

    Children who place at lesson 11 should require only about fifteen days to complete lessons 11 through 40 of *Language for Learning*. Children who place at lesson 21 should complete lessons 21 through 40 in less than ten days, and those who place at lesson 31 should require only a few days to complete lessons 31 through 40.

3. When children complete lesson 40, administer the lesson 40 program assessment (Assessment 4). Groups that sore 90 percent or better are ready to begin reading instruction. You then convert one of the two daily language periods into a daily reading period. Continue to teach one period of language and one period of reading each day. Do not have language and reading periods back to back.

4. See page 11 of this Teacher's Guide for a procedure for accelerating children who place at lesson 41 in *Language for Learning*. These children receive a daily period of language instruction and a daily period of reading instruction each day.

Teaching Effectively

How to Set Up a Group

To organize children for *Language for Learning* instruction, follow these directions:

1. Seat children in a curved row. Sit so that you can observe every child in the group as well as the other members of the class. For larger groups, seat the children in two rows.

2. Arrange children according to their instructional needs. Seat the children who need the most help directly in front of you (in the first row if there is more than one row). Seat the children who are likely to need the least help at the ends of the first row (or in the second row). You will naturally look most frequently at the children seated directly in front of you. If you are constantly aware of these children, you will be in a position to know when their responses are firm. When their responses are firm, you can be sure that the rest of the group is firm.

3. Assign the seats. The children should sit in their assigned seats every day.

4. Sit close to the children. Position the children as close together as possible. There will be times during the lesson that you will want to shake a child's hand or have a child touch a picture in the presentation book. This will be possible when children are within arm's reach.

5. Make sure the children can see the pictures. Because many exercises require the children to look at the pictures, check that they all can see the book. Hold your head next to the book, and see whether you can see the eyes of all the children. If you have to look almost sideways from the book to see a child's eyes, that child won't be able to see what is on the page.

Getting into the Lesson

The children respond with enthusiasm when your lesson is well prepared and presented with good pacing. Here are some suggestions that will help you present the lesson:

1. Practice the exercises. Rehearse the exercises before you present them to the children.

2. Get into the lesson quickly. Present the first actions exercise in the lesson, even if the group is shy or has some behavioral problems. Repeat the exercise until all the children are responding without hesitation. Then quickly present the next exercise. Actions exercises get the children responding. You can return to the "stand up—sit down" Actions exercises whenever the children's attention lags during a lesson.

3. Follow the scripted directions. Present each exercise as it appears in the presentation book. If you change the vocabulary of a particular exercise, the children may have difficulty on future exercises that build on the vocabulary specified in the exercise.

4. Use clear signals. A signal is a motion you make to get a simultaneous response from the group. All signals have the same purpose—to give the children a moment to think and to then enable them to respond together. All signals have the same rationale—if you can get the group to respond simultaneously (with no one child leading the others), you will get information about the performance of all the children, not just those who happen to answer first. Also, all of the children will maximize their opportunities to respond and practice.

5. Practice the signals. Work on signals until they are natural and you can do them without concentrating on them. Your clear, easy-to-follow signals will help the children follow the steps in the exercises and the sequences of instruction. More information about signals appears in the following section, Teaching Techniques, pages 21–26.

6. React to the children's performance. Work with the children until their responses are firm and assured. The children should know that they do something important, that you are pleased when they do a good job, and that you will help them when they need help.

7. Pace exercises appropriately. Pacing is the rate at which different parts of the exercises are presented. You and the children should have a

sense of moving quickly through the steps of the exercise. The parts of an exercise that are easy for children should be done very briskly. On the other hand, steps in an exercise that are difficult for the children—steps that require them to figure something out—should be presented more slowly. Sometimes the word *pause* appears in the directions to the teacher. This indicates to you that you should pause an extra second or two to let the children think before you signal the response.

Here are some general guidelines for well-paced instruction:

- Speak quickly and with expression.
- Stress words that are important by saying them a little louder, but not slower.
- Follow the instructions about pausing that appear in the exercise.
- If you miss a line, stumble over words, or rush a signal, repeat that part of the exercise. Tell the children, Stop. Let's try that again.
- Move quickly from one exercise to the next, pausing no longer than three or four seconds between exercises. When the children have done well on the exercise, let them know about it: You really did a good job on that part. Then say, New exercise, and go on to the next exercise.
- If the children are making a lot of errors, slow your pace, and pause longer before signaling. This pause gives children more time to think.

What Is Good Performance?

1. The group is performing well and deserves praise when
   - All children respond on signal.
   - All children give the correct answer.
2. When the children respond appropriately, you should acknowledge it:
   - Praise children when they complete all the steps in an exercise on signal and without making a mistake.
   - Praise children after they have been corrected. Let them know that now they are right. If the exercise has been particularly difficult and they have worked hard to do it successfully, act particularly pleased: That was hard. But now you can do it. Good for you.

- Praise children only when they perform according to your standard. If you reward a child for poor performance, that child won't be motivated to improve. Furthermore, you will lose your credibility with the other children in the group.
3. Tell the children why you are praising them. After the children have done an entire exercise correctly, say, That was good. You did the whole exercise, and it was hard.
4. Challenge the children. A challenge often motivates an uninterested child to become an eager participant.

   If two children in a group perform particularly well, praise them, and challenge the other children. Wow! Henry and Myrna really can do it. Aren't they good! Just listen to how well they do.
5. Use tangible rewards if the children do not respond well to verbal praise. Use pieces of chalk, crackers, raisins, stars, points accumulated toward a small toy—something the children are willing to work for. If you use tangible rewards, always tell the children why they are receiving them. Pair verbal praise with the tangible reward. When the children have learned to work, you will probably want to drop the tangible rewards and use only verbal praise.

Firm Responses Throughout the program you will encounter the following instruction to the teacher: "Repeat until all children's responses are firm." This instruction means that at the conclusion of every exercise, every child should be able to perform the exercise without any need for correction. Children's responses are firm when they give the correct answers at every step of an exercise.

It is easier to bring the children to this standard of performance at the first introduction of an exercise than it will be in a later lesson after they have made the same mistakes many times. It is much more efficient to teach, correct, and repeat until all responses are firm the first time an exercise is presented.

Let the children know what your standard is. Stay with an exercise until you can honestly say to them, Good. Everybody can do this exercise.

Statement Repetition It is particularly important to work on statement repetition with some children.

Children who are able to repeat statements (aloud or to themselves) are more readily able to follow directions successfully and learn from teaching demonstrations that present definitions or rules. Remember, the ability to repeat statements accurately the first time or after only a few practice trials is a good indicator of success in future academic work, including the ability to read and comprehend.

Apply the following standard to evaluate children's statement repetition skill:

The child can repeat the statement with every word pronounced acceptably and with all words included. Do not accept responses in which endings are omitted from words, words are missing, or word order is reversed. Evidence that children have the general idea of the statement is not good enough. They must demonstrate that they have the skill to precisely repeat any statement in each exercise.

The statements in the program have been carefully selected. In the early lessons the children repeat simple three- and four-word statements: *I am standing. This is a cup.* As the children progress through the program, the statements they learn to use gradually increase in both length and complexity. By the end of the program the children are comfortable with such statements as *A bird has feathers, but an airplane does not have feathers.*

Handling Responses Different from Those in the Book

Although the responses the children are to make are indicated in each exercise, it is quite possible that individual children will make other responses that are equally correct. You should acknowledge all correct responses; you want to let the child who gives another answer know that his or her observation is a good one. But in teaching the exercise, you will usually have the children respond as the exercise is written.

Here is an example of how to handle a different response: In a parts exercise a child might call the point of a pencil a *tip.* You say, Right. Some people call this part a *tip.* But it's also called a *point.* Let's use *point.* What part is this? Continue with the exercise.

There are two reasons for following this practice:

1. Many responses occur across many lessons. The children review them in daily practice.
2. In some tracks a later exercise builds on a response made in an earlier exercise.

Individual Turns

Individual turns are specified at the end of most exercises. Here are several suggestions for giving individual turns:

1. Give individual turns only after the group's responses are firm. If you wait until the children are firm on group responses, the chances are much better that each child will be able to give a firm response when answering alone.
2. Do not give every child an individual turn for every exercise—two or three individual turns are sufficient unless the exercise is an unusually difficult one. Present individual turns quickly and naturally. You do not need to use a signal; simply ask a question, or give an instruction to one child. If you get a correct response, praise the child, and then immediately present another question to another child. Don't call on children in a predictable order, starting at one end of the row and calling on every child in turn. Instead, skip around the group.
3. Give most of the turns to the lowest-performing children—those seated directly in front of you. By watching those children during the group practice of the exercise, you can tell when they are ready to respond individually. When they can do the exercise without further correction, you can safely assume that the other children will be able to do it as well.
4. When a child makes a mistake on an individual turn, present the correction to the entire group. When one child makes a particular mistake, there is probably another child who will make the same mistake. The most efficient remedy, therefore, is to correct the entire group. Then give another individual turn to the child who made the mistake.
5. If you feel doubtful about the responses of any of the children, give individual turns even when they are not specified. On the other hand, if a group does well on an exercise, you may wish to skip individual turns for that exercise.

Group Progress

Here are some questions and answers about the children's progress through *Language for Learning*:

1. How much should you teach each day? Your objective should be to complete at least one lesson

a day with each group. When new concepts are introduced, however, you may not always complete an entire lesson. When the choice is between making sure all the children's responses are firm or completing the lesson in one day, choose firm responses, and complete the lesson the next day.

You should not have to make this choice often; the number of lessons that cannot be completed during your scheduled time should be small compared to those that can be successfully completed. On the other hand, whenever you finish a lesson before the language period is over, start the next lesson. Children in the fast cycle may be able to complete two lessons of starred exercises each day.

2. What about skipping exercises within lessons? In general, children not in the fast cycle should be taught every exercise in each lesson. Occasionally, however, you may observe that the children have already learned particular skills or information. For example, all the children in a group may know their first names and whole names before the end of that track. In that case you do not need to present the names exercise in every lesson where it appears. For example, children frequently find the opposites exercises very easy. You can skip some of these exercises or present them as a challenge, saying, I know you know this. Let's see how quickly we can do this exercise.

How to Make the Program Succeed

Here are some general procedures for making the program work in your classroom:

1. Follow the program. The lessons are carefully organized and sequenced.

2. Follow the suggestions in this Teacher's Guide for implementing the program and teaching effectively. Study the section of the guide titled The Program to learn about the major exercises in each track. Study the correction procedures. Practice presenting the exercises before working with the children.

3. Be sure that every child is responding. Follow the instructions "Repeat until all children's responses are firm."

4. Make sure that the children in the group respond together on signal and that some children are not leading the others. Evaluate the children's responses to determine from their errors if any corrections or additional practice is necessary.

5. Make allowances for regional differences in some of the vocabulary in the exercises. What is referred to as a pop bottle in the Midwest may be called a soda bottle on the East Coast. Some people call a garbage can a trash can. Do not hesitate to make such local substitutions for the words that are used in the program.

6. Relate what the children are learning in the language lesson to what is being done the rest of the day in school. You will find that you will become very conscious of the kind of language you are teaching. Use this language in everyday situations. For example, when you are teaching *or*, you might say, Who will go get the milk? John or Dexter or Angela? I'll tell you. It will be the one who is not a boy. When you are teaching if-then rules, you might say, I'm going to give puzzles to children if they are sitting down. If you're sitting down, then you get a puzzle.

Seat-work activities, music, stories, play periods with toys, and indoor and outdoor games can all support the concepts and skills the children are learning in the program. You want the children to understand that the language they are learning works with many people in many situations—its use and effectiveness are not confined to the pages of the books used in the language lessons.

Teaching Techniques

★ EXERCISE 5 **Concept Application**

1. You're going to figure out which boy is big.
  - Listen to the rule. The boy wearing a hat is big. Listen again. The boy wearing a hat is big. Everybody, say the rule about the boy wearing a hat. **(Signal.)** *The boy wearing a hat is big.*
  - Again. **(Signal.)** *The boy wearing a hat is big.*
    (Repeat until all children can say the rule.) Remember, the boy wearing a hat is the only boy that is big.

2. Let's use the rule.
  a. (Point to a.) Is this boy wearing a hat? **(Touch.)** *Yes.*
    So is this boy big? **(Touch.)** *Yes.*
  b. (Point to b.) Is this boy wearing a hat? **(Touch.)** *No.*
    So is this boy big? **(Touch.)** *No.*
  c. (Point to c.) Is this boy wearing a hat? **(Touch.)** *No.*
    So is this boy big? **(Touch.)** *No.*

3. Here are some more questions.
  a. (Point to a.) Is this boy wearing a hat? **(Touch.)** *Yes.*
    So, what else do you know about this boy? **(Touch.)** *This boy is big.*
  b. (Point to b.) Is this boy wearing a hat? **(Touch.)** *No.*
    So, what else do you know about this boy? **(Touch.)** *This boy is not big.*
  c. (Point to c.) Is this boy wearing a hat? **(Touch.)** *No.*
    So, what else do you know about this boy? **(Touch.)** *This boy is not big.*

4. (Call on two children.) Show me the boy who is big. **(Wait.)** Let's see if you are right.
    (Turn the page quickly.)

How the Exercises Are Organized

Each of the exercises in *Language for Learning* presents a carefully organized sequence of instruction. Most of the exercises are divided into parts and steps. Each part is indicated by a number and each step by a letter or a bullet. The organization of each exercise into parts and steps makes it easier for you to follow the instructional plan of each exercise and to learn the patterns of the different types of exercises. The exercises are easy to teach because they are organized to make instructional sense to you and to the children.

The page layout also contributes to the ease of teaching the program. In exercises with pictures, the text is almost always in the left column, and the pictures are almost always to the right of the text. This arrangement makes it easy for you to keep track of where you are in the text and to point to the specified parts of the pictures.

Most of the picture exercises are organized so that the letter of the step in the exercise corresponds to the letter of the picture you will point to. Above is an example from lesson 48.

The letters of the steps in parts 2 and 3 correspond to the letters of the pictures. For example, in part 2, step b, you point to picture b. In part 3, step c, you point to picture c. These conventions are used in most of the picture exercises throughout the program.

Exercises that don't use pictures are grouped on one or two pages at the beginning of each lesson. You can hold the teacher's presentation book in your lap as you teach these exercises.

EXERCISE 5 Object Identification

1. I'll tell you about these pictures.
   a. (Point to a.) A boy.
   b. (Point to b.) A girl.
   c. (Point to c.) A cat.
   d. (Point to d.) A dog.

2. Again. (Repeat part 1.)

3. Now it's your turn.
   a. (Point to a.) What is this? (Touch.)
      A boy.
   b. (Point to b.) What is this? (Touch.)
      A girl.
   c. (Point to c.) What is this? (Touch.)
      A cat.
   d. (Point to d.) What is this? (Touch.)
      A dog.

4. Let's name these things again.
   (Repeat part 3 until all children's responses
   are firm.)

5. Now let's do something else.
   a. (Ask a girl in the group to stand up.)
      Everybody, what is this? (Signal.) *A girl.*
   b. (Ask a boy in the group to stand up.)
      Everybody, what is this? (Signal.) *A boy.*

6. (Repeat part 5 until all children's responses
   are firm.)

Individual Turns
(Repeat parts 3 and 5, calling on different
children for each step.)

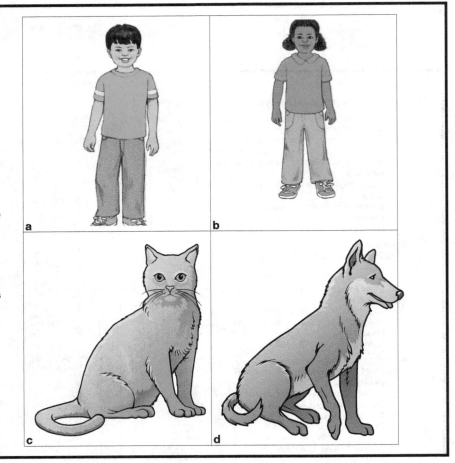

Signaling the Children's Responses

Why signals? To maximize language practice, it is important for all the children to respond at once. Signals are used so that the children will respond as a group. You will use two signaling techniques to present the exercises and workbook activities—a touch signal and a hand signal.

A touch signal is used with picture exercises. You touch a picture or a part of a picture to signal the children's response. A hand signal is used in exercises without pictures. You hold out your hand, then drop it. The directions in the teacher's presentation books indicate which signal to use at each step of each exercise. "Touch" indicates a touching signal. "Signal" indicates a hand signal.

The Touch Signal Part of an exercise in which the touch signal is used appears above. The word touch after a question or an instruction tells you to use the touch signal. This signal has two parts: pointing and touching.

Pointing

■ Look at the picture to demonstrate to the children that they too should be looking at it.

■ Point to the picture by holding your finger about an inch from the page, just over the letter. Be careful not to cover the picture—all children must be able to see it.

■ Ask the question, or give the instruction.

■ Hold your finger in the point position for about one second.

Touching

■ At the end of the one-second interval, quickly and decisively touch the letter a.

■ As your finger touches the page, the children should respond.

■ Continue touching the picture for the duration of the children's response.

■ Drop your finger when they finish responding.

Note: When pointing to or touching the pictures, watch to see that you are not covering any important part of the picture with your arm, hand, or finger.

Practicing the Touch Signal

Use the exercise on page 22 to practice the touch signal. Have some other adults play the role of the children. Keep presenting the exercise until they respond in unison to your signal.

Watch for these common pointing problems:

- Touching the picture instead of pointing to it as you ask the question or give the instruction
- Not holding your point for at least one second after you finish talking

Watch for these common touching problems:

- Touching the picture before you finish your instructions
- Touching the picture indecisively
- Covering the picture as you touch it
- Not touching the picture for as long as the children are responding

The Hand-Drop Signal The following actions exercise uses hand-drop signals. The word *signal* after a question or an instruction tells you to drop your hand to signal the children's response.

Below are the guidelines for giving the hand-drop signal:

- At the beginning of each step of the exercise hold out your hand. Keep your hand perfectly still.
- Ask the question, or give the instruction.

- Pause about one second, and then quickly drop your hand. (The interval between the question or the instruction and the hand drop is the same as that between the question and the touching when using the touch signal.)
- The instant your hand drops, the children are to respond.

Note: If it is easier or more natural for you to clap your hands to signal the children's response, do so. Just be sure that the timing is the same as that described above.

Practicing the Hand-Drop Signal

Use the previous exercise to practice the hand-drop signal until the children are responding together. Watch for these common signaling problems:

- Not holding out your hand from the beginning of each step
- Not pausing for one second after you finish talking
- Dropping your hand while you are still talking
- Dropping your hand too slowly

Touch Signals and Hand-Drop Signals in One Exercise Occasionally a hand-drop signal is used in a picture exercise, if pointing to the picture will give away an answer the children are supposed to be figuring out. On page 24 is an exercise that uses both a hand-drop signal and a touch signal. Practice moving quickly from one step to another.

EXERCISE 1 Actions — Following Directions

1. Get ready to do some actions. Watch my hand. Remember to wait for the signal.
   a. Everybody, stand up. (Signal. Children are to stand up.)
      Everybody, sit down. (Signal. Children are to sit down.) ● ◆
   b. (Repeat step a until all children respond to your signal.)

2. Let's do those actions again.
   a. Everybody, stand up. (Signal.)
      My turn. What are you doing?
      Standing up.
      Your turn. What are you doing? (Signal.)
      Standing up. ▲
   b. Everybody, sit down. (Signal.) What are you doing? (Signal.) *Sitting down.* ■

3. Let's do those actions some more.
   (Repeat part 2 until all children can perform the actions and say what they are doing.)

EXERCISE 9 **Tense**

1. These pictures show what a monkey is doing.
   a. (Point to a.) What is the monkey doing? (Touch.) *Carrying a box.*
      Say the whole thing about what the monkey is doing. (Touch.) *The monkey is carrying a box.*
   b. (Point to b.) What is the monkey doing now? (Touch.) *Opening the box.*
      Say the whole thing about what the monkey is doing. (Touch.) *The monkey is opening the box.*

2. (Repeat part 1 until all children's responses are firm.)

3. Listen.
   • What did the monkey do before it opened the box? (Signal. Do not touch the picture.) *Carried the box.*
     Say the whole thing about what the monkey did. (Touch.) *The monkey carried the box.*
   • (Point to b.)
     Now say the whole thing about what the monkey is doing in this picture. (Touch.) *The monkey is opening the box.*
   • Say the whole thing about what the monkey did before it opened the box. (Signal. Do not touch the picture.) *The monkey carried the box.*

4. (Repeat part 3 until all children's responses are firm.)

Individual Turns
(Repeat the exercise, calling on different children for each step.)

a

b

Differentiated Instruction

The purpose of differentiated instruction is to individualize instruction so that all the children meet the instructional objectives. In *Language for Learning*, differentiated instruction is achieved in several ways:

■ Through the daily individual turns, which provide you with detailed information about how each student performs

■ Through both the specified and general correction procedures, which are often directed to the entire group but which focus on specific problems individual children in the group are experiencing

■ Through the Extra Help remedies associated with each of the fifteen program assessments. These remedies are tied to specific skills that individual children have not learned thoroughly.

Corrections

All children make mistakes. The mistakes children make provide you with important information about the difficulties they are having. It is important to correct mistakes immediately. Knowing how to effectively correct children's mistakes helps you help the children in your language groups. Three kinds of correction procedures are used in the program: general corrections, specific corrections, and statement corrections. Each of these is discussed in this section.

General Corrections Children's responses that call for general corrections include not attending, not answering, and responding before or after the signal. Here are some ideas for correcting these problems:

Not Attending Not attending occurs when children are not looking where they should be looking during an exercise—for example, not looking at the picture to which you are pointing. Correct not attending by looking at these children and saying, Watch my finger. Let's try it again. Then return to the beginning of the exercise. Returning to the beginning of the exercise will help the children understand your standard: Everyone has to pay attention.

Not Responding Not responding occurs when the children don't answer when you signal a response. Some children may learn not to listen the first time a question is asked and then join in later. They may become dependent on the other children's responses and may get the idea they don't have to initiate their own responses. If children are not responding, correct not answering by saying, I have to hear everybody. Then return to the beginning of the exercise.

Responding Before or After the Signal Remember that the purpose of a signal is to orchestrate a group response. When children do not respond on time (responding before your signal or too long after your signal), they are not attending to your signal, and you are not getting information from every child.

The children will learn to attend to your signal if you consistently return to the beginning of the exercise after each correction. When the children learn that you will repeat the exercise until they are all responding on signal, they will pay more attention to your signal.

If you find that you are spending a lot of time correcting children who are not attending, not answering, and answering before or after the signal, your pacing of the exercise or the signal is probably too slow. Remember that the objective of a signal is not to keep the children sitting on the edges of their seats, never knowing when they will have to respond next. Rather, the pacing of signals should be predictable and occur at a rate that permits children to think and then respond with assurance.

Specific Corrections To correct specific response errors, follow the correction procedures that appear in some of the exercises of the teacher's presentation book, as well as suggestions for corrections that appear in the Program section of this guide. Corrections for specific response errors vary from exercise to exercise because these corrections deal with the specific content of a given exercise and the types of errors the children are likely to make.

Practicing Corrections It is very important to practice making corrections. You must be able to present a correction without hesitation when the mistake occurs. By practicing the corrections, you will be well prepared for the mistakes that children will commonly make.

Have other adults play the role of the children and make the specified mistake. Then present the correction. Practice it until you can do it quickly and naturally. Also practice returning to the beginning of the exercise and presenting the entire exercise. Your group is firm when they respond correctly to every step of the exercise.

Statement Corrections The correction procedure for statement errors is consistent from exercise to exercise, even though the statements themselves will vary. You will find that the model, lead, test, and retest correction procedure that is described below really helps children who have trouble making statements.

Here is an example of the statement correction procedure. (Several children have had trouble saying the full statement *This is a cup*.)

1. **The model** (Teacher: My turn. Listen. This is a cup.) In this step you demonstrate the statement the children are to make.

2. **The lead** (Teacher: Let's say it together. You and the children: This is a cup.) Leading gives the children the benefit of responding with you until they are confident. Some statements require a number of leads to produce a firm, correct response from the children. Don't be afraid to continue leading until the children can produce the statement with you. But remember, the lead step should be used only when the children cannot produce the statement. If they can produce the statement after the model, skip the lead step.

3. **The test** (Teacher: Your turn. Say the whole thing. Children: *This is a cup*.) If the children say the statement correctly, you know the correction has been effective. If they still have trouble, you know that you must repeat the model and lead steps until all the children can pass the test step.

4. **The retest** This involves going back to an earlier part of the exercise and presenting the subsequent steps to make sure the children can make the statement when it occurs in the context of the entire exercise.

The retest step applies to specific response errors as well. After the children can respond to the specific question or instruction they had previously missed, you should return to an earlier part of the exercise and present the subsequent steps in sequence. The retest is very important. The children will learn that the various steps they take in learning are not isolated, but rather fit together in a sequence.

Additional Statement Corrections What follows are statement correction procedures for children who require many repetitions before they are able to produce a statement precisely. The best procedure presents a small-step progression of tasks that require the child to say parts of a sentence.

Example: The child has trouble placing the word *not* in the statement, *The cup is not on the table*. Here are the steps of the correction procedure:

1. You say most of the statement, and the child says only the last part.
   Listen: The cup is not on the table.
   Once more: The cup is not on the table.
   Listen again: The cup is not on . . . (Signal.) *the table*.
   After the child is firm on this part, increase the number of words the child says.
2. Listen: The cup is not . . . (Signal.) *on the table*.
   Continue until the child can say the entire sentence.
3. Listen: The cup is . . . (Signal.) *not on the table*.
4. Listen: The cup . . . (Signal.) *is not on the table*.
5. Say the whole thing. (Signal.) *The cup is not on the table*.

Note: Do not require the child to say more than a dozen responses at a time. After a dozen responses, do something else, and then come back to the problem statements. Do not act as if you're disappointed with the child's performance. Praise the child for trying, and assure the child that he or she will get it if he or she keeps trying. Give praise when the child successfully says the entire sentence.

The Program

This section presents the rationale, some teaching information, and sample exercises for each track of the program. The groups of tracks are displayed on the Scope and Sequence Chart (page 7).

The purpose of this overview is to give you an understanding of the concepts and skills presented in each group of tracks, to explain why they are included in the program, and to discuss problems children may have with specific exercises. The discussions of the tracks also present teaching techniques and corrections that are useful in solving more common problems.

This table lists when the tracks first appear in the lessons and gives the page numbers on which key exercises from these tracks are discussed in the Teacher's Guide.

Actions

Actions exercises help children learn concepts by performing actions and by describing actions illustrated in the teacher's presentation books.

The actions exercises

- Provide a clear demonstration of many language concepts and word meanings.

- Provide practice that the children enjoy (actions exercises are fun).

- Introduce concepts that the children use in everyday activities.

- Provide you with immediate feedback about the children's performance (if the children don't understand the instructions for performing an action, you can identify their problem immediately).

- Allow for a review of many important concepts and words that are presented in sequences of actions (not only do the children learn the concepts, but they also practice them until their use becomes natural and easy).

- Establish foundations for teaching more difficult language-usage conventions such as those associated with pronouns and tenses.

Schedule of Exercises	Starting with Lesson	Page in Teacher's Guide
Basic Actions		
Beginning Actions	1	28
Actions—Parts of the Body	4	32
Actions—Pictures	17	32
Actions—Pronouns	23	34
Tense	55	35
Tense—Pictures	59	37
Actions—Review	51	38
Descriptions of Objects		
Object Identification	1	40
Identity Statements	3	41
Common Objects	7	45
Missing Objects	23	46
Opposites	24	47
Plurals	51	50
Comparatives	131	54
Information and Background Knowledge		
Names	1	57
School Information	1	57
Days of the Week	35	58
Months of the Year	92	59
Seasons	128	60
Part/Whole	28	61
Materials	62	64
Common Information	71	67
Locations	127	69
Signs	143	71
Instructional Words / Problem-Solving Concepts		
Spatial and Temporal Relations	17	73
Prepositions	27	75
And—Actions	60	79
Same/Different	89	80
Some, All, None	92	88
Actions—Or	102	91
First/Next and Before/After	103	92
If-Then Rules	125	95
Where, Who, When, What	121	101
Classification		
Classification	51	103
Problem-Solving Strategies and Applications		
Review	38	110
Concept Applications	43	111
Absurdities	125	118

This guide divides the actions exercises into two types: basic actions and actions used in the development of concepts in the other tracks. The items in the first column are basic actions. The rest are actions associated with other concepts.

Basic Actions	Other Actions
Beginning Actions	Actions—Prepositions
Actions—Parts of the Body	Actions—Spatial and Temporal Relations
Actions—Pictures	Actions—Plurals
Actions—Pronouns	Actions—And
Actions—Tense	Actions—Some, All, None
Tense—Pictures	Actions—Same/Different
Review Actions	Actions—Or
	Actions—First/Next and Before/After
	Actions—If-Then Rules

Basic actions exercises focus on specific actions such as "stand up" and "touch the floor." In these first actions exercises, the children perform simple actions and label these actions. In subsequent lessons, they learn to produce the full statements that describe the actions. As children progress through the basic actions exercises, they also learn the names of parts of the body and the uses of various pronouns. In addition, they also practice the words and statements for expressing differences in tense.

Most basic actions exercises require children to perform actions. But in Actions—Pictures exercises, children analyze pictures of people and animals performing actions. (The children learn to describe what the people and animals are doing, what they were doing, and what they will do.) Tense actions and tense pictures give children practice in describing events that happen in present time, past time, and future time.

Review exercises provide children with opportunities to practice what they have learned. These exercises occur on a regular basis throughout the lessons of the program.

Other actions exercises are also used in the development of concepts in other tracks. Most of these tracks contain both actions and pictures exercises. For example, the teaching of prepositional concepts involves actions exercises (Hold your hand *in front of* your nose) as well as pictures exercises (Show me the man *in front of* the house). The introduction of the concepts *some, all, none* involves actions exercises: Hold up *all* of your fingers; Hold up *some* of your fingers; Hold up *none* of your fingers. Part of the teaching of *and, or,* and *if-then* involves actions (You will touch your nose *or* stand up). Discussions of actions for *same/different, first/next and before/after, prepositions,* and *if-then* appear in the descriptions of various tracks. The basic actions exercises are discussed below. Other actions are discussed in different sections of this guide.

Beginning Actions
Lessons 1–22

Lesson 1: Actions—Following Directions

In the first actions exercises, the children respond on signal to your instructions. The children do not make full statements in these early exercises; rather, they learn to follow your directions and to then label their actions (for example, *Standing up, Sitting down*). Here is the first exercise from lesson 1.

EXERCISE 1 Actions — Following Directions

1. Get ready to do some actions. Watch my hand. Remember to wait for the signal.

   a. Everybody, stand up. (Signal. Children are to stand up.)
   Everybody, sit down. (Signal. Children are to sit down.) ● ◆
   b. (Repeat step a until all children respond to your signal.)

2. Let's do those actions again.

   a. Everybody, stand up. (Signal.)
   My turn. What are you doing?
   Standing up.
   Your turn. What are you doing? (Signal.)
   Standing up. ▲
   b. Everybody, sit down. (Signal.) What are you doing? (Signal.) *Sitting down.* ■

3. Let's do those actions some more.
(Repeat part 2 until all children can perform the actions and say what they are doing.)

CORRECTIONS

EXERCISE 1

● **Error**
(Children respond before you signal.)
Correction
1. You have to wait for my signal.
2. Let's try it again.
3. (Repeat part 1a until all children respond.)

◆ **Error**
(Children respond late.)
Correction
1. You have to do it as soon as I signal.
2. Let's try it again.
3. (Repeat part 1a until all children respond.)

▲ **Error**
(Children don't say *Standing up.*)
Correction
1. Standing up. Say it with me. (Signal. Respond with children.) *Standing up.*
2. Again. (Signal. Respond with children.) *Standing up.*
3. All by yourselves. Say it. (Signal. Do not respond with children.) *Standing up.*
4. (Have children sit down.)
5. (Repeat part 2a.)

■ **Error**
(Children don't say *Sitting down.*)
Correction
1. Sitting down. Say it with me. (Signal. Respond with children.) *Sitting down.*
2. Again. (Signal. Respond with children.) *Sitting down.*
3. All by yourselves. Say it. (Signal. Do not respond with children.) *Sitting down.*
4. (Have children stand up.)
5. (Repeat part 2b.)

Teaching Techniques

■ Keep your pacing brisk—say your lines quickly. A brisk pace will become even more important when the instructions become more complicated in later exercises.

■ Follow each step with a hand-drop signal to show the children **when** to respond. Make your signal precise. A good signal is essential to the pacing of the exercise.

■ In step a, after giving the instructions, pause only long enough for the children to stand or sit. Then immediately ask the question What are you doing? so the children realize they are to label the action they just performed.

■ Do not allow the children to lead you. If you do not require them to respond on signal, you will find yourself slowing the pace of the exercise, waiting for each child to perform the action before presenting the next instruction.

■ Make sure the children are responding on signal before leaving this exercise on the first day it is presented.

Corrections

Follow one or more of the corrections that appear in the corrections box of this exercise. If the children don't respond to your signal, select those children who are responding to your signal. Say, Watch them. They can do it. Repeat parts 1 and 2 with those children. Praise them for good performance. Then repeat the exercise with all the children until all respond to your signal.

EXERCISE 1 Actions — Statements

1. Get ready to do some actions. Watch my hand. Remember to wait for the signal.
  a. Everybody, stand up. (Signal. Wait.)
  Everybody, sit down. (Signal. Wait.)
  Everybody, touch your head. (Signal. Wait.)
  Put your hand down. (Signal. Wait.)
  Everybody, touch your head. (Signal. Wait.)
  Put your hand down. (Signal. Wait.)
  b. (Repeat step a until all children's responses are firm.)
  c. Everybody, stand up. (Signal. Wait.)
  What are you doing? (Signal.) *Standing up.*
  Everybody, sit down. (Signal. Wait.)
  What are you doing? (Signal.) *Sitting down.*
  Everybody, touch your head. (Signal. Wait.)
   What are you doing? (Signal.) *Touching my head.*
  Put your hand down. (Signal.)
  d. (Repeat step c until all children's responses are firm.)

2. Now let's try this.
  a. Everybody, touch your head. (Signal. Wait.)
  What are you doing? (Signal.) *Touching my head.* ●
  b. Watch me. (Touch your head. Keep touching it.) I'll say the whole thing. I am touching my head.
  c. Let's all say the whole thing. (Signal. Respond with children.) *I am touching my head.*
  d. Again. (Repeat the sentence with children until they can all say it with you.)
  e. Your turn. Say the whole thing. (Signal. Do not respond with children.) *I am touching my head.*
  f. Again. (Signal.) *I am touching my head.*
  g. (Repeat step e until all children's responses are firm.)
  Everybody, put your hand down. (Signal.)

3. Let's go a little faster.
  a. Everybody, touch your head. (Signal. Wait.)
  What are you doing? (Signal.) *Touching my head.*
  b. Say the whole thing. (Signal.) *I am touching my head.*
  (Repeat step b until all children can make the statement.)
  Put your hand down. (Signal.)

4. (Repeat part 3 until all children's responses are firm.)

Individual Turns
(Repeat part 3, calling on different children for each step.)

CORRECTIONS

EXERCISE 1

● **Error**
(Children say the entire sentence when you ask, *What are you doing?*)
Correction
1. Stop. My turn. Listen. What are you doing? Touching my head.
2. Your turn. What are you doing? (Signal.) *Touching my head.*
3. Now say the whole thing. (Signal.) *I am touching my head.*
4. (Repeat part 2a until all children answer correctly.)

Lesson 7: Actions—Statements

In this exercise, the children learn to "say the whole thing"—that is, to make a statement about what they are doing. In part 1, step a, the children perform actions without responding verbally. In step c, they label their actions. In part 2, they learn to make an actions statement.

Teaching Techniques

■ In part 1, make sure the children can perform all actions in step a, on signal, before you go to step c.

■ Make sure the children do not respond with a complete statement in step c. (They should say, *Standing up*, not *I am standing up*.)

■ In part 2, lead the children through the statement as many times as necessary so that at steps e and f they can make the statement without your help.

■ In part 2, make sure the children continue to do the action as they talk about it. They should keep touching their heads from the beginning of step c until the end of step f, for example. The words and statements may not have meaning unless the children are simultaneously **doing** the action they are talking about.

Corrections

■ Sometimes children say the entire statement in response to What are you doing? Follow the correction specified in the corrections box.

■ If a child does not follow your instructions correctly (for example, he doesn't touch his head), point to a child who has followed and say, Look, John is touching his head. If necessary, help the child by moving his hand to his head.

■ Some children may have trouble with the response *Touching my head*. If you say, Touch your head . . . What are you doing? and they respond, *Touching your head*, they have made a mistake. To correct this error, use a model, a lead, and a test.

1. Have another child model the response:
Linda's turn. Touch your head. (Wait.)
What are you doing? *Touching my head.*

2. Lead the children:
Let's all do it. Everybody, touch your head. (Wait.)
What are you doing? (Signal. Respond with the children.) *Touching my head.*
Repeat this step until all children can say, *Touching my head.*

3. Test the children:
All by yourselves. Touch your head. (Wait.)
What are you doing? (Signal. Do not respond with the children.) *Touching my head.*

EXERCISE 1 Actions — Statements

1. Get ready to do some actions.

   a. My turn. I can touch my ear. Watch.
(Touch your ear.) Your turn. Touch your ear.
(Signal. Children touch their ears.)
Good. Put your hand down. (Signal.)

   b. Everybody, stand up. (Signal. Wait.)
What are you doing? (Signal.) *Standing up.*
Everybody, sit down. (Signal. Wait.)
What are you doing? (Signal.) *Sitting down.*

   c. Everybody, touch your nose. (Signal. Wait.)
What are you doing? (Signal.) *Touching my nose.*
Say the whole thing. (Signal.)
I am touching my nose.
Put your hand down. (Signal.)

   d. Everybody, touch your head. (Signal. Wait.)
What are you doing? (Signal.)
Touching my head.
Say the whole thing. (Signal.)
I am touching my head.
Put your hand down. (Signal.)

   e. Everybody, touch your ear. (Signal. Wait.)
What are you doing? (Signal.) *Touching my ear.*
Say the whole thing. (Signal.)
I am touching my ear.
Put your hand down. (Signal.)

2. Let's do those actions again.
(Repeat part 1 until all children's responses are firm.)

Lesson 10: Actions—Statements

This exercise establishes a pattern that is followed in many of the actions exercises throughout the program.

Teaching Techniques

- Always make sure that the children are doing the action while they are answering the question What are you doing? They must still be doing it when they "say the whole thing."
- Present each instruction quickly, emphasizing the critical word or words: Touch your nose.
- Make each signal crisp and clear. It is essential that these action routines be done in a brisk manner.
- If the children do not perform the action, help them. For example, take a child's hand, and move it to his or her nose.

Corrections

If the children are hesitant to respond or are being led by some of the group, return to the beginning of the exercise. Give the instruction, and then give a very precise signal. Repeat until all the children are responding on signal. This is very important as the routines become more complicated—and more fun—as the children proceed through the program.

EXERCISE 1 Actions—Parts of the Body

[**Note:** If children make a mistake, demonstrate the correct action and have children do it. Then return to step a in part 2 and repeat the exercise.]

1. It's time for some actions.
   a. I can touch my chin. Watch. (Touch your chin.)
   b. What am I doing? (Signal.) *Touching your chin.*

2. Now it's your turn.
   a. Everybody, smile. (Signal. Wait.)
   What are you doing? (Signal.) *Smiling.*
   Say the whole thing. (Signal.) *I am smiling.*
   b. Everybody, touch your chin. (Signal. Wait.)
   What are you doing? (Signal.) *Touching my chin.*
   Say the whole thing. (Signal.) *I am touching my chin.*
   c. Everybody, touch your leg. (Signal. Wait.)
   What are you doing? (Signal.) *Touching my leg.*
   Say the whole thing. (Signal.) *I am touching my leg.*
   d. Everybody, touch your head. (Signal. Wait.)
   What are you doing? (Signal.) *Touching my head.*
   Say the whole thing. (Signal.) *I am touching my head.*
   e. Everybody, touch your hand. (Signal. Wait.)
   What are you doing? (Signal.) *Touching my hand.*
   Say the whole thing. (Signal.) *I am touching my hand.*
   f. Put your hand down. (Signal.)

3. Let's do that again.
   (Repeat part 2 until all children's responses are firm.)

Lesson 25: Actions—Parts of the Body

The children learn the names of parts of the body in many of the beginning actions exercises.

Teaching Techniques

- You identify your chin in part 1. Make sure the children are watching you.
- Make sure the children are pointing to the right body part as they respond to your instructions.
- Move quickly through these steps. The children like these routines. Correct any mistakes, and return to the beginning of the exercise.

For the exercises in this track, the children are introduced to pictures of actions they have been performing. Children describe actions illustrated in the presentation book.

The first exercises use action words that have already been practiced in the actions exercises. In later exercises, children respond to new action words and pronouns.

EXERCISE 5 Action Statements — Pictures

1. We're going to talk about some actions.
   a. (Point to the girl.) Everybody, what is this? (Touch.) *A girl.*
   Say the whole thing. (Touch.) *This is a girl.*
   b. Listen. What is this girl doing? (Touch.) *Standing.*
   c. Let's say the whole thing about what this girl is doing. (Touch. Respond with children.) *This girl is standing.*
   d. Again. (Touch.) *This girl is standing.*
   e. All by yourselves. Say the whole thing about what this girl is doing. (Touch.) *This girl is standing.*
   f. (Repeat steps a through e until all children's responses are firm.)

2. Now we'll talk about some more actions.
   a. (Point to the dog.) Everybody, what is this? (Touch.) *A dog.*
   Say the whole thing. (Touch.) *This is a dog.*
   b. What is this dog doing? (Touch.) *Sitting.*
   c. Say the whole thing about what this dog is doing. (Touch. Do not respond with children.) *This dog is sitting.*
   d. Again. (Touch.) *This dog is sitting.*
   e. (Repeat steps a through d until all children's responses are firm.)

3. Get ready to do some more.
   a. (Point to the cat.) Everybody, what is this? (Touch.) *A cat.*
   Say the whole thing. (Touch.) *This is a cat.*
   b. What is the cat doing? (Touch.) *Standing.*
   c. Say the whole thing about what this cat is doing. (Touch.) *This cat is standing.*
   d. Again. (Touch.) *This cat is standing.*
   e. (Repeat steps a through d until all children's responses are firm.)

4. Let's do those again.
   a. (Point to the girl.) Everybody, what is this? (Touch.) *A girl.*
   b. What is this girl doing? (Touch.) *Standing.*
   c. Say the whole thing about what this girl is doing. (Touch.) *This girl is standing.*

5. (Repeat parts 2 and 3 until all children's responses are firm.)

Individual Turns
(Repeat the exercise, calling on different children for each step.)

Lesson 17: Action Statements—Pictures

This exercise from lesson 17 is the first exercise in the Actions—Pictures track. In part 1, you lead the children by responding with them as they say the whole thing about what the girl is doing. The objective is for the children to be able to respond to parts 2, 3, and 4 in sequence, without mistakes, and without your help.

Teaching Techniques

■ Emphasize the words this dog when you say, Say the whole thing about what **this dog** is doing. This will alert the children to the difference between the action-statement form that begins with "This dog" and the identity-statement form "This is a dog."

■ Because this is a pictures exercise, you will use different signals than in the action routines. You will point to and touch the pictures as indicated.

■ Remember to keep touching the picture as long as the children are responding. When the children say, *Sitting*, your finger must be on the picture while they are saying the word. When the children say,

This dog is sitting, your finger should be on the picture while they are saying the entire statement.

■ Recognize that parts 2 and 3 follow the same pattern and that part 4 is a simpler version of that pattern.

Corrections

Some children may have trouble saying the whole thing about what the dog is **doing**. They may say, *This is a dog*. Stop them as soon as you hear them say, *This is . . .* Say, You have to tell me what **this dog** is doing. Then do a model-lead-and-test correction.

1. Model the response:
   My turn. This dog is sitting.

2. Lead the children:
   Let's say the whole thing about what **this dog** is doing. (Signal.) This dog is sitting.

3. Test the children:
   Your turn. Say the whole thing about what **this dog** is doing. (Signal.) *This dog is sitting.*

Repeat parts 2 and 3 until all children can say the statement.

EXERCISE 6 Action Statements — Pictures

1. Look at these pictures.
   Let's see which girl is eating.
   (Point to each picture, one at a time.) Is this
   girl eating? (Children are to answer *yes* or *no.*)

2. We're going to talk about each picture.
   a. (Point to a.) Is this girl eating? (Touch.) *Yes.*
      Say the whole thing. (Touch.) *This girl is
      eating.*
      Again. (Touch.) *This girl is eating.*
      (Repeat until all children's responses are
      firm.)
   b. (Point to b.) Is this girl eating? (Touch.) *No.*
      Say the whole thing. (Touch.) *This girl is
      not eating.*
      Again. (Touch.) *This girl is not eating.*
      (Repeat until all children's responses are
      firm.)
   c. (Point to c.) Is this girl eating? (Touch.) *No.*
      Say the whole thing. (Touch.) *This girl is
      not eating.*
      Again. (Touch.) *This girl is not eating.*
      (Repeat until all children's responses are
      firm.)

3. (Point to b.) We're going to talk some more
   about this girl.
   Is this girl walking? (Touch.) *No.*
   Is this girl sitting? (Touch.) *Yes.*
   Is this girl standing? (Touch.) *No.*
   What is this girl doing? (Touch.) *Sitting.*
   Say the whole thing. (Touch.) *This girl is
   sitting.*

4. Let's do those again.
   (Repeat part 3 until all children's responses
   are firm.)

Individual Turns
(Repeat parts 1 through 3, calling on different
children for each step.)

Lesson 24: Action Statements— Pictures

In this action statements—pictures exercise the children
make a *not* statement about actions. (They have already
learned in object identification exercises to make *not*
statements in the form *This is not a . . . .*) In action
exercises, the form is *This _____ is not _____.*

Teaching Techniques

■ Make sure that the children can answer *yes* or *no* to
   all the pictures in part 1.

■ Then proceed to part 2, moving quickly from one
   picture to the next. Recognize that each step in part
   2 follows the same pattern.

Corrections

If children have trouble in steps b and c in part 2, use
the model-lead-and-test correction.

1. **Model:** My turn. Say the whole thing about **this
   girl.** (Pause.) **This girl** is not eating.

2. **Lead:** Let's say the whole thing about **this girl.**
   (Signal.) *This girl is not eating.*

3. **Test:** All by yourselves. Say the whole thing about
   this girl. (Signal.) *This girl is not eating.*

4. **Retest:** Return to the beginning of part 2, and
   repeat until the children's responses are firm.

Actions—Pronouns Lessons 23–52

Because it is less confusing for children to use pronouns
in real-life situations than in book situations, all
pronoun exercises are first presented as part of the
daily actions exercises. Before lesson 23 the children
have already used the pronouns *I* and *my;* the other
pronouns are formally introduced according to the
following schedule:

I—you	Lesson 23	she—her	Lesson 37
you—your	Lesson 24	he—his	Lesson 38
I—my	Lesson 26	they—their	Lesson 45
we	Lesson 28	our	Lesson 51

After lesson 51, pronouns are integrated into actions
review exercises as well as into a variety of other
exercises.

34   Teacher's Guide

EXERCISE 1 **Actions — Pronouns**

1. Get ready to do some actions.
   a. Everybody, touch the floor. (Signal. Wait.) What are you doing? (Signal.) *Touching the floor.*
   Say the whole thing about what you are doing. (Signal.) *I am touching the floor.*
   b. Everybody, stand up. (Signal. Wait.) What are you doing? (Signal.) *Standing up.* Say the whole thing about what you are doing. (Signal.) *I am standing up.*
   c. Everybody, sit down. (Signal. Wait.) What are you doing? (Signal.) *Sitting down.* Say the whole thing about what you are doing. (Signal.) *I am sitting down.*
   d. (Repeat part 1 until all children can make the statements.)

2. We're going to talk about what I am doing.
   a. My turn. I am going to touch my ear. (Touch your ear, and keep touching it.) What am I doing? (Signal. Respond with children.) *Touching your ear.*
   Let's say the whole thing about what I am doing. (Signal. Respond with children.) *You are touching your ear.*
   Again. (Signal.) *You are touching your ear.* (Repeat with children until they all respond correctly.)

   b. All by yourselves. Say the whole thing about what I am doing. (Signal. Do not respond with children.) *You are touching your ear.*
   Again. (Signal.) *You are touching your ear.* (Repeat until all children can make the statement.)

3. Let's do some more.
   a. I'm going to touch the floor. (Touch the floor.) What am I doing? (Signal.) *Touching the floor.*
   Say the whole thing about what I am doing. (Signal.) *You are touching the floor.*
   Again. (Signal.) *You are touching the floor.* (Repeat until all children can make the statement.)
   b. I'm going to stand up. (Stand up.) What am I doing? (Signal.) *Standing up.*
   Say the whole thing about what I am doing. (Signal.) *You are standing up.*
   Again. (Signal.) *You are standing up.* (Repeat until all children can make the statement.)
   c. I'm going to sit down. (Sit down.) What am I doing? (Signal.) *Sitting down.*
   Say the whole thing about what I am doing. (Signal.) *You are sitting down.* (Repeat until all children can make the statement.)
   d. (Repeat part 3 until all children's responses are firm.)

Individual Turns
(Repeat part 3, calling on different children for each step.)

Lesson 24: Actions—Pronouns

In this exercise, from lesson 24, the children use the pronouns **I** and **you** to answer questions about what each child is doing and about what you are doing.

Teaching Techniques

■ If the children have done well in previous exercises in which you ask them, say the whole thing about what are you doing? and they reply *I am . . .* , then they will have little trouble with this exercise.

■ Stress the words **I, your,** and **you** in part 2. (Saying **you** with the children when referring to yourself does not actually confuse them.)

■ In part 2 repeat step a only until the children can make the statement at step b without your lead.

Corrections

If children respond *We are . . .* instead of *I am . . .* , let them know their response is reasonable, but say, When I ask about **you,** you say "I." (In later exercises the children will learn to respond with **we** when you ask, What are **we** doing? and to distinguish between instructions that call for the response *I am touching the floor* and those that call for *We are touching the floor*.)

Tense
Lessons 55–100

Tense changes in verbs present difficulties for many young children. Children must learn an entire set of language conventions to describe events in the past, present, and future. There are several ways to express past time, present time, and future time. Children must deal with irregular past-tense verbs (*I ate, I sat, I ran*) and must learn vocabulary for the past progressive. For the past progressive, irregular verbs are eliminated.

In the tense exercises, children not only learn the words and statements for expressing differences in tense but also are given demonstrations of the **concept** of tense. The children learn

1. present-tense actions and identity statements.
2. demonstrations of the concepts involved in changing tense—present to past and present to future.

3. the statement patterns for describing their own actions in past, present, and future tense, using both singular and plural forms.

4. to describe pictures using past-, present-, and future-tense statements.

5. a large number of verbs, both regular and irregular, in past-, present-, and future-tense forms.

⭐ **EXERCISE 4** **Actions—Tense** **(Demonstration)**

[**Note:** You will need a pencil and a cup.]

1. We're going to talk about a pencil and a cup.
   a. (Hold up the pencil.)
      What is this? (Signal.) *A pencil.*
      (Hold up the cup.)
      What is this? (Signal.) *A cup.*
   b. Watch. (Put the pencil in the cup and point to the pencil.)
      Where is the pencil? (Signal.) *In the cup.*
   c. Now watch. (Hold the pencil over the cup.)
      Listen. My turn. Is the pencil in the cup? No.
      Was the pencil in the cup? Yes.
   d. Listen. Your turn.
      Is the pencil in the cup? (Signal.) *No.*
      Was the pencil in the cup? (Signal.) *Yes.*
      Where was the pencil? (Signal.)
      In the cup. ●

2. Let's do it again.
   a. (Put the pencil in the cup.)
      Where is the pencil? (Signal.) *In the cup.*
      Say the whole thing. (Signal.) *The pencil is in the cup.*
   b. (Hold the pencil over the cup.)
      Listen. Where was the pencil? (Signal.)
      In the cup.
      Say the whole thing. (Signal.) *The pencil was in the cup.*

c. Again. Say the whole thing. (Signal.)
   The pencil was in the cup.
d. (Repeat steps a through c until all children's responses are firm.)

Individual Turns
(Repeat parts 1 and 2, calling on different children for each step.)

┌ **CORRECTIONS** ───────────────────────────┐
EXERCISE 4

● **Error**
(Children say *Over the cup.*)
Correction
1. The pencil is over the cup. I asked where was the pencil.
2. Let's do it again.
   (Repeat step d.)
└──┘

Lesson 55: Actions—Tense (Demonstration)

This exercise from lesson 55 demonstrates the difference in meaning between present tense and past tense. The only difference between the present-tense statement and the past-tense statement is the verbs **is** and **was**.

Teaching Techniques

■ Practice the presentation before presenting it to the children. Stress the words **is** and **was** whenever they occur.

■ Make sure that the children are firm in saying the statement at the end of part 2.

Corrections

In part 1, if the children don't respond correctly to the question Was the pencil in the cup? follow the correction in the corrections box.

In part 2, step b, if the children say, *The pencil is in the cup* instead of *The pencil was in the cup,* correct as follows:

1. Was in the cup. Say that. (Repeat until children's responses are firm.)

2. The pencil was in the cup. Say it with me. *The pencil was in the cup.* (Repeat until children's responses are firm.)

3. (Repeat part 2 of the exercise.)

★ **EXERCISE 4** Tense—Pictures

1. Look at these pictures. They show what a cat does.
   a. (Point to a.)
      This picture shows where the cat is first.
      The cat is on the floor.
      Say the whole thing.
      (Touch.) *The cat is on the floor.*
   b. (Point to b.)
      This picture shows where the cat is next.
      Where is it?
      (Touch.) *On the couch.*
      Yes, the cat is on the couch.
      Say the whole thing.
      (Touch.) *The cat is on the couch.*

2. Listen.
   • Where was the cat before it got on the couch?
     (Signal. Do not touch the picture.) *On the floor.*
   • Say the whole thing about where the cat was.
     (Signal.) *The cat was on the floor.*

3. (Repeat parts 1 and 2 until all children's responses are firm.)

Individual Turns
(Repeat the exercise, calling on different children for each step.)

┌─ **CORRECTIONS** ──────────
│ EXERCISE 4
│   (Correct all mistakes immediately; then
│   return to the beginning of the exercise.)
└────────────────────────────

Tense—Pictures
Lessons 59–98

Lesson 59: Tense

The first picture presentation in the tense track appears in lesson 59. The children practice using the present and past tense of verbs in a number of contexts. In this exercise they talk about a cat, telling what the cat did **first** and **next**.

Teaching Techniques

■ If the children do not give the response *On the floor* in part 2, acknowledge any other correct response (They might say, *In front of the couch*, for example.) Say, Yes, the cat is in front of the couch. Is it also on the floor? The children reply, *Yes,* and you say, Let's say that it is on the floor. Where is the cat in this picture? The exercise will be easier to teach if you use the responses in the exercise.

■ Part 2 is critical. Remember to stress the last three words of your instructions: Say the whole thing about where **the cat was.** These are the first words the children say in their response.

■ In part 2 do not point to the picture of the cat on the floor. You want the children to respond on the basis of the information the words and pictures give them. Do not give away the answer by pointing to the picture.

Corrections

If the children make an error at step a in part 2, stop them, and point to picture a. Then say, This is where the cat **was.** Where was the cat? Wait for the children to respond, and repeat the sequence from part 1.

If the children have trouble saying the past-tense statement, model the statement, lead them through it, and test them on it. Repeat this procedure until they all can say it. It is important that the children be able to say every statement in the tense exercises.

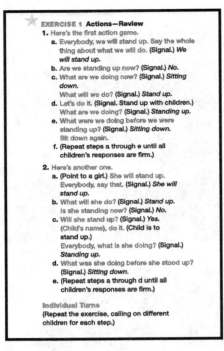

Lesson 121: Actions

Future tense is introduced in an actions exercise after the children have received plenty of practice in handling past- and present-tense statements. The exercise is similar to the one used to demonstrate the past tense.

Teaching Techniques

■ Make sure that the children are saying the word **will** correctly in step a before presenting the next steps.

■ Stress the word **will** in step a, part 1.

■ If the children are having trouble, stress the word **were** in step e, part 1.

■ Repeat part 1 until the children's responses are firm; then go to part 2.

Corrections

If children say the wrong verb in part 1, step a, follow the model-lead-and-test procedure to firm the children's responses.

To correct mistakes in step e, repeat that step, pausing before each *were* and stressing it. Then quickly tell the children the answer: You were sitting down. That's what you were doing. Repeat step e until the children's responses are firm, and then return to the beginning of part 1.

Concepts introduced in other tracks are incorporated into the daily actions exercises. These exercises provide a continual review of the concepts and of the statement patterns taught in the program.

Lesson 63: Actions

This exercise reviews the preposition **on** and the past-tense verb **was**.

Teaching Techniques

■ This exercise and all the review exercises in the actions track should be done briskly. You and the children should be moving along at a good pace. Your signals should be precise and easy to follow. Pause briefly at the end of each part.

■ The task should be fun for both you and the children. As you begin, challenge them to get all the way through the exercise without a mistake. Let them know when they have done particularly well—responded correctly, clearly, and at a normal speaking rate.

■ Correct any errors in a perfunctory manner, and then return to the beginning of the part in which the error occurred.

Descriptions of Objects

The purpose of the exercises in Descriptions of Objects is to help children learn the language concepts and sentence production required to answer the following kinds of questions:

1. What is the object's name? "A cup."
2. How do you make a statement that incorporates that name? "This is a cup."
3. What are some of the ways that you can describe the cup? "This cup is big. This cup is wet. This cup is yellow."
4. How can you compare two cups of different sizes? "This cup is big," "This cup is small," or "This cup is bigger than this cup."
5. How do you describe the presence of more than one cup? "These are cups. The cups are on the table. These cups are green."
6. What are the names of common objects in and out of the classroom?

The tracks discussed in this part of the guide all relate to the language used to describe these basic features of objects. Below is a list of these tracks and the range of lessons in which they occur:

Track	Lesson
Object Identification	1–8
Identity Statements	3–38
Common Objects	7–33
Missing Objects	23–34
Opposites	24–150
Plurals	51–70
Comparatives	131–146

The ability to respond to questions and to make statements is essential to using and understanding the language of instruction. The purpose of these tracks is to acquaint children with some of the language conventions associated with identifying and describing objects.

In the Object Identification and Identity Statement tracks, the children learn

1. to give the name of an object when asked, What is this? *A dog.*
2. to produce complete statements in response to the instruction Say the whole thing. *This is a dog.*
3. to respond to the question Is this a . . . by answering either *yes* or *no*.
4. to produce *not* statements for questions that are answered *no.* Is this a ball? *No.* Say the whole thing. *This is not a ball.*

The language skills taught in these tracks are used throughout the program.

In the Common Objects track, the children learn the names of common objects in the classrooms and learn to make statements about those objects. In the Missing Objects track, the children play a memory game. In later lessons they work with opposites, plurals, and comparatives.

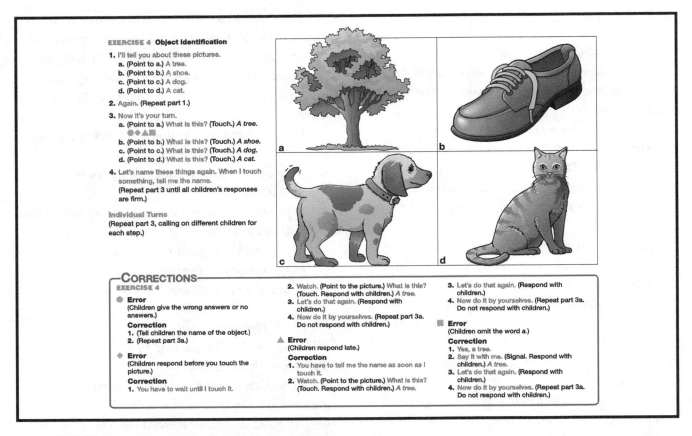

EXERCISE 4 Object Identification

1. I'll tell you about these pictures.
   a. (Point to a.) A tree.
   b. (Point to b.) A shoe.
   c. (Point to c.) A dog.
   d. (Point to d.) A cat.

2. **Again.** (Repeat part 1.)

3. Now it's your turn.
   a. (Point to a.) What is this? (Touch.) *A tree.*
      ●◆▲■
   b. (Point to b.) What is this? (Touch.) *A shoe.*
   c. (Point to c.) What is this? (Touch.) *A dog.*
   d. (Point to d.) What is this? (Touch.) *A cat.*

4. Let's name these things again. When I touch
   something, tell me the name.
   (Repeat part 3 until all children's responses
   are firm.)

Individual Turns
(Repeat part 3, calling on different children for
each step.)

CORRECTIONS
EXERCISE 4

● **Error**
(Children give the wrong answers or no
answers.)
Correction
1. (Tell children the name of the object.)
2. (Repeat part 3a.)

◆ **Error**
(Children respond before you touch the
picture.)
Correction
1. You have to wait until I touch it.

2. Watch. (Point to the picture.) What is this?
   (Touch. Respond with children.) *A tree.*
3. Let's do that again. (Respond with
   children.)
4. Now do it by yourselves. (Repeat part 3a.
   Do not respond with children.)

▲ **Error**
(Children respond late.)
Correction
1. You have to tell me the name as soon as I
   touch it.
2. Watch. (Point to the picture.) What is this?
   (Touch. Respond with children.) *A tree.*

3. Let's do that again. (Respond with
   children.)
4. Now do it by yourselves. (Repeat part 3a.
   Do not respond with children.)

■ **Error**
(Children omit the word a.)
Correction
1. Yes, a tree.
2. Say it with me. (Signal. Respond with
   children.) *A tree.*
3. Let's do that again. (Respond with
   children.)
4. Now do it by yourselves. (Repeat part 3a.
   Do not respond with children.)

Object Identification Lessons 1–8

Lesson 1: Object Identification

This exercise from lesson 1 requires the children to identify common objects by producing two-word responses. The children do not make full statements in this exercise.

Teaching Techniques

You will use the point-and-touch signal described on pages 22–23 to teach this exercise.

■ Be sure to point to the letter **before** asking the question.

■ Pause about one second after completing the question before touching the letter a.

■ When you touch letter a, look at the tree. If you look at the children, they may look at you, not at the tree.

■ As soon as the children begin to respond, quickly look at them to see who is (and who is not) responding.

■ Be sure to keep touching the picture for as long as the children are responding. When they finish a response, lift your finger, and point to the next picture.

■ Move rapidly from picture to picture. Ask the questions quickly, and avoid long pauses between the pictures. The children will stay on task better if your pacing is relatively fast.

Corrections

On any of the pictures the children may make these errors:

1. respond before you touch the picture
2. fail to respond immediately after you touch the picture
3. misidentify the object or fail to respond at all
4. omit the article

The corrections for each of these errors appear in the corrections box. Follow the steps in the correction you are using. Remember, an error has not been corrected until **all** the children can respond correctly. Also remember to return to the beginning of part 3 after correcting any error, and repeat all the questions in sequence. The children should be able to answer each of your questions correctly and on signal before you turn to the next page.

EXERCISE 7 **Identity Statements**

1. We're going to talk about a dog. When I touch it, you tell me about it.
   a. (Point to the dog.) Everybody, what is this? (Touch.) *A dog.*
      Yes, a dog.
   b. My turn. I can say the whole thing. This is a dog. Listen again. This is a dog. Say the whole thing with me. (Touch. Respond with children.) *This is a dog.*
   c. Again. (Touch. Respond with children.) *This is a dog.*
      (Repeat until all children can make the statement with you.)
   d. Your turn. All by yourselves. Say the whole thing. (Touch. Do not respond with children.) *This is a dog.*
      Again. (Touch. Do not respond with children.) *This is a dog.*

2. (Repeat part 1 until all children can make the statement.)

3. We're going to talk about a cat. When I touch it, you tell me about it.
   a. (Point to the cat.) Everybody, what is this? (Touch.) *A cat.*
      Yes, a cat.
   b. My turn. I can say the whole thing. This is a cat. Listen again. This is a cat. Say the whole thing with me. (Touch. Respond with children.) *This is a cat.*
   c. Again. (Touch. Respond with children.) *This is a cat.*
      (Repeat until all children are making the statement with you.)
   d. Your turn. All by yourselves. Say the whole thing. (Touch. Do not respond with children.) *This is a cat.*
   e. Again. (Touch. Do not respond with children.) *This is a cat.*

4. (Repeat part 3 until all children can make the statement.)

Individual Turns
(Call on different children to say the whole thing about each picture.)

In these exercises the children identify a pictured object with a two-word response and then make the whole identification statement about the object.

Lesson 5: Identity Statements

Teaching Techniques

In part 1, step b, you are modeling the kind of response called for by the instruction Say the whole thing.

■ Maintain a one-second pause after saying, I can say the whole thing and, Listen again.

■ Point to the picture as you say the whole thing, but do not touch it. You want the children to learn that your touch is the signal for them to respond.

Remember that in step b you are modeling the statement. You want the children to imitate your model, so it is important to say the statement at exactly the same rate you will say it in step c. The rate should be medium slow.

In step c, do the following:

■ Point to the picture before saying, Again.

■ Pause after your instruction for the same length of time you paused in step b. Then touch the picture to signal that the children are to respond.

■ Lead the children at the same rate you used to model the statement.

- Keep touching the picture as long as you and the children are making the statement. You want them to know that the entire statement is about that picture.
- Lead the children through the statement until they are firm at saying each word and saying the words at an appropriate rate. You may need to lead them several times—as many as seven times for some lower-performing children. Praise the children who are saying it correctly, and encourage those who are trying hard.

In step d the children say the statement by themselves. Do not respond with them.

- If children are not responding correctly after seven trials, move to another exercise, and return to the identification exercise later.
- Point before saying, Your turn . . . .
- Maintain your one-second pause.
- Keep touching the picture as the children respond.
- Make sure they make an acceptable response. An acceptable response is one in which the children begin responding the instant you touch the picture and produce all the words in the statement at the rate you established in steps b and c.

Corrections

The children may leave out words or confuse the order of words in a statement.

If you hear mistakes at step c when you are leading the children, model the response for them. Say the statement several times so that the children operate from your lead and not from the lead of other children. Then repeat the step.

If the children are having a great deal of trouble producing the statement, you may be saying it too quickly. Return to step b, and say it more slowly; you will be providing the children with a new model of how to say it. Maintain the same slower pacing when doing steps c and d. In subsequent lessons gradually increase the rate at which you model and lead the responses. Your goal is to get the children to respond at a normal speaking rate.

If children persistently omit one or more words from the statement, stress these words when you say the statements with them. You can also have the children pat their knees or clap their hands together as you emphasize those words.

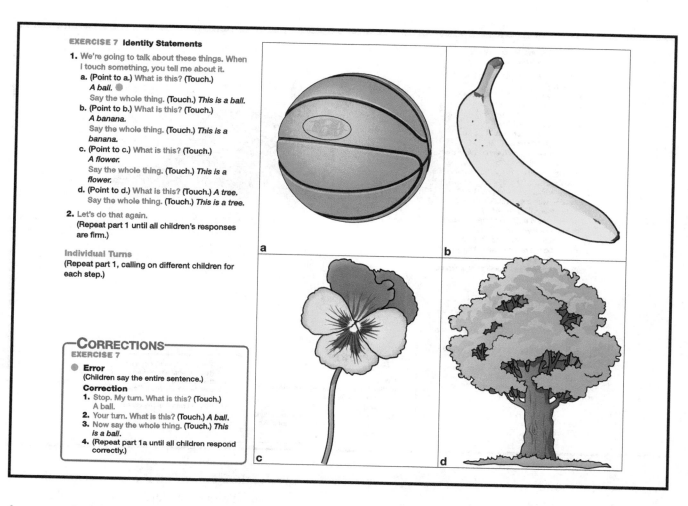

EXERCISE 7 Identity Statements

1. We're going to talk about these things. When I touch something, you tell me about it.
   a. (Point to a.) What is this? (Touch.)
      A ball. ⬤
      Say the whole thing. (Touch.) *This is a ball.*
   b. (Point to b.) What is this? (Touch.)
      A banana.
      Say the whole thing. (Touch.) *This is a banana.*
   c. (Point to c.) What is this? (Touch.)
      A flower.
      Say the whole thing. (Touch.) *This is a flower.*
   d. (Point to d.) What is this? (Touch.) *A tree.*
      Say the whole thing. (Touch.) *This is a tree.*

2. Let's do that again.
   (Repeat part 1 until all children's responses are firm.)

Individual Turns
(Repeat part 1, calling on different children for each step.)

CORRECTIONS
EXERCISE 7

⬤ **Error**
(Children say the entire sentence.)

Correction
1. Stop. My turn. What is this? (Touch.) A ball.
2. Your turn. What is this? (Touch.) *A ball.*
3. Now say the whole thing. (Touch.) *This is a ball.*
4. (Repeat part 1a until all children respond correctly.)

Lesson 8: Identity Statements

In lesson 8 the children again identify objects by giving two-word responses and then saying the whole thing. The difference between this exercise and the preceding ones is that you do not model or lead any of the children's responses.

Teaching Techniques

■ Make sure the children make the responses indicated in the exercise. These conventions of responding will be used throughout the program. The question What is this? is answered with a word or phrase. Say the whole thing indicates that the children make an entire statement.

■ The children are to respond at a normal or near-normal speaking rate—not in a drone or with a shout.

■ In teaching the exercise, it is important to establish a predictable and rhythmic pace for going from one picture to another. When the children make mistakes, you must slow down and correct them,

but when they are performing well, you can move rapidly.

Corrections

If the children make the whole statement in response to the question What is this? follow the correction specified in the corrections box. Don't wait for them to complete the statement. As soon as you hear them say, *This,* stop them. Then model the response called for. Say, A ball. What is this? A ball. Your turn. What is this?

If children don't say the whole statement in step 3 of the correction, again stop them, and model the kind of response called for: Stop. My turn to say the whole thing. Listen. This is a ball. Then say, Your turn. Say the whole thing. Then repeat the correction.

If children produce statement responses in a drone, stop them, and show them the rate at which you want them to say the statement: My turn to say the whole thing. This is a ball. Your turn to say the whole thing.

EXERCISE 6 Yes-and-No Questions
with "Not" Statements

1. We're going to talk about this picture. (Point to the cat.)
   a. Everybody, what is this? (Touch.) *A cat.*
      Is this a car? (Touch.) *No.*
      Is this a cat? (Touch.) *Yes.*
      Is this a dog? (Touch.) *No.*
      Is this a fish? (Touch.) *No.*
   b. What is this? (Touch.) *A cat.*
      Say the whole thing. (Touch.) *This is a cat.*
   c. Is this a fish? (Touch.) *No.*
      I can say the whole thing. This is not a fish.
      Listen again. This is not a fish.
   d. Say the whole thing with me. (Touch.
      Respond with children.) *This is not a fish.*
      Again. (Touch.) *This is not a fish.*
      (Repeat step d until all children can make the statement with you.)
   e. All by yourselves. Say the whole thing.
      (Touch. Do not respond with children.) *This is not a fish.* ●
      (Repeat steps d and e until all children can make the statement.)

2. Let's do that again.
   a. What is this? (Touch.) *A cat.*
      Say the whole thing. (Touch.) *This is a cat.*
   b. Is this a fish? (Touch.) *No.*
      Say the whole thing. (Touch.) *This is not a fish.*
   c. (Repeat part 2 until all children can make both statements.)

Individual Turns
(Repeat part 2, calling on different children for each step.)

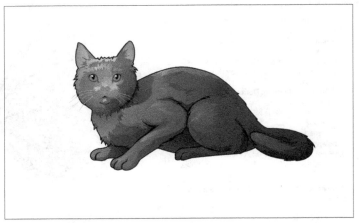

CORRECTIONS
EXERCISE 6

● **Error**
(Children don't say the entire sentence or don't say it correctly.)
Correction
1. Listen. Not a fish. Say it with me. (Signal.)
   (Repeat until all children say *not a fish* with you.)

2. This is . . . (signal) *not a fish.*
   (Repeat until all children say *not a fish* by themselves.)
3. Say the whole thing. (Touch.) *This is not a fish.*
4. (Repeat part 1 of the exercise.)

Lesson 21: Yes-or-No Questions and "Not" Statements

This is one of the exercises that demonstrates the relationship between **yes** and positive identity statements and between **no** and negative identity statements. In this exercise the children will produce a **not** statement.

Teaching Techniques

■ Pacing is important in presenting this exercise. Ask the questions quickly to keep the children's attention on the picture. But if they start making mistakes, slow the rate at which you ask questions.

■ Be precise with your pointing and touching signals. Hold your finger about an inch from the picture as you ask a question. Then pause, lift your finger, and touch the picture. After the children respond, quickly lift your finger, and point for the next question.

■ When modeling the statement in part 1, step c, pause after the word **is,** and stress the word **not.** This is (pause) not a fish. The pause shows the children that the first part of the statement is the same as the familiar This is a cat. Stressing the word **not** allows the children to focus on placing the word **not** appropriately in the sentence.

■ In part 2 the children pair the response **a cat** with the statement *This is a cat* and pair the response **no** with the statement *This is not a fish*. The objective of this exercise is to have the children say the positive and negative statements in sequence and without error.

Corrections

In part 1, expect some children to have trouble saying the statement with you. If they do, follow the correction in the box.

If the children have trouble in step 3 of the correction, have them pause after **is** and stress **not.** Do this by holding up your finger after they say **is** and by touching the picture again for the last part of the statement.

If the children make mistakes in part 2, firm their responses on both the answer **no** and the statement. Then present steps a and b in sequence until the children are firm on both steps.

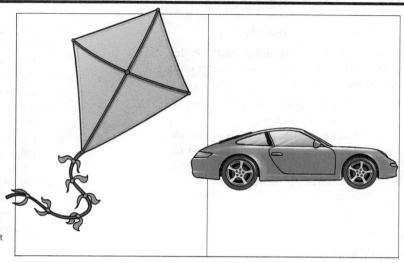

EXERCISE 6 Yes-or-No Questions
with "Not" Statements

1. (Point to the kite.) Let's look at this picture.
   a. Everybody, what is this? (Touch.) *A kite.*
      Say the whole thing. (Touch.) *This is a kite.*
   b. Get ready to answer some questions.
      Is this a ball? (Touch.) *No.*
      Is this a bottle? (Touch.) *No.*
      Is this a kite? (Touch.) *Yes.*
      Is this a cat? (Touch.) *No.*
      (Repeat until all children's responses are
      firm.)
   c. One more time. Is this a kite? (Touch.) *Yes.*
      Say the whole thing. (Touch.) *This is a kite.*
      Is this a car? (Touch.) *No.*
      Say the whole thing. (Touch.) *This is not a
      car.* ●

2. (Point to the car.) Now look at this picture.
   a. Everybody, what is this? (Touch.) *A car.*
      Say the whole thing. (Touch.) *This is a car.*
   b. Get ready to answer some questions about
      this picture.
      Is this a kite? (Touch.) *No.*
      Is this a car? (Touch.) *Yes.*
      Is this a bottle? (Touch.) *No.*
      (Repeat until all children's responses are
      firm.)
   c. One more time. Is this a car? (Touch.) *Yes.*
      Say the whole thing. (Touch.) *This is a car.*
      Is this a kite? (Touch.) *No.*
      Say the whole thing. (Touch.) *This is not a
      kite.*

CORRECTIONS
EXERCISE 6

● **Error**
(Children say *This is a car.*)
Correction
1. We're talking about a kite.
2. Is this a car? (Touch.) *No.*
3. Let's say the whole thing. (Touch.
   Respond with children.) *This is not a car.*

4. All by yourselves. (Touch. Do not respond
   with children.) *This is not a car.*
   (Repeat until all children's responses are
   firm.)
5. (Return to part 1 of the exercise.)

Lesson 23: Yes-or-No Questions with "Not" Statements

In this exercise the children say the *not* statement without the teacher first modeling and leading it.

Corrections

Sometimes children respond as follows at the end of step c in part 1. When you ask, Is this a car? they answer, *This is a kite*. What they are saying is correct, but repeating that statement will not give them the practice they need in making the *not* statement. Follow the correction specified in the exercise. Say, I asked about a car. So you have to tell me about the car. The idea is that they must learn that if you ask about a **car,** they must use the word **car** in their answer. This response convention is used throughout the program.

Remember to repeat part 1 after correcting the mistake. The children are considered firm on the exercise when they respond without error to the sequence of steps in each exercise.

Common Objects
Lessons 7–33

In the common objects exercises, children learn to identify and make statements about the various objects they see and use in the classroom. The children learn

1. The vocabulary of the classroom so that they can follow instructions.

2. That everything around them has a name. When they have this understanding, they will know how to ask questions about things they don't know about.

3. That the language in the exercises can be used to describe what they see and use in the classroom.

EXERCISE 5 Common Objects

[**Note:** You will find a pointer helpful in this exercise. Touch the objects in any order that is convenient for you.]

1. I'm going to touch some objects in this room and tell you what they are.
   a. (Touch a chalkboard.) This is a chalkboard. What is this? (Touch.) *A chalkboard.*
   b. (Touch a door.) This is a door. What is this? (Touch.) *A door.*
   c. (Touch a window.) This is a window. What is this? (Touch.) *A window.*

2. Tell me what I touch.
   a. (Touch a chalkboard.) Everybody, what is this? (Signal.) *A chalkboard.*
   b. (Touch a door.) Everybody, what is this? (Signal.) *A door.*
   c. (Touch a window.) Everybody, what is this? (Signal.) *A window.*

3. (Repeat part 2 until all children's responses are firm.)

4. Let's do those objects again.
   a. (Touch a chalkboard.) Everybody, what is this? (Signal.) *A chalkboard.*
      Say the whole thing. (Signal.) *This is a chalkboard.*
   b. (Repeat step a until all children's responses are firm.)
   c. (Touch a door.) Everybody, what is this? (Signal.) *A door.*
      Say the whole thing. (Signal.) *This is a door.*
   d. (Touch a window.) Everybody, what is this? (Signal.) *A window.*
      Say the whole thing. (Signal.) *This is a window.*

5. (Repeat part 4 until all children's responses are firm.)

Individual Turns
(Repeat part 4, calling on different children for each step.)

Lesson 7: Common Objects

Teaching Techniques

The first time you introduce an object, you should actually touch it, as the exercise specifies. Walking around your classroom to touch objects may be somewhat disruptive in your classroom, so after you have introduced an object and the children are familiar with its name, you can point to it with your finger, or a yardstick, or a pointer. But if the children are having trouble with a name, continue to actually touch the object.

You may vary the order of touching objects according to their location in your classroom. Initially, you might prefer to walk the children around the classroom to show them the objects. If this routine presents management problems, drop it.

Corrections

If children don't know the name of an object,
1. tell them the name of the object: A chalkboard,

touch the chalkboard, and repeat the question. If children are mispronouncing the word, have them repeat the correct pronunciation until firm.

2. use a model-lead-and-test correction:
   My turn. Chalk (pause) board.
   Say it with me. (Signal.) *Chalk* (pause) *board.*
   (Repeat until all children's responses are firm.)
   All by yourselves. (Signal.) *Chalkboard.*

   Repeat this procedure until all children can pronounce the word correctly. Then point to the chalkboard, and present the original question.

Missing Objects
Lessons 23–34

The track is designed to teach children about missing objects so they can do a variety of workbook exercises that involve missing objects.

EXERCISE 3 Missing Objects

[Note: You will need a ruler and a piece of chalk for this exercise.]

1. You're going to learn about missing objects.
   a. (Show ruler and chalk.) I have a ruler. I have chalk. Do I have a ruler? (Signal.) *Yes.*
      Point to the ruler. (Signal. Children point.)
      Do I have chalk? (Signal.) *Yes.*
      Point to the chalk. (Signal. Children point.)
   b. Let's do it again.
      (Repeat step a until all children's responses are firm.)

2. I'm going to try to fool you. I'm going to take away one of these objects. See if you can tell which object is missing.
   a. Everybody, close your eyes. Don't look.
      (Remove the ruler. Show chalk.) Everybody, open your eyes. What object do I have now? (Signal.) *Chalk.*
      Do I have the ruler anymore? (Signal.) *No.*
   b. I don't have the ruler anymore, so the ruler is missing. Which object is missing? (Signal.) *The ruler.*
      Yes, the ruler is missing.

3. Let's do it again. (Show the ruler and chalk.)
   a. Do I have the ruler? (Signal.) *Yes.*
      Do I have chalk? (Signal.) *Yes.*
   b. Close your eyes. (Remove chalk.) Open your eyes. What object do I have now? (Signal.) *The ruler.*
      Do I still have the chalk? (Signal.) *No.*
   c. I don't have the chalk anymore, so the chalk is missing. Which object is missing? (Signal.) *The chalk.*

4. Once more. (Show ruler and chalk.) I have the ruler and I have chalk.
   a. Close your eyes. (Remove chalk.) Open your eyes.
   b. Which object do I still have? (Signal.) *The ruler.*
      Which object is missing? (Signal.) *The chalk.*

5. (Repeat exercise until all children's responses are firm.)

Lesson 23: Missing Objects

Teaching Techniques

If some children have trouble keeping their eyes closed when you are removing an object, tell children to Put your head down. Children are to maintain a facedown position so they can't see which object you remove.

If children have trouble identifying the missing object, ask these questions:

Do I have a ruler?

Do I have chalk?

I don't have _____. So which object is missing?

Opposites
Lessons 24–150

In *Language for Learning*, certain descriptive words that have clearly defined opposites are treated as polar concepts—the objects described are either **long** or **short, wet** or **dry, big** or **little.** Later, in the comparative track, the children build on this fundamental language structure to make judgments about things that are, for example, **bigger** or **taller** than other things.

In the first exercises in the opposites track, the children learn only one of the two opposite words that can be used to describe an object. For example, they do not learn **long** and **short** in the same lesson. Instead, instruction begins with **long** and **not long.** After they have practiced using **long** and **not long** for several lessons, they are introduced to a word that means the same as **not long: short.**

The presentation for each opposite concept is similar, with similar demonstrations and statements:

1. The children learn the word for one member of an opposite pair and demonstrate the meaning of that word.

2. The children generate statements using opposites: for example, *the woman is tall; the woman is not tall.* *

3. After the children are firm on the first member of the opposite pair, they learn the opposite word.**

In addition, the children practice a variety of opposite pairs in different exercises that run to the end of the program.

A list of the opposites the children learn is shown below, along with the number of the lesson where each opposite first appears.

Opposites*	Lesson
full/not full	24
wet/not wet	30
big/not big	37
long/not long	50
old/not old	58

Opposites**	Lesson	Opposites**	Lesson
full/empty	41	awake/asleep	130
big/small	43	late/early	132
wet/dry	45	fast/slow	134
long/short	53	sick/well	136
tall/short	91	hard/soft	141
old/young	60	daytime/nighttime	143
hot/cold	123	clean/dirty	145
sad/happy	125	lose/win	147
open/close	128	quiet/noisy	149

1. Look at these jars.
   (Point to a.) What is this?
   (Signal.) *A jar.*
   (Point to b.) What is this?
   (Signal.) *A jar.*

2. We'll talk some more about these jars.
   a. (Point to a.) This jar is full.
   b. (Point to b.) This jar is not full.
   • Your turn. (Point to each jar and ask,)
     Is this jar full? (Children are to answer *yes*
     or *no*.) ●

3. Now we're going to say the whole thing.
   a. (Point to a.) Is this jar full? (Touch.) *Yes.*
      My turn to say the whole thing. This jar is
      full.
   b. (Point to b.) Is this jar full? (Touch.) *No.*
      Say the whole thing. (Signal.) *This jar is not
      full.*
   c. (Point to c.) Is this jar full? (Touch.) *No.*
      Say the whole thing. (Signal.) *This jar is not
      full.*
   d. (Point to d.) Is this jar full? (Touch.) *Yes.*
      Say the whole thing. (Signal.) *This jar is full.*

4. Let's do that again.
   (Repeat part 3 until all children's responses
   are firm.)

Individual Turns
(Repeat part 3, calling on different children for
each step.)

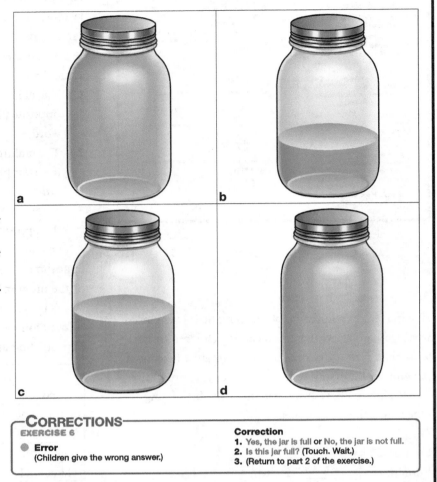

a   b

c   d

CORRECTIONS

EXERCISE 6

● **Error**
(Children give the wrong answer.)

Correction
1. Yes, the jar is full or No, the jar is not full.
2. Is this jar full? (Touch. Wait.)
3. (Return to part 2 of the exercise.)

Lesson 24: Opposites—Full/Not Full

The first concept, **full** and **not full,** is introduced in
lesson 24. The first exercise (not shown here) is a
demonstration in which you fill an empty glass with
water to show the difference between a "not full" glass
and a full glass. Be sure that you have the real objects
necessary for the demonstration. Your demonstration
should go very quickly—the quicker the better.

The exercise from lesson 25 (shown above) is
the picture presentation of the same concept. In this
exercise, the children use the word **full** in statements.

Teaching Techniques

▪ In part 2, point quickly to each jar in turn, and
ask, Is this jar full?

▪ In part 3, allow the children to examine each
picture as you ask, Is this jar full? Then pause a
second, and touch the picture. After the children
answer *yes* or *no,* quickly give the instruction Say
the whole thing.

Corrections

If the children were firm on preceding exercises, they
should have no problems with this exercise. If they have
trouble with the not statement, use the model-lead-and-
test correction.

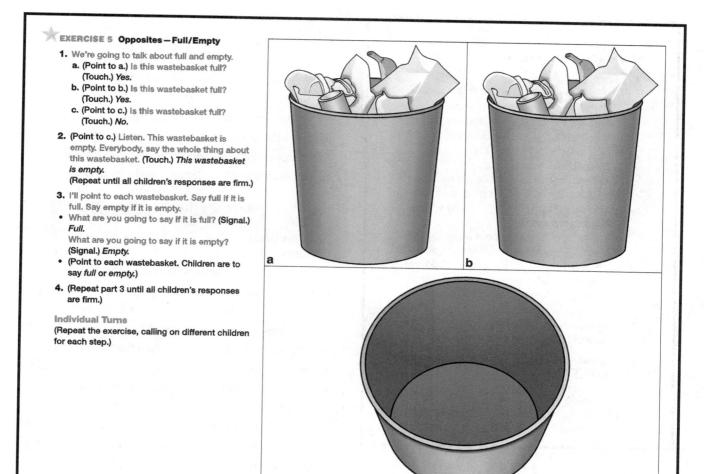

★ **EXERCISE 5** **Opposites—Full/Empty**

1. We're going to talk about full and empty.
   a. (Point to a.) Is this wastebasket full? (Touch.) *Yes.*
   b. (Point to b.) Is this wastebasket full? (Touch.) *Yes.*
   c. (Point to c.) Is this wastebasket full? (Touch.) *No.*

2. (Point to c.) Listen. This wastebasket is empty. Everybody, say the whole thing about this wastebasket. (Touch.) *This wastebasket is empty.*
   (Repeat until all children's responses are firm.)

3. I'll point to each wastebasket. Say full if it is full. Say empty if it is empty.
   • What are you going to say if it is full? (Signal.) *Full.*
   What are you going to say if it is empty? (Signal.) *Empty.*
   • (Point to each wastebasket. Children are to say *full* or *empty*.)

4. (Repeat part 3 until all children's responses are firm.)

Individual Turns
(Repeat the exercise, calling on different children for each step.)

After six opposite words have been introduced and practiced, the children are introduced to the first opposite pair exercise in lesson 41. This exercise shows them that an object that is not full can be called **empty**.

Lesson 41: Opposites—Full/Empty

Teaching Techniques

■ When a new opposite word is introduced, give the children thinking time for steps that involve that word. In part 2 the children "say the whole thing" about an empty wastebasket.

■ When presenting part 3, ask the two questions, and then point to one of the wastebaskets. Pause before touching it. This will help the children think about what they must say; without the pause, they may make mistakes.

Corrections

If children make the wrong statement in part 2, let them know that what they say is reasonable but that you want to hear about **empty.**

If the children give wrong answers in part 3 (*This wastebasket is not full*), pause for a longer period before touching each wastebasket. If they still make mistakes, repeat the entire exercise.

EXERCISE 5 Opposites

1. Listen.
   a. If something is not old, it is the opposite of old, so it's young. If something is not wet, it's the opposite of wet, so it's dry. If something is not big, it's the opposite of big. So what do you know about it? (Signal.) *It's small.*
   b. Listen. I'm thinking about a television set that is not big. It's the opposite of big. So what do you know about it? (Pause. Signal.) *It's small.*
   c. Listen. I'm thinking about frogs that are not young. They're the opposite of young. So what do you know about them? (Pause. Signal.) *They're old.*
   d. Listen. I'm thinking about windows that are not dry. They're the opposite of dry. So what do you know about them? (Pause. Signal.) *They're wet.*

2. (Repeat part 1 until all children's responses are firm.)

Individual Turns
(Repeat the exercise, calling on different children for each step.)

Lesson 101: Opposites

This is the review exercise—a series of questions without pictures using opposite words to describe a variety of objects, animals, and people.

Teaching Techniques

Treat this exercise as a game. You are thinking of something, and the children have to figure out what it is. Read each statement forcefully, emphasizing the words at the end (not big, not young, not dry). Ask the question quickly. Hold up your hand, pause, and signal. The children should respond together.

Corrections

If the children say, *Small* instead of *It's small,* say, That's right. It's small. Let's all say that. (Signal.) *It's small.* Then repeat step a until all children are saying, *It's small.*

If the children give a wrong answer or no answer, tell them the correct answer (It's small) immediately. Then repeat the step. Repeat the exercise until they can answer each question correctly and on signal.

Plurals
Lessons 51–70

Children must understand the difference between references to singulars and plurals if they are to follow instructions accurately and fully understand demonstrations. The only difference between the two instructions Circle the word and Circle the words is the ending **-s** on **words.** Some children have not learned to attend to the noun endings and possible verb variations that indicate whether the speaker is referring to one object or more than one.

Plurals are introduced with actions exercises. After the children have learned to distinguish between the words used to describe singular and plural actions, pictures exercises are introduced.

In the plurals track, the children learn

1. to attend to the endings of matched singular and plural nouns: *Touch your ears. Touch your ear.*

2. to make action statements that contain singular and plural words: *I am touching my knees. I am touching my knee.*

3. to learn singular and plural nouns and statements that describe pictures of objects: *You are touching the dogs. These are dogs. These are not dogs. These dogs are sleeping. These dogs are not sleeping.*

★ **EXERCISE 2** **Actions—Plurals**

[Note: Pronounce ssss as zzzz.]

1. My turn. I'll tell you if I hold up my hand or my hands.
   (Hold up one hand.) Hand.
   (Hold up the other hand.) Hand.
   (Hold up both hands.) Handssss.
   (Hold up both hands.) Handssss.

2. Your turn. Tell me if I hold up my hand or my hands.
   a. (Hold up both hands.) Tell me. (Signal.) *Hands.*
   b. (Hold up one hand.) Tell me. (Signal.) *Hand.*
   c. (Hold up both hands.) Tell me. (Signal.) *Hands.*
   d. (Hold up one hand.) Tell me. (Signal.) *Hand.*
   e. (Hold up the other hand.) Tell me. (Signal.) *Hand.*

3. (Repeat part 2 until all children's responses are firm.)

Individual Turns
(Repeat part 2, calling on different children for each step.)

Lesson 52: Actions—Plurals

This introductory exercise gives children practice in hearing and saying singular and plural nouns. Children who aren't used to saying the **ssss** or **zzzz** sound at the end of words often have difficulty hearing the difference between singular and plural nouns in instructions.

Teaching Techniques

■ Exaggerate the **zzzz** sound in **hands.**

■ Make sure that the children are saying the final **zzzz** sound in the word **hands.**

■ Have the children repeat the exercise several times. The more practice they receive at the beginning of the track, the less they will need in subsequent exercises.

Corrections

If some children answer the first question in part 2 incorrectly, follow the model-lead-and-test correction.

1. Model the response: Handssss.

Exaggerate the final sound of the word.

2. Lead the children: Say it with me. *Handssss.* Repeat until firm.

3. Test the children: Repeat the instruction.

4. Call on individual children. Praise those who are saying the endings correctly.

EXERCISE 2 Actions—Plurals

1. Watch what I do. Let's see if I can fool you. Listen carefully.
   a. Hold up your hands. (Pause. Signal. Wait.) Put your hands down.
   b. Hold up your hand. (Pause. Signal. Wait.) Put your hand down.
   c. Hold up your hand. (Pause. Signal. Wait.) Put your hand down.
   d. Hold up your hands. (Pause. Signal. Wait.) Put your hands down.

2. (Repeat part 1 until all children's responses are firm.)

3. Watch me again. See if I can fool you. Listen carefully.
   a. Touch your ears. (Pause. Signal. Wait.) Put your hands down.
   b. Touch your ears. (Pause. Signal. Wait.) Put your hands down.
   c. Touch your ear. (Pause. Signal. Wait.) Put your hand down.

4. (Repeat part 3 until all children's responses are firm.)

Individual Turns
(Repeat parts 1 and 3, calling on different children for each step.)

Lesson 56: Actions—Plurals

In this exercise in the plurals track, the children respond to instructions that require them to hold up or touch one or more than one thing. Their actions will be correct only if they can hear the difference between singular and plural nouns.

Teaching Techniques

Notice that the exercise calls for you to pause between the instruction and the signal calling for the children's responses. Your pause must be long enough to give the children time to think about their responses. Pausing will reduce the number of errors. As the children become more proficient at distinguishing between plural and singular endings, you can reduce the length of the pause.

Corrections

Expect some children to have trouble with this exercise. If you think some of your children are going to make the mistake of touching only one ear when you say, Touch your ears, follow this pre-correction procedure before step b.

1. Listen. Earssss. Say it. (Signal.) *Earssss.*
2. Ear. Say it. (Signal.) *Ear.*
3. Touch your ears. Do it. (Signal. Wait.)
4. Touch your ear. Do it. (Signal. Wait.) Then start step b.

If they make the mistake of touching both ears when you instruct them to touch your ear, say:

1. Ear. Just one ear. Touch your ear.
2. Now touch your earssss. (Signal.)

If children make more than one or two errors on the exercise, repeat the entire exercise. (A good idea is to go on to another exercise in the lesson, then return to this exercise before the end of the lesson.)

If the children are weak in these plurals exercises, make sure that they practice plurals at other times of the day. For example, when they are leaving for recess, present an exercise to each child: Hold up your handssss or Hold up your hand. Present the instructions in random order, sometimes giving the singular instruction two or three times in a row. Don't alternate singular and plural instructions from child to child, or some children will learn that every **other** time you ask the questions, both hands should be held up.

EXERCISE 6 Plurals

1. Tell me if I touch carsssss.
   a. (Touch one car.) Am I touching carsssss? (Signal.) *No.*
   b. (Touch two cars at the same time.) Am I touching carsssss? (Signal.) *Yes.*
   c. (Touch three cars at the same time.) Am I touching carsssss? (Signal.) *Yes.*
   d. (Touch one car.) Am I touching carsssss? (Signal.) *No.*
   e. (Touch two cars at the same time.) Am I touching carsssss? (Signal.) *Yes.*
   f. (Repeat part 1 until all children's responses are firm.)

2. Watch.
   a. (Touch one car.) Am I touching carsssss? (Signal.) *No.*
   What am I touching? (Signal.) *A car.*
   Say the whole thing about what I am doing. (Signal.) *You are touching a car.*
   b. (Touch two cars.) Am I touching carsssss? (Signal.) *Yes.*
   What am I touching? (Signal.) *Cars.*
   Say the whole thing about what I am doing. (Signal.) *You are touching cars.*
   c. (Repeat part 2 until all children's responses are firm.)

Individual Turns
(Repeat the exercise, calling on different children for each step.)

CORRECTIONS
EXERCISE 6

[**Note:** Use this correction for all wrong responses.]

Correction
1. (Tell the correct answer.)
2. (Have children say it with you.)
3. (Repeat the exercise from the beginning.)

Lesson 54: Plurals

Teaching Techniques

In the first pictures exercise, you touch either a car or cars. The children are to respond by saying *car* or *cars*. At the end of part 2 you touch some cars and ask, Am I touching cars? After the children answer, you say, Say the whole thing about what I am doing. The children are to say, *You are touching cars.* They should have no trouble with this statement, because they practiced a similar statement, *I am touching my ears,* in the preceding exercise.

⭐ **EXERCISE 7** **Plurals**

Look at this picture.

a. (Point to a boy.) What is this? (Touch.)
   A boy.
   Say the whole thing. (Touch.) *This is a boy.*

b. (Point to all the boys at the same time.)
   What are these? (Touch.) *Boys.*
   Say the whole thing. (Touch.) *These are boys.*

c. (Point to a girl.) What is this? (Touch.)
   A girl.
   Say the whole thing. (Touch.) *This is a girl.*

d. (Point to all the girls at the same time.)
   What are these? (Touch.) *Girls.*
   Say the whole thing. (Touch.) *These are girls.*

Individual Turns
(Repeat the exercise, calling on different children for each step.)

Lesson 62: Plurals

In this exercise the children are introduced to the plural statement form "These are boys."

Teaching Techniques

Expect some children to have trouble saying the statement *These are boys.* Typical mistakes include adding words and omitting the word **are,** and saying **or** instead of **are.** You can help reduce errors by emphasizing the word **are** in step b and by saying the statement in a rhythm that has three distinct beats: These (pause) are (pause) boys.

Corrections

If children have trouble making the statement, repeat the model-lead-and-test procedure until the children's responses are firm. With some groups you may have to provide many repetitions before the children are saying the statement appropriately.

⭐ **EXERCISE 7** **Comparatives**

1. Look at the picture.
- (Point to a.) What is this? (Touch.) *A ball.*
- (Point to b, c, and d.) What are these? (Touch.) *Apples.*
  Say the whole thing. (Signal.) *These are apples.*
- (Point to e.) What is this? (Touch.) *A cup.*
- (Point to a and e.) Which is bigger, the ball or the cup? (Touch.) *The ball.*
  Yes, the ball is bigger than the cup. Say that. (Signal.) *The ball is bigger than the cup.*
- (Repeat part 1 until all children's responses are firm.)

2. One of these apples is bigger than the ball. I'll point to the apples. You tell me which apple is bigger than the ball.
- (Point to b.) Everybody, is this apple bigger than the ball? (Touch.) *Yes.*
- (Point to c.) Everybody, is this apple bigger than the ball? (Touch.) *No.*
- (Point to d.) Everybody, is this apple bigger than the ball? (Touch.) *No.*
- (Repeat part 2 until all children's responses are firm.)

3. (Point to b.) Listen. This apple is bigger than the ball. Say that. (Touch.) *This apple is bigger than the ball.*
(Repeat part 3 until all children can make the statement.)

Individual Turns
(Repeat parts 2 and 3, calling on different children for each step.)

Comparatives
Lessons 131–146

Comparatives are an extension of opposites. In the opposites track, the children describe pairs of objects, for example, **big** and **small.** In the comparatives track the children learn to compare two objects by using the words **bigger** or **smaller,** for example. They learn the conventional way of stating the comparison: *This object is bigger (smaller) than that object.*

The objectives of the comparatives track are

1. to teach comparative forms of familiar opposites: **bigger, smaller, taller, shorter, longer.**

2. to teach the statements for comparing two objects: *The rock is bigger than the box; the box is smaller than the rock.*

Lesson 131: Comparatives

Comparatives are introduced beginning in lesson 131. In the exercise shown above, the children compare objects and then "say the whole thing," using the word **bigger.**

Teaching Techniques

■ Remember to stress the word **bigger** in the statement.

Corrections

The children may have trouble saying the statement. Use this procedure to help them:

1. Listen. Bigger than. Everybody, say it with me. *Bigger than.* Again. All by yourselves. (**Signal.**)

2. Listen. The rock is bigger than the box. Say the whole thing. (**Signal.**)

3. If the children have trouble, lead them on the whole statement. Then test them by having them say it by themselves.

Information and Background Knowledge

The objectives of the information and background knowledge tracks are

1. to make sure that the children have the basic information that relates to school routines, their names, the names of their teacher and school, the days of the week, and the months and seasons of the year.

2. to teach the children the relationship between objects and their parts, the names of parts of the body, and the names and functions of the parts of some common objects—a table, a toothbrush, an umbrella, and so on.

3. to teach the children to identify the materials of which common objects are made.

4. to present background knowledge about some occupations, natural phenomena, and locations.

Basic Information
Lessons 1–135

The tracks that relate to basic school information are

Names (of children)	Lessons 1–23
Information (about school and community)	Lessons 1–34
Days of the Week	Lessons 35–74
Months	Lessons 92–115
Seasons	Lessons 128–138

In these tracks, the children learn

1. the first names and whole names of each child in the group and the difference between their first name and whole name.

2. the name of their teacher, the name of their school, and the name of the city or county where they live.

3. the number and names of the days of the week, the months of the year, and the seasons of the year.

4. the meanings of **today** and **tomorrow.**

5. some characteristics of the four seasons.

EXERCISE 2 Information—Names

1. We're going to learn names.
   a. (Ask one child to stand up. Say child's whole name—John Jones, for example.) _____ _____, stand up. Your first name is _____. What's your first name? (Child responds.)
   b. Everybody, what's his/her first name? (Signal. Children say the child's first name.) Good. _____, sit down.

2. (Repeat part 1 with several children.)

Lesson 1: Information—Names

Teaching Techniques

This is a simple but important exercise. If some children have trouble learning names, do only three or four names the first day and the rest in the second lesson. By the fourth day, every child should know the name of every other child in a group of six to eight children.

Corrections

1. If children give their whole name when asked for their first name, say, You're telling me your whole name. I want just your first name.
Listen. Your first name is _____. What's your first name?

2. When the child responds correctly, go to step b.
If children are not firm on first names, they will have trouble with the exercises in which they use whole names. If they need help, try to present games during other parts of the day that incorporate children's names. These games require a child to call on another by name. Praise children who correctly use the names of other children in these games.

EXERCISE 3 Information—School

1. Here are some things you should know.
   a. Listen. I'm your teacher. My name is _____. Everybody, what's your teacher's name? (Pause. Signal. Children say the teacher's name.)
   b. (Repeat step a until all children's responses are firm.)
   c. Listen. You go to _____ School. Everybody, what's the name of the school you go to? (Pause. Signal. Children say the name of their school.)
   d. (Repeat step c until all children's responses are firm.)

2. Let's try those questions again.
   a. Everybody, what's your teacher's name? (Pause. Signal.)
   b. What's the name of the school you go to? (Pause. Signal.)

3. (Repeat part 2 until all children's responses are firm.)

Individual Turns
(Repeat part 2, calling on different children for each step.)

Lesson 1: Information—School

Teaching Techniques

- If there is more than one adult in the classroom, teach the children the name of each adult.
- Be sure the children are looking at you as you start the exercise. After you ask the question in part 1, pause for about a second, and then use a hand-drop signal. Let the children know they are to respond to your signal. Repeat step a until all children answer correctly and on signal. Follow the same procedure for step c.
- In later lessons the children are asked, What city do you live in? If the children live in a rural area, substitute What county do you live in?

Corrections

If the children confuse the two answers in part 2,
1. help them by pointing to yourself and to the classroom.
2. pause between the two questions, and stress the words **school** and **teacher.**
When the children are able to answer the two questions correctly, stop pointing.

EXERCISE 2 Information — Days of the Week

1. Let's do the days of the week.

   a. There are seven days in a week. How many days are there in a week? **(Signal.)** *Seven.*

   b. My turn. I'll say the days of the week. Listen: Sunday, Monday, Tuesday, Wednesday, Thursday, Friday, Saturday. I said the days of the week.

   c. Listen: Sunday, Monday. Say those days with me. **(Signal. Respond with children.)** *Sunday, Monday.*

   d. Again. **(Signal. Respond with children.)** *Sunday, Monday.*

2. All by yourselves.

   a. Say those days of the week. **(Signal. Do not respond with children.)** *Sunday, Monday.*

   b. (Repeat step a until all children can say the days.)
Good. Next time we'll say the days of the week again.

Lesson 35: Information—Days of the Week

The children learn to name the days of the week over a seven-lesson period. In this first exercise, they listen to the sequence of days and learn to say the first two days in order.

Teaching Techniques

■ In step a you ask how many days there are in a week. Make sure all the children answer.

■ In step b you say the names of all the days in the week. Make it sound interesting by giving a definite cadence to the sequence. For example, you might clap three times to establish a cadence, then say, Sunday, Monday, Tuesday (pause), Wednesday, Thursday, Friday (pause), Saturday. The more distinctive you make the names of some of the days, the easier it will be for the children to learn the sequence.

■ For some children, this may be new learning. Do not try to teach more than what each exercise requires. But if the children already know some of the days, you can do these exercises quickly.

■ It is important for the children to say new days by the end of the exercise in which they are introduced. This will require increasing practice as more days are included. If too many repetitions seem necessary, give the children additional practice at other times of the school day.

EXERCISE 2 Information—Days, Months

1. We're going to talk about days and months.
   a. Everybody, how many days are in a week? (Signal.) *Seven.*
      Name them. (Signal.) *Sunday, Monday, Tuesday, Wednesday, Thursday, Friday, Saturday.*
   b. Listen. There are twelve months in a year. Listen again. There are twelve months in a year. How many months in a year? (Signal.) *Twelve.* ●
      Say the whole thing. (Signal.) *There are twelve months in a year.*
   c. (Repeat step b until all children's responses are firm.)

2. I'll name some months of the year.
   a. Listen to the first three months: January, February, March. Everybody, say the first three months of the year with me. (Signal. Respond with children.) *January, February, March.*
      (Repeat step a until all children's responses are firm.)
   b. All by yourselves. Say the first three months of the year. (Signal.) *January, February, March.*
      (Repeat step b until all children's responses are firm.)
   c. Listen. How many months are in a year? (Signal.) *Twelve.*
      Say the whole thing. (Signal.) *There are twelve months in a year.*
   d. Everybody, say the first three months of the year. (Signal.) *January, February, March.*
      (Repeat step d until all children's responses are firm.)

CORRECTIONS
EXERCISE 2

● **Error**
(Children say *Seven.*)
Correction
1. You're telling how many days there are in a week. I want to know how many months in a year.

2. How many months in a year? (Signal.) *Twelve.*
3. How many days in a week? (Signal.) *Seven.*
4. Again.
   (Return to the beginning of step a.)

Lesson 92: Information—Days, Months

Teaching Techniques

■ On different days, the order Days—Months is reversed. It is important to let the children know that they must listen carefully to the beginning question of each exercise. To prevent errors, stress the critical words in the question about **days** of the week and the question about **months** of the year.

■ As with the days of the week, recite the months so that you give some of them a distinctive personality.

Corrections

Follow the corrections in the box if children confuse the numbers of days and months.

If the children have not learned the days of the week when they start work on months, they may become confused. If your children start making mistakes, firm them on the days of the week and the answer to the question How many days are in a week? Then ask how many months in a year.

If children continue to have trouble, change the form of the instructions:

1. Say, Listen. Tell me how many **days** are in a **week**. Then say, Get ready. Pause three seconds to allow children time to think. Then signal. The children respond, *Seven.*

2. Say, Listen. Tell me how many **months** are in a **year**. (Signal.) Then say, Get ready. Pause three seconds. The children respond, *Twelve.*

With this procedure you are providing the children with thinking time and correcting these information mistakes immediately.

⭐ **EXERCISE 7 Seasons**

1. These pictures show the same place at different seasons of the year.
   - (Point to a.) This picture shows winter. Snow is on the ground. Snow is on the mountain. There are no plants in the field. Look at the tree. There are no leaves on the tree.
   - (Point to b.) This picture shows spring. Spring comes after winter. Say that. (Signal.) *Spring comes after winter.* See the little plants coming up in the field? The tree has little leaves. There is still snow on the mountain.
   - (Point to c.) This picture shows summer. Summer comes after spring. Say that. (Signal.) *Summer comes after spring.* Look at the plants in the field. They're big. The tree has leaves. There is no snow on the mountain.
   - (Point to d.) This picture shows fall. Fall comes after summer. Say that. (Signal.) *Fall comes after summer.* The farmer has cut the plants in the field. The leaves on the tree are falling. There is some snow on the mountain.

2. My turn. I'll touch the picture and say the seasons. Here I go.
   - (Point to a.) Winter. (Point to b.) Spring. (Point to c.) Summer. (Point to d.) Fall.
   - Say the seasons with me. (Touch each picture in order, and say the seasons with children.)
   - Your turn. All by yourselves. Say the seasons. (Touch each picture in order. Children are to say the seasons.)
   - (Repeat part 2 until all children can say the four seasons.)

a | b
c | d

Seasons
Lessons 128–138

Lesson 128: Seasons

Teaching Techniques

In part 1 point to and quickly describe each of the pictures. Don't drag out the descriptions. Make sure the children are looking at the picture you're talking about.

Part 2 contains the critical steps. When presenting part 2, say the names so that each has a personality. For example: Wiinter, **spring** (pause), sssummer, **fall.**

Corrections

Correct mistakes in part 2 by modeling and leading (using the cadence you have worked out).

Lesson 129: Seasons

In the next seasons exercise, beginning at lesson 129 (not shown here), the children are introduced to the rule *There are four seasons in a year.*

Emphasize the words **four** and **seasons** so that the children will understand that this rule differs from the ones for days of the week and months of the year.

After you review the names of the seasons, ask the children about each of the four pictures in turn, calling on individuals to make observations about the picture and discuss the characteristics of the seasons in their own communities. Having the entire group repeat each child's good observations will help children remember the characteristics of the different seasons.

Some children have trouble with the idea that an object can be described in more than one way. These children seem to think that, after the object has been labeled, nothing more can be said about it. Yet that object is an example of hundreds of different concepts. A pencil is an example not only of **pencil** but also of something yellow, a writing instrument, a hard object, something with a point, and so on.

One primary purpose of the part/whole track is to show the children that we can do a double-take with objects. We can identify the whole object; we can also name the parts of the object. This double-take idea is further amplified as children do exercises with opposites, colors, shapes, and classification in which attention is called to some other property of an object after it has been identified.

In the first exercise of the part/whole track, the children learn the parts of the head through actions exercises. Next they identify parts of the head in a picture. Starting in lesson 29 they learn the parts of a common object—a table. Below is a list of the objects presented, with the number of the lesson where each first appears.

head	28	body	86
table	30	house	91
pencil	32	shoe	96
toothbrush	35	nail	101
elephant	41	pin	102
wagon	44	chair	106
tree	49	cabinet	111
umbrella	59	hammer	111
car	65	saw	112
flower	68	broom	117
coat	79	belt	117

The part/whole track provides the children with practice in organizing information. The important thing is that children learn **how** to learn new names, remember them so they aren't confused with other names, and use them. Because some of the vocabulary taught in the track is used in other tracks, it is important for children to learn the vocabulary used in the part/whole exercises.

Lesson 25: Actions—Parts of the Body

EXERCISE 1 Actions—Parts of the Body

[**Note:** If children make a mistake, demonstrate the correct action and have children do it. Then return to step a in part 2 and repeat the exercise.]

1. It's time for some actions.
   a. I can touch my chin. Watch. **(Touch your chin.)**
   b. What am I doing? **(Signal.)** *Touching your chin.*

2. Now it's your turn.
   a. Everybody, smile. **(Signal. Wait.)**
      What are you doing? **(Signal.)** *Smiling.*
      Say the whole thing. **(Signal.)** *I am smiling.*
   b. Everybody, touch your chin. **(Signal. Wait.)**
      What are you doing? **(Signal.)** *Touching my chin.*
      Say the whole thing. **(Signal.)** *I am touching my chin.*
   c. Everybody, touch your leg. **(Signal. Wait.)**
      What are you doing? **(Signal.)** *Touching my leg.*
      Say the whole thing. **(Signal.)** *I am touching my leg.*
   d. Everybody, touch your head. **(Signal. Wait.)**
      What are you doing? **(Signal.)** *Touching my head.*
      Say the whole thing. **(Signal.)** *I am touching my head.*
   e. Everybody, touch your hand. **(Signal. Wait.)**
      What are you doing? **(Signal.)** *Touching my hand.*
      Say the whole thing. **(Signal.)** *I am touching my hand.*
   f. Put your hand down. **(Signal.)**

3. Let's do that again.
   (Repeat part 2 until all children's responses are firm.)

Lesson 25: Actions—Parts of the Body

Parts of the body are introduced in an actions exercise.

Teaching Techniques

If children already know the names of the parts of the body introduced in part 1, move quickly to part 2. Some children, however, will need to be taught carefully from the beginning. You may have to repeat some of the part names more often than is indicated in the exercise.

Corrections

If the children have trouble with any step, either show or tell them the answer. Then repeat the step. Then repeat the entire exercise. Be sure to present some individual turns.

EXERCISE 8 Part/Whole—Table

1. Today we're going to learn the parts of a table. (Circle the top table with your finger.)
   a. Everybody, what is this? (Touch.) *A table.*
   b. Say the whole thing. (Touch.) *This is a table.*

2. (Point to the bottom table.) Here's a table that is in parts. I'll name the parts.
   a. (Point to the legs.) These are legs. (Point to the top.) This is a top.
   b. (Point to the legs.) What are these parts called? (Touch.) *Legs.* (Point to the top.) What is this part called? (Touch.) *A top.*
   c. (Repeat steps a and b until all children's responses are firm.)

3. (Point to the top table.) Let's see if you can name the parts of this table.
   a. (Point to the legs.) What are these parts called? (Touch.) *Legs.*
   b. (Point to the top.) What is this part called? (Touch.) *A top.*
   c. (Circle the table.) Legs and a top are parts of a . . . (touch) *table.* Yes. What's the whole object called? (Touch.) *A table.*
   d. (Repeat part 3 until all children's responses are firm.)

4. (Point to a table in the room.)
   a. Now let's name the parts of this table. (Children are to name each part as you point to it.)
   b. What's the whole object called? (Touch.) *A table.*

5. (Ask different children:) What do you do on a table? (Praise reasonable responses.)

Lesson 30: Part/Whole

Most part/whole objects are introduced by means of an "exploded" picture. This is the first such exercise. It gives the children a vivid demonstration of the separate parts of a table. Later in the exercise the children work from a picture of the whole object. They see that the part names they have learned can also be used in describing the whole object.

Teaching Techniques

■ Do part 1 quickly. In part 2 point to the parts, and name them in an important-sounding way. Emphasize the words **legs** and **top.**

■ Repeat part 3 until the children can respond correctly. Make sure that your signals are precise so that the children will know what part you are asking about and will be able to respond together.

■ In part 3 the children must identify the whole object. This step is important. The children must be able to give the object's name as well as the names of its parts.

■ Looking at and naming the parts of a real table demonstrates that the part names can be used with real objects.

■ Move at a brisk pace through this exercise but, where necessary, allow the children some thinking time. At the end of each part/whole exercise, the children should be able to respond perfectly to each step.

Corrections

If the children have trouble, tell them the answer. Then return to the beginning of the exercise, and present the remaining steps in sequence.

Review Exercises

All of the objects introduced in the track are presented again in review exercises. If the children are firm on the part/whole exercises, they will be able to do the review exercises quickly. You will find that they enjoy "rattling off" these answers. The question What do we usually do with a . . . ? appears at the end of most of the review exercises. Call on different children to answer this question. The question is designed to start the children thinking about how different objects are used.

If the children forget the name of a part, give them the correct answer. Then repeat the exercise.

Materials
Lessons 62–148

In the materials track, children learn to identify common materials. This information is important because it shows children a new aspect of objects and, in this way, helps them to build their fund of information. For some of the exercises, you will need to bring objects made of different materials to the lesson.

A list of the materials the children learn is shown below, along with the number of the lesson where each material first appears.

Material	Lesson
cloth	62
paper	62
plastic	62
leather	66
glass	72
wood	75
metal	83
concrete	89
rubber	106
paper	121
brick	126

Lesson 62: Materials

For this exercise you will need a cloth shirt with plastic buttons.

This exercise is particularly important because it helps the children differentiate between the name of a part and the material that part is made of.

Teaching Techniques

■ Let the children feel the parts of the shirt you use in the task before you begin.

■ Present the steps in part 2 until the children are firm. You should do these steps very quickly.

Corrections

If the children name a material when they should name a part, correct them by saying, You told me the material of this part. But I asked for the name of this part. What's the name of this part? If children fail to respond correctly, tell them the answer, and repeat the question.

★ EXERCISE 5 Materials

[Note: You will need a cloth shirt with plastic buttons.]

1. We're going to talk about this shirt.
   a. (Hold up a shirt, or point to a child's shirt. Point to the collar.) A shirt has a collar.
   b. (Point to the front.) A shirt has a front.
   c. (Point to a button.) A shirt has buttons.

2. Now it's your turn.
   a. (Hold up the shirt, or point to it.) Everybody, get ready to name each part of this shirt. (Touch the collar.) What is the name of this part? (Signal.) *The collar.*
   b. (Touch the front.) What is the name of this part? (Signal.) *The front.*
   c. (Touch a button.) What is the name of this part? (Signal.) *A button.*

3. Listen carefully.
   a. (Touch a button.) What part am I touching? (Signal.) *A button.*
      Listen. The button is made of plastic. What's it made of? (Signal.) *Plastic.*
   b. (Touch the front.) What part am I touching? (Signal.) *The front.*
      Listen. The front is made of cloth. What's it made of? (Signal.) *Cloth.*
   c. And what's the button made of? (Signal.) *Plastic.*
      And what's the front made of? (Signal.) *Cloth.*

★EXERCISE 4 Materials—Demonstration

[Note: Prepare three circles, each approximately 5 inches in diameter. One is to be made of plastic, one of paper, and one of cloth. You should have a lapboard or a large book on which to put the three circles.]

1. We're going to learn what things are made of.
   a. (Point to the circles.) Everybody, what are these? (Signal.) *Circles.*
   Yes, circles.
   b. (Point to the paper circle.) This circle is made of paper. What is it made of? (Touch.) *Paper.*
   c. (Point to the cloth circle.) This circle is made of cloth. What is it made of? (Touch.) *Cloth.*
   d. (Point to the plastic circle.) This circle is made of plastic. What is it made of? (Touch.) *Plastic.*
   e. (Repeat part 1 until all children's responses are firm.)

2. I'll point to each circle. You tell me what it is made of.
   a. (Point to the plastic circle.) What is this circle made of? (Signal.) *Plastic.*
   (Point to the cloth circle.) What is this circle made of? (Signal.) *Cloth.*
   (Point to the paper circle.) What is this circle made of? (Signal.) *Paper.*
   b. Let's do those again.
   (Repeat step a until all children's responses are firm.)

Individual Turns
(Repeat part 2, calling on different children.)

Lesson 62: Materials—Demonstration

For this exercise, you will need to prepare three circles, each the same size and ideally the same color. One should be plastic, one paper, and the third cloth.

Teaching Techniques

■ Display the t hree circles on a flat surface. Point to each circle, and identify the material.

■ If the children have trouble in part 1, repeat part 1, presenting the circles in a different order.

■ You may want to have the children hold or touch each of the circles.

Corrections

If the children make mistakes in part 2, tell them the correct answer, and then repeat part 2.

★ **EXERCISE 6** **Materials**

1. Look at the objects in this picture. All of these objects are made of plastic. When I touch each object, you name it. **(Point to each object. The children are to respond *a bag, a bottle, a comb, a tablecloth, a wastebasket, a bucket*.)**

2. Take a good look at the objects and see how many you can remember. **(Let children look at the book for about ten seconds.)**

3. **(Remove the picture from children's view.)** See if you can name at least three things in the picture that are made of plastic. **(Call on three or four children to name different objects made of plastic. Each child should name at least three things.)**

4. Can anyone think of anything else made of plastic? **(Accept all reasonable answers.)**

Lesson 70: Materials

This is an exercise that children find enjoyable. They first identify the objects made of a specific material in a picture. Then they see how many objects they can name when the picture is not visible. Similar exercises are used with all the materials taught in the program.

Teaching Techniques

- Present this exercise as a challenge. After the children have identified the objects, put down the book and say, Now you get to see how many things you can remember.

- Praise the children who name at least three objects. Act astonished if a child can name five or all six objects.

Corrections

- If a child is unable to name three objects, say, I'll let you look at the picture again, but then you'll have to name **four** things in the picture. Allow the child to examine the picture for about five seconds. Then remove it, and ask the child to name four objects that are made of plastic.

- If the child names objects that are made of plastic but are not in the picture, say, That is made of plastic, but it isn't in the picture. Name only objects that are in the picture.

- If most of the children do not do well, show the entire group the picture again. Call on several children to tell what they see. Then say, I'll come back to this picture later. I'll see who can remember at least three objects in this picture. Do the next exercise in the lesson, and then return to the materials exercise. Ask the question again, without showing the picture. Praise children who can name three objects from the picture.

1. Think of things that are made of wood. Let's see who can name at least three things made of wood.
   (Call on different children to name objects made of wood. Each child should name at least three things.)

2. Think of things that are made of cloth. Let's see who can name at least three things made of cloth.
   (Call on different children to name objects made of cloth. Each child should name at least three things.)

3. Think of things that are made of plastic. Let's see who can name at least three things made of plastic.
   (Call on different children to name objects made of plastic. Each child should name at least three things.)

Lesson 75: Materials

This review exercise appears frequently throughout the program. It requires the children to name objects made of different materials.

Teaching Techniques

Call on two or three children for each part. Move quickly from one child to another. Praise all appropriate responses.

Corrections

■ If children name only objects that have appeared in picture exercises, say, You can name **any** object that is made of wood. I'll name some—fence, tent stake, boat, window frame, pencil shaft, cane, chair, table. Your turn. When I call on you, name at least three things made of wood.

■ If children name only those objects that somebody has just named, say, Yes, those are good objects. But see if you can name some new ones.

Praise children who name novel things. However, do not accept questionable items. For example, if a child says that a boot is made of wood, say, I guess somebody could make a boot of wood, but I don't think that boots are made of wood. Name something else that is made of wood.

Common Information Lessons 71–150

In the common information track, the children learn about a variety of occupations, places, and natural phenomena. Information is presented through both pictures and simple explanations. New words are introduced in the track every two to seven lessons. Every word is reviewed at least five times. These are the words introduced and the lesson where each word first appears.

dentist	71	jungle	116
dental assistant	71	driver	117
city	71	passenger	118
farm	73	beach	120
store	74	ship	121
sky	75	thermometer	121
sun	75	grocery store	122
clouds	75	painter	125
firefighter	79	airport	131
teacher	80	pilot	132
earth	83	fire station	133
forest	85	lumberjack	134
ocean	87	library	136
orchard	94	librarian	137
carpenter	95	restaurant	138
doctor	107	customer	140
nurse	108	waiter	141
patient	109	engine	145
medicine	112	mechanic	146
police officer	113	garage	147

★ **EXERCISE 3** Common Information

. Get ready for some new information.
  a. Listen. A dentist is a person who fixes teeth. What do we call a person who fixes teeth? (Signal.) *A dentist.*
     Say the whole thing about a dentist. (Signal.) *A dentist is a person who fixes teeth.*
  b. Again. (Signal.) *A dentist is a person who fixes teeth.*
     (Repeat step b until all children can make the statement.)
  c. Listen. A dental assistant is a person who helps a dentist. What do we call a person who helps a dentist? (Signal.) *A dental assistant.*
     Say the whole thing about a dental assistant. (Signal.) *A dental assistant is a person who helps a dentist.*
  d. Again (Signal.) *A dental assistant is a person who helps a dentist.*
     (Repeat step d until all children can make the statement.)
  e. Listen. A city is a place with lots of people. What do we call a place with lots of people? (Signal.) *A city.*
     Say the whole thing about a city. (Signal.) *A city is a place with lots of people.*
  f. Again. (Signal.) *A city is a place with lots of people.*
     (Repeat step f until all children can make the statement.)

2. Let's see how much information you remember.
  a. What do we call a person who fixes teeth? (Signal.) *A dentist.*
     Say the whole thing about a dentist. (Signal.) *A dentist is a person who fixes teeth.*
  b. What do we call a place with lots of people? (Signal.) *A city.*
     Say the whole thing about a city. (Signal.) *A city is a place with lots of people.*
  c. (Repeat part 2 until all children's responses are firm.)

3. I'll turn the page, and we'll see a picture of a dentist.
   (Turn the page quickly.)

EXERCISE 3 Common Information (cont.)

4. (Show the picture to children. Ask different children the following questions.)
   • What do you see in this picture?
   • What else do you see in this picture?
   • How do you think the man in the chair feels?
   • What do you think the dentist will do?
   (Praise all good responses.)

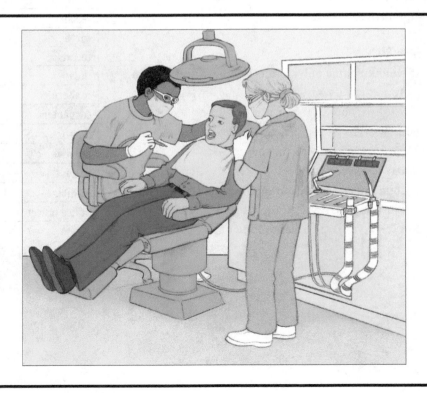

Lesson 71: Common Information

The first exercise presents information about the concepts **dentist** and **city**. The information is presented on the first page of the exercise. The children then identify a picture of a dentist on the next page.

Teaching Techniques

The children may have to practice the new statements introduced. After they have learned to make the statements, return to the beginning of the exercise, and present the entire routine briskly. Do not accept slow, draggy responses.

- Don't leave a common information exercise until you are sure that every child can answer correctly at every step. Every statement taught in the track is reviewed many times in subsequent lessons. If you leave an exercise before the children's responses are firm, they will have problems in later lessons. If they perform well every day, the exercises will be more enjoyable as they progress through the program.

- Many of the common information exercises have a picture on the second page. Have fun with the children as they answer your questions and discuss what they see in the picture.

Corrections

Some children may have trouble making the statements. These procedures will make it easier for them:

1. As you ask the questions in part 1, stress the words that they will use in the response: What do we call (pause) a person who fixes teeth?

2. If necessary, lead the children until their responses are firm. Then test them by having them say the statement without your lead.

3. Repeat the question after the children say the statement appropriately: Yes, a dentist. Listen again. What do we call (pause) a person who fixes teeth? After the children reply, move quickly to the next instruction: Say the whole thing about a dentist.

Locations
Lessons 127–150

Some of the locations included in this track have been chosen because they are familiar to most young children (a city, a park). Others have been chosen because they may be unfamiliar to the children (a jungle, an airport) but important to their general knowledge. Most of the locations that are taught have been previously introduced in the common information track.

In the locations track, the children learn

1. the name and primary function of thirteen locations.

2. the names of some things that are observed in each location.

3. the names or titles of people often found in these locations.

4. the function of some of the things and people found in these locations.

These are the locations taught and the lesson in which each is introduced.

farm	127	jungle	141
grocery store	129	airport	143
dentist's office	132	fire station	145
doctor's office	133	library	147
city	136	garage	147
ocean	138	restaurant	149
forest	138		

1. Today we're going to learn about a farm.
What do we call a place where food is grown?
(Signal.) *A farm.*

2. Here's a picture of a farm. I'll name some of
the things you see on a farm. Watch. (Point to
each item in turn.)
   • This a cow. What is this? (Touch.) *A cow.*
     Cows live on farms and give us milk.
   • These are sheep. What are these?
     (Touch.) *Sheep.*
     Sheep give us wool.
   • This is a barn. What is this? (Touch.)
     A barn.
     A barn is where farm animals live.
   • This is a tractor. What is this?
     (Touch.) *A tractor.*
     The farmer is plowing the field with the
     tractor.
   • These are chickens. What are these?
     (Touch.) *Chickens.*
     Chickens give us eggs.

3. Let's see if you remember the names of those
things.
   • (Point to a cow.) What is this?
     (Touch.) *A cow.*
   • (Point to the sheep.) What are these?
     (Touch.) *Sheep.*
   • (Point to the barn.) What is this?
     (Touch.) *A barn.*
   • (Point to the tractor.) What is this?
     (Touch.) *A tractor.*
   • (Point to the chickens.) What are these?
     (Touch.) *Chickens.*
   • (Repeat part 3 until all children's responses
     are firm.)

4. What else do you see in the picture? (Call on
different children.)

• (Circle the entire picture.) What do we call
the place you see in this picture?
(Touch.) *A farm.*

• Can you think of something else you
would see on a farm? (Accept reasonable
responses.)

Lesson 127: Locations

Teaching Techniques

▪ Make sure you are pointing so that the children
can see which part of the picture you are asking
about.

▪ Go over part 2 until the children can identify all
the objects without error.

▪ In part 4 you ask the children to name the **place**
where these objects are found. You are no longer
asking them to name the objects. When you ask
the question, emphasize the word **place.** Pause a
moment to give the children a chance to "switch
gears." Then touch the picture.

Corrections

Immediately correct any errors in part 2. Tell the
children the correct answer, repeat the question, and
then return to the beginning of part 2.

If the children identify one of the objects in the
picture when asked about the place, say, You're telling
me about the . . . . I w ant to know the name of the
place. What do we call the **place** we see in this picture?

Children are introduced to signs in lesson 143. They learn about signs that have words and signs that have icons or symbols. The exercise from lesson 143 appears below.

Teaching Techniques

- If children make mistakes, simply tell them the correct answer, and repeat the step they missed.
- New signs are introduced in lessons 145 and 147. Here are the additional signs that children learn.

EXERCISE 8 Signs

1. These are signs. I'll tell you what each sign says.
  a. (Point to the danger sign.) This sign says danger. What does it say? (Signal.) *Danger.* You may see this sign near places where a bridge is out or where workers are building something and a person could get hurt.
  b. (Point to the stop sign.) This sign says stop. What does it say? (Signal.) *Stop.* A stop sign tells a driver not to keep on going. The driver has to stop at the stop sign and look for other cars before going on.
  c. (Point to the no smoking sign.) This sign doesn't have any words, but the line through it is just like a cross-out mark. The line through the sign means don't do this. This sign tells you no smoking. What does it tell you? (Signal.) *No smoking.*
  d. (Point to the no bike riding sign.) This sign tells you no bike riding. What does this sign tell you? (Signal.) *No bike riding.*
  e. (Point to the no dogs sign.) What does this sign tell you? (Signal.) *No dogs.*

2. Let's go over the signs again. I'll point to each sign. You tell me what it tells you or what it says.
  a. (Point to the danger sign.) What does this sign say? (Signal.) *Danger.*
  b. (Point to the stop sign.) What does this sign say? (Signal.) *Stop.*
  c. (Point to the no smoking sign.) What does this sign tell you? (Signal.) *No smoking.*

  d. (Point to the no bike riding sign.) What does this sign tell you? (Signal.) *No bike riding.*
  e. (Point to the no dogs sign.) What does this sign tell you? (Signal.) *No dogs.*

3. (Repeat part 2 until all children's responses are firm.)

EXERCISE 8 Signs

1. These are signs. I'll tell you what each sign says.
   a. (Point to the danger sign.) This sign says danger. What does it say? (Signal.) *Danger.* You may see this sign near places where a bridge is out or where workers are building something and a person could get hurt.
   b. (Point to the stop sign.) This sign says stop. What does it say? (Signal.) *Stop.* A stop sign tells a driver not to keep on going. The driver has to stop at the stop sign and look for other cars before going on.
   c. (Point to the no smoking sign.) This sign doesn't have any words, but the line through it is just like a cross-out mark. The line through the sign means don't do this. This sign tells you no smoking. What does it tell you? (Signal.) *No smoking.*
   d. (Point to the no bike riding sign.) This sign tells you no bike riding. What does this sign tell you? (Signal.) *No bike riding.*
   e. (Point to the no dogs sign.) What does this sign tell you? (Signal.) *No dogs.*

2. Let's go over the signs again. I'll point to each sign. You tell me what it tells you or what it says.
   a. (Point to the danger sign.) What does this sign say? (Signal.) *Danger.*
   b. (Point to the stop sign.) What does this sign say? (Signal.) *Stop.*
   c. (Point to the no smoking sign.) What does this sign tell you? (Signal.) *No smoking.*

   d. (Point to the no bike riding sign.) What does this sign tell you? (Signal.) *No bike riding.*
   e. (Point to the no dogs sign.) What does this sign tell you? (Signal.) *No dogs.*

3. (Repeat part 2 until all children's responses are firm.)

EXERCISE 11 Signs

1. You've seen all these signs before. You'll tell me what each sign says or what it tells you.
   a. (Point to the stop sign.) What does this sign say? (Signal.) *Stop.*
   b. (Point to the no smoking sign.) What does this sign tell you? (Signal.) *No smoking.*
   c. (Point to the no dogs sign.) What does this sign tell you? (Signal.) *No dogs.*
   d. (Point to the exit sign.) What does this sign tell you? (Signal.) *Exit.*
   e. (Point to the no swimming sign.) What does this sign tell you? (Signal.) *No swimming.*

2. (Repeat part 1 until all children's responses are firm.)

The purpose of this group of tracks is to teach the meanings and uses of a number of words and concepts important to following instruction, solving logical problems, and answering questions. Below is a list of the tracks with the lesson in which each one starts.

Track	Lesson
Spatial and Temporal Relations	17–48
Prepositions	27–88
And—Actions	60–67
Same/Different	89–150
Some, All, None	92–105
First, Next and Before, After	98–117
Actions—Or	102–118
Where, Who, When, What	121–150
If-Then Rules	125–150

The program presents these important concepts in many contexts. In all but one track, the concepts are first introduced in actions exercises. They appear in later actions reviews. The concepts also appear in pictures exercises, and later in track reviews and in applications and absurdities exercises. Most of these concepts also appear as workbook activities.

Spatial and Temporal Relations
Lessons 17–48

Children learn a variety of temporal sequencing skills and vocabulary. Early in the program, they learn **first** and **next** as words that describe temporal events—what a person does first, what the person does next. Later, children learn how to apply those words to "static" pictures—for instance, a picture of three dogs in line walking toward a door. The dog first in line is the dog that will reach the door first. Children do a variety of workbook activities that require knowledge of **first, next,** and **last.** (See pages 129–131 in this guide.)

Much later in the program, starting with lesson 103, children are introduced to **before** and **after.** These

words parallel **first** and **next.** If a person smiles and then claps, the clapping occurs after the person smiles. The smiling occurs before the person claps.

The sequencing-events track begins in lesson 17 with the introduction of **first** and **next.**

EXERCISE 3 **Actions—First, Next**

1. Listen. Here's a new game.
   a. First I'm going to clap. Next I'm going to smile. Once more. First I'm going to clap. Next I'm going to smile.
   b. What am I going to do first? (Signal.) *Clap.* What am I going to do next? (Signal.) *Smile.*
   c. (Repeat step b until all children's responses are firm.)
   d. My turn. Here I go. (Clap. Pause. Smile.) What did I do first? (Signal.) *Clapped.* What did I do next? (Signal.) *Smiled.*
   e. Your turn. First you'll clap. Next you'll smile.
      Show me what you'll do first. Get ready. (Signal. Children clap.)
   f. Show me what you'll do next. Get ready. (Signal. Children smile.)
      Good. First you clapped. Next you smiled.
   g. I'll tap two times. Show me the thing you do first and the thing you do next. Get ready. (Tap two times. Children clap, then smile.)

2. (Repeat part 1 until all children's responses are firm.)

Lesson 17: Actions—First, Next

Teaching Techniques

In steps e and f, the children are to show you what they do first and next. Be careful that some of the children don't lead the others and show them what to do. Say, All together. Wait for my signal. Show me what you do first.

Get ready. (Signal.)

Good. Now show what you do next. Get ready. (Signal.)

Lesson 24: Actions—First, Next

After the children have worked on exercises like this one for several lessons, they will do workbook activities that apply **first** and **next** to illustrations of actions. For these exercises, children follow the arrow and identify what to do first and what to do next. Note that **first** and **next** are related to pictures that are not actually ordered in time; both boys are present at the same time. But by following a sequencing rule (following the arrow), one of the objects becomes the first one you'll touch. The other object becomes the next one you'll touch. This notion is important for reading where the first letter is not really temporally first. It is first only if you follow the sequencing rule of moving from left to right as you identify the letters.

Lesson 39: Actions—First, Next, Last

Later, children do an expanded version of the **first-next** exercises that incorporates **last.** The expanded version helps the children learn more about the relationship between sequencing events in space and sequencing events in time. For these activities, several children line up. You ask which child would reach the door first if the line moved toward you. This type of activity is similar to arrow exercises except that the line actually moves.

⭐ EXERCISE 2 Actions—First, Next, Last

[Note: You will need a chair for this exercise.**]**

1. We're going to do first, next, and last. (Ask three children to stand in front of the group. Place a chair to the right of the children and stand at the other end of the children. Direct the children in line to turn and face the chair.)
   a. Everybody, if these children walk to the chair, who will get to the chair first? (Signal. Children respond.)
      So, who is first in line now? (Signal. Children respond.)
   b. Who is next? (Signal. Children respond.)
      Who is last? (Signal. Children respond.)

2. (Ask the three children to turn so they face you.)
   a. Everybody, if these children stay in line and walk to me, who will get to me first? (Signal. Children respond.)
   b. So, who is first in line? (Signal. Children respond.)
      Who is next in line? (Signal. Children respond.)
      Who is last? (Signal. Children respond.)

3. You said that _____ will get to me first if the children walk toward me. Let's see if you are right.
   a. [Name the three children], stay in line and walk toward me.
   b. So, who got to me first? (Signal. Children respond.)
      Who got to me next? (Signal. Children respond.)
      Who got to me last? (Signal. Children respond.)

In part 2, make sure that children are firm on their prediction about which child will reach you first before you present part 3. Once children see the relationship between standing in line and reaching a point by moving, they should have no trouble with this activity.

A more advanced version of this exercise starts in lesson 46. It requires children to analyze **first, next,** and **last** from pictures.

> ## Prepositions
> ## Lessons 27–88

On, in, over, and **under** frequently occur in directions. If children are to understand and follow directions, they need a precise understanding of prepositions.

The objectives of the prepositions track are

1. to demonstrate the meaning of prepositions with real objects.
2. to teach children to perform actions that involve prepositions (Put your hand **over** your head).
3. to teach children to use prepositions to describe the relationship of objects in a picture.

Each preposition is introduced in a demonstration or actions exercise, then presented in pictures exercises. Here is a schedule of the prepositions taught in the program.

Prepositions	Lesson
on	27
over	30
in front of	35
in	51
in back of	57
under	67
next to	76
between	87

EXERCISE 3 Prepositions — On
                    (Demonstration)

[**Note:** You will need a pencil and a table for this exercise.]

1. We're going to talk about a pencil and a table.
   a. (Hold up the pencil.) What is this? (Signal.) *A pencil.*
   b. (Point to the table.) What is this? (Signal.) *A table.*

2. My turn. I'll tell you if I hold the pencil on the table.
   a. (Hold the pencil on the tabletop.) Is the pencil on the table? Yes.
      (Hold the pencil on another part of the tabletop.) Is the pencil on the table? Yes.
      (Hold the pencil over the tabletop.) Is the pencil on the table? No.
      (Hold the pencil next to the table.) Is the pencil on the table? No.
      (Hold the pencil near the floor.) Is the pencil on the table? No.
   b. Your turn. Tell me if the pencil is on the table.
      (Repeat step a, with children answering the questions.)

3. Now we're going to say the whole thing. Watch. (Put the pencil on the table.)
   Is the pencil on the table? (Signal.) *Yes.*
   Say the whole thing with me. (Signal.) *The pencil is on the table.*
   All by yourselves. Say the whole thing about where the pencil is. (Signal.) *The pencil is on the table.*

4. (Repeat part 3 until all children can make the statement.)

Lesson 27: Prepositions—On (Demonstration)

In this first exercise, the children learn the difference between **on** and **not on**.

Teaching Techniques

For demonstrations of this kind to be successful, you must move very quickly. In part 2a you are showing the children the difference between **on** and **not on**. If your pacing is slow, they will tend to forget what you have just shown, and they will make mistakes.

Study the instructions so that you can present part 2 without having to read from the book. For your first two demonstrations, you will position the pencil on different parts of the tabletop. You will present three demonstrations of **not on**; your pencil will be **over**, **next to**, and **near** the table. For each demonstration, first position the pencil, and then quickly ask the question Is this pencil on the table? Answer each of the questions yes or no. Your answer must follow your question quickly to keep the children from responding. Make it clear that step a is your turn. Then in step b, repeat step a with the children answering the questions.

When all the children respond correctly, move quickly to statement production in part 3. Lead the children through the statement in a natural tone of voice, but emphasize the word **on**.

Corrections

Some children have trouble saying preposition statements. Often they omit the word **is**. They may also slur the preposition word—which may mean that they will later confuse **on** and **under**.

To firm the children on saying the statement in part 3, say it with a pause: The pencil is (pause) on the table. The pause helps the children see that the first part of the statement is similar to familiar statements, such as The boy is running. By stressing **on**, you help children place the word in the sentence.

If children have trouble saying the statement with you,
Model the response:
My turn. The pencil is (pause) on the table.
Lead the response:
Say the whole thing with me. *The pencil is* (pause) *on the table.*
Test the response:
All by yourselves. Say the whole thing about where the pencil is. (Signal.) *The pencil is on the table.*

By stressing the first words the children will say in their response, you make it easier for them to respond correctly.

The children must be firm on saying these statements and all the subsequent preposition statements. If you are not sure of some of the children's responses, test them individually.

★EXERCISE 5 **Prepositions—On/Over**

1. We're going to talk about this picture.
   (Point to a leaf.) What is this? (Touch.) *A leaf.*
   (Point to the dog.) What is this? (Touch.)
   A dog.

2. One of these leaves is over the dog.
   (Point to each leaf and ask,) Is this leaf over
   the dog? (Children answer *yes* or *no*.) ●
   (Repeat until all children's responses are firm.)

3. (Point to a.)
   Everybody, where is this leaf? (Touch.) *Over*
   the dog.
   Say the whole thing about where this leaf is.
   (Touch.) *This leaf is over the dog.*
   (Repeat until all children can make the
   statement.)

4. One of these leaves is on the dog. (Point to
   each leaf and ask,) Is this leaf on the dog?
   (Children answer *yes* or *no*.) ●
   (Repeat until all children's responses are
   firm.)

5. (Point to b.) Everybody, where is this leaf?
   (Touch.) *On the dog.*
   Say the whole thing about where this leaf is.
   (Touch.) *This leaf is on the dog.*
   (Repeat until all children can make the
   statement.)

Individual Turns
(Repeat parts 2 through 5, calling on different
children.)

─**CORRECTIONS**─
EXERCISE 5

● **Error**
(Children give the wrong answer.)

Correction
1. (Give the correct answer.)
2. (Repeat the question.)
3. (Return to the exercise.)

Lesson 31: Prepositions—On/Over

This first pictures exercise follows the introduction
of **on** and **over** in actions exercises. For the first time,
the children discriminate between two prepositions.
The picture shows a dog and some leaves—two on the
ground, one on the dog's back, and one hovering over
the dog.

In parts 2 and 3 the children work on the
preposition **over** by answering a series of **yes/no**
questions and then making a statement about the leaf
that is **over** the dog. In parts 4 and 5 the children work
on the preposition **on.**

★ EXERCISE 4 Actions—Prepositions: In Front Of

EXERCISE 4 Actions—Prepositions: In Front Of

[Note: You will need a chair for this exercise.]

1. I'm going to put a chair in front of me.
   a. (Place the chair directly in front of you.) The chair is in front of me. Where is the chair? (Signal.) *In front of you.*
   b. (Turn so that the chair is to your right.) Is the chair in front of me now? (Signal.) *No.*
   c. (Turn so the chair is to your left.) Is the chair in front of me now? (Signal.) *No.*
   d. (Turn so the chair is directly in front of you.) Is the chair in front of me now? (Signal.) *Yes.* Where is the chair now? (Signal.) *In front of you.*

2. (Repeat part 1 until all children's responses are firm.)

3. Let's do something harder.
   a. (Call on a child.) Put the chair in front of me. (The child responds.) Everybody, where is the chair? (Signal.) *In front of you.* Say the whole thing. (Signal.) *The chair is in front of you.*
   b. (Turn so the chair is in back of you. Call on a child.) Put the chair in front of me. (The child responds.) Everybody, where is the chair? (Signal.) *In front of you.* Say the whole thing. (Signal.) *The chair is in front of you.*
   c. (Turn so the chair is to your side. Call on a child.) Put the chair in front of me. (The child responds.) Everybody, where is the chair? (Signal.) *In front of you.* Say the whole thing. (Signal.) *The chair is in front of you.*

4. (Repeat part 3 until all children's responses are firm.)

Lesson 35: Actions—Prepositions: In Front Of

In front of is introduced with a demonstration. It is always used with objects that have fronts and backs.

Teaching Techniques

Practice this exercise before presenting it to the children so that it will go smoothly.

- In part 1, place a chair in front of you. Then turn different ways, and ask the children, Is this chair in front of me now? Move quickly through this series of steps.

- In part 3, call on different children to place the chair in front of you. These steps should be done rapidly. Don't let a child take too long to place the chair, or the attention of the group will stray.

Corrections

If children have trouble making the statement, follow the statement correction procedure. Pause after **is,** and stress the prepositional words **in front of.**

If the children have trouble in part 3,

1. show them your front, and say, Here is my front.
2. point straight ahead, and say, Here's in front of me.
3. say, Put the chair so that it is in front of me. Put it so that I am pointing to it.
4. after the child places the chair appropriately, say, Let's do another one. Turn so that the chair is no longer in front of you, and say, Put the chair in front of me. Do not point unless the child has trouble.

EXERCISE 4 Prepositions—In Front Of, On, Over

1. One of these dogs is in front of the bike. One of these dogs is on the bike. One of these dogs is jumping over the bike.

2. Get ready to tell me where each dog is.
   a. (Point to a.) Everybody, where is this dog? (Touch.) *Over the bike.*
   b. (Point to b.) Everybody, where is this dog? (Touch.) *On the bike.*
   c. (Point to c.) Everybody, where is this dog? (Touch.) *In front of the bike.*
   (Repeat part 2 until all children's responses are firm.)

3. We're going to talk about one of the dogs. (Point to b.)
   • Where is this dog? (Touch.) *On the bike.*
   Say the whole thing about where this dog is. (Touch.) *This dog is on the bike.*
   • Is this dog in front of the bike? (Touch.) *No.*
   Say the whole thing. (Touch.) *This dog is not in front of the bike.* ●

4. Now we'll talk about another dog. (Point to c.)
   • Where is this dog? (Touch.) *In front of the bike.* ■
   Say the whole thing about where this dog is. (Touch.) *This dog is in front of the bike.*
   • Is this dog on the bike? (Touch.) *No.*
   Say the whole thing. (Touch.) *This dog is not on the bike.*

Individual Turns
(Repeat parts 3 and 4 until all children can make the statements.)

CORRECTIONS
EXERCISE 4

● **Error**
(Children respond incorrectly.)
Correction
1. Is this dog in front of the bike? (Touch.) *No.*
2. Say the whole thing. (Touch.) *This dog is not in front of the bike.*
(Repeat until children respond correctly.)
3. (Repeat part 3 of the exercise.)

■ **Error**
(Children say, *This dog is on the bike.*)
Correction
1. (Point to dog c.) We're talking about in front of.
2. Is this dog in front of the bike? (Touch.) *Yes.*
3. Let's say the whole thing. (Touch. Respond with children.) *This dog is in front of the bike.*
4. All by yourselves. (Touch. Do not respond with children.) *This dog is in front of the bike.*
5. (Repeat part 4 of the exercise.)

Lesson 39: Prepositions—In Front Of, On, Over

When this exercise appears, the children have had **on, over,** and **in front of** in both actions and pictures exercises. This pictures exercise consolidates what they have learned. A similar exercise is used with other prepositions in later lessons.

Teaching Techniques

Children sometimes confuse the responses called for by the questions What is this? and Where is this? To reduce errors, it is important to stress the words **what** and **where** whenever they appear in an exercise.

The pacing in this exercise is important. But do not hurry the children when asking the **where** question.

In parts 3 and 4 the children should be able to answer each question and make each statement without error. Don't let them shout the statements or make them in a droning manner. This part of the exercise should be done quickly, and the children's responses should be confident and natural-sounding.

Corrections

If the children make mistakes on **in front of,** follow the correction used when **in front of** was introduced:

1. Show me the front of the bike.
2. Now show me what's in front of the bike.
3. Repeat the questions.

And—Actions
Lessons 60–67

The meaning and use of the word **and** are taught in two actions exercises and used in a variety of exercises throughout the program.

The particular usage of **and** emphasized in the program is illustrated by this example: The ball is little and green. The same meaning could also be phrased as The ball is green and little. The word **and** joins the two descriptive terms; the order in which the terms are mentioned doesn't matter.

★ **EXERCISE 3** Actions—And

1. It's time for some actions.

   a. Everybody, stand up. (Signal. Wait.)
     What are you doing? (Signal.) *Standing up.*
     Say the whole thing. (Signal.) *I am standing up.*
     Sit down.

   b. Everybody, stand up and touch your head. Get ready. (Signal. Wait.)
     What are you doing? (Signal.) *Standing up and touching my head.*
     (Repeat step b until all children can make the statement.)

   c. Say the whole thing with me. (Signal. Respond with children.)
     I am standing up and touching my head.
     (Repeat step c until all children's responses are firm.)

   d. All by yourselves. Say the whole thing. (Signal. Do not respond with children.)
     I am standing up and touching my head.

   e. Again. (Signal.) *I am standing up and touching my head.*
     (Repeat step e until all children can make the statement.)
     Sit down.

2. Let's do that again.

   a. Everybody, stand up and touch your head. Get ready. (Signal. Wait.)
     What are you doing? (Signal.) *Standing up and touching my head.*

   b. Say the whole thing. (Signal.) *I am standing up and touching my head.*

3. Here's another one.

   a. Everybody, sit down and touch your nose. Get ready. (Signal. Wait.)
     What are you doing? (Signal.) *Sitting down and touching my nose.*

   b. Say the whole thing. (Signal.) *I am sitting down and touching my nose.*

4. (Repeat part 3 until all children's responses are firm.)

Lesson 60: Actions—And

Teaching Techniques

Note that the instructions for these tasks don't involve things that happen first and next. If, for example, the instruction says, Touch your foot and touch your wrist, the child must be touching his or her foot and wrist at the same time. It doesn't matter which is touched first.

The children are to continue performing the actions until you present the next instructions. Watch them carefully to make sure they are not copying responses from other children. If in doubt, call on individual children.

Corrections

Expect some children to have trouble with the statements. For example, to firm their responses in part 3, do the following:

1. Model: Sitting down (pause) and touching my nose. Note the pause and the emphasis on the word **and**.

2. Lead: Say it with me. *Sitting down* (pause*) and touching my nose.* The lead should contain the same pause and emphasis as the model. Repeat the lead until the children's responses are firm.

3. Test: Your turn. The children are to make the response with the pause and emphasis.

4. Call on individual children. If any children have trouble, return to the lead step and repeat the lead and test until all the children's responses are firm.

Same/Different
Lessons 89–150

Typically, early school exercises refer to things as being the same only when they are identical. The problem with limiting the concept **same** to "identical" is that **same** is frequently used in other senses, such as "the same color," "the same shape," or "the same size." In these exercises the children learn that **same** can mean that something about two or more things is identical but it is not necessary that everything be identical.

The concept of **same** involves comparing objects. When we say, for example, that two boys are doing the same thing, we are not making a statement about what either boy is doing; we are simply saying that if you observe the actions of both boys, you will be able to make the same observations about them. Similarly, when we say that two girls are wearing something that is the same, we are not saying what they are wearing; we are simply calling attention to the fact that some article of clothing worn by one girl is also worn by the other.

In the same/different track the children learn

1. to perform the **same** action the teacher performs.

2. to identify, in pictures, the **same** action performed by different characters.
3. the concept that things with the same label are the same. For example, all birds can be the same because all are labeled **birds.**
4. that people and animals may be "the same" in many ways: Two elephants may be the same because they both have hats, because they are both sitting, and because they are both elephants.
5. that objects can be described as "the same" because they have the same function, because they are

found in the same place, because they have the same parts, or because they do the same thing.
6. that **different** is the opposite of **same.**
7. to compare objects, people, and animals, and make observations about how they are the same and how they are different.

In the same/different track, children first learn to apply the concepts **same** and **not same.** Later they learn **different** as a word that means **not same.**

⭐ **EXERCISE 1 Actions—Same**

1. We're going to play a game.
   a. Everybody, I'm going to do something. Then you're going to do the same thing. My turn. **(Tap your head once.)** I did it.
   b. Your turn. Do the same thing I did. Get ready. **(Signal. Children are to tap their heads once.)**
      Good. You did the same thing I did.
   c. **(Repeat part 1 until all children's responses are firm.)**

2. Here's another one.
   a. I'm going to do something. Then you're going to do the same thing. My turn. **(Clap your hands twice.)** I did it.
   b. Your turn. Do the same thing I did. Get ready. **(Signal. Children are to clap their hands twice.)**
      Good. You did the same thing I did.
   c. **(Repeat part 2 until all children's responses are firm.)**

3. New game.
   a. Your turn. Get ready to touch the floor. **(Signal. Children are to touch the floor.)** Stop touching the floor.
   b. Watch me. Tell me if I do the same thing you did. **(Touch your nose.)**
      Am I doing the same thing you did? **(Signal.)** *No.*
   c. Tell me what to do. **(Signal.)** *Touch the floor.*
      (Touch the floor.)
      Now am I doing the same thing you did? **(Signal.)** *Yes.*
      (Keep touching the floor.)
   d. What did you do? **(Signal.)** *Touched the floor.*
      What am I doing? **(Signal.)** *Touching the floor.*
      (Lift your hand from the floor.)
   e. We did something that was the same. Tell me what we did that was the same. **(Signal.)** *Touched the floor.*
      Yes, we touched the floor.
   f. **(Repeat part 3 until all children's responses are firm. Then praise children.)**

Individual Turns
(Repeat the exercise, calling on different children for each step.)

Lesson 89: Actions—Same

The first exercise in the track introduces the idea of doing the same thing.

Teaching Techniques

Like other actions exercises that teach concepts, the demonstrations in parts 1 and 2 must be executed smoothly. Watch your pacing. Make sure that you can present the steps without looking at the book.

Go very rapidly in part 3 to keep the children from forgetting the action that you are trying to match.

The slower you go, the greater the possibility that the children will make mistakes in this part of the exercise.

Ignore any wording errors, such as children saying *touch the floor* instead of *touched the floor.* You are teaching **same.** Don't confuse the children with corrections on other details.

Corrections

If the children make mistakes in part 3, tell them the answer, and then return to the beginning of part 3.
Let's do that last part again. Your turn . . . .

⭐ **EXERCISE 5** **Same**

1. Look at these boys.
   (Point to each boy, and ask:) What is this boy doing? (Touch. Children are to answer *running, climbing, running, swinging.*)

2. We'll talk about each boy.
   a. (Point to a.)
   Is this boy tall? (Touch.) *Yes.*
   What is this boy doing? (Touch.) *Running.*
   One of the other boys is doing the same thing. We're going to find out which boy is doing the same thing.
   b. (Point to b.)
   Is this boy doing the same thing the tall boy is doing? (Touch.) *No.* ⬤
   c. (Point to c.)
   Is this boy doing the same thing the tall boy is doing? (Touch.) *Yes.*
   d. (Point to d.)
   Is this boy doing the same thing the tall boy is doing? (Touch.) *No.*

3. Look at this boy again.
   • (Point to a.)
   What is this boy doing? (Touch.) *Running.*
   • (Point to a and c.)
   What are they doing that is the same? (Touch.) *Running.*
   • These boys are the same because they are running. Why are these boys the same? (Touch.) *Because they are running.*
   • Let's say the whole thing about why these boys are the same. (Signal. Respond with children.) *These boys are the same because they are running.*
   Your turn. Say the whole thing about why these boys are the same. (Signal. Do not respond with children.) *These boys are the same because they are running.*

4. (Repeat part 4 until all children's responses are firm.)

CORRECTIONS
EXERCISE 5

⬤ **Error**
(Children say *Yes.*)
Correction
1. What's the tall boy doing? (Touch.) *Running.*
2. Is this boy running? (Touch.) *No.*
So this boy is not doing the same thing the tall boy is doing. Climbing is not the same as running.
3. (Repeat step b.)

Lesson 92: Same

This is the first pictures exercise in the same/different track. It is similar to the actions exercises in that it focuses on doing the same thing.

Teaching Techniques

The children will catch on to this exercise more easily if you move quickly from step to step. If they don't make any mistakes, you shouldn't have to slow down until part 3 where they make the statements.

Corrections

If children make mistakes in step b, follow the correction in the corrections box.

Expect some children to have some trouble saying the statements in part 3. You can help them by presenting the statement in this way: These boys are the same (pause) **because** they are **running.** You can say the first part of the statement, These boys are the same. . . . Then have them say the second part, *because they are running,* until their responses are firm. Then have them say the entire statement.

⭐ **EXERCISE 6 Same**

1. (Point to the balls.) Look at the picture.
   (Point to each ball, and ask:) What is this?
   (Touch. Children are to answer *a ball*.)

2. I know why these things are the same.
   Because they are balls.
   • Everybody, why are these things the same?
     (Touch.) *Because they are balls.*
     Yes, they are the same because they are balls.
   • Say the whole thing about why they are the same. (Touch.) *They are the same because they are balls.*
     (Repeat until all children can make the statement.)

3. (Point to the dogs.) Look at the picture.
   (Point to each dog, and ask:) What is this?
   (Touch. Children are to answer *a dog*.)

4. I know why these things are the same.
   Because they are dogs.
   • Everybody, why are these things the same?
     (Touch.) *Because they are dogs.*
     Yes, they are the same because they are dogs.
   • Say the whole thing about why they are the same. (Touch.) *They are the same because they are dogs.*
     (Repeat until all children can make the statement.)

5. Let's do it again.
   • (Point to the balls.) Everybody, why are these things the same? (Touch.) *Because they are balls.*
   • (Point to the dogs.) Everybody, why are these things the same? (Touch.) *Because they are dogs.*
   • (Repeat part 5 until all children can make the statement.)

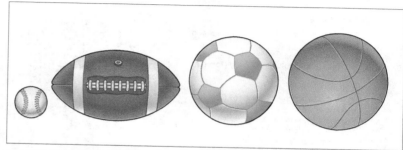

Individual Turns
(Repeat the exercise, calling on different children for each step.)

Lesson 92: Same

This is the second same/different exercise introduced in lesson 92. It teaches the children that things can be labeled "the" same if they have the same name.

Corrections

In part 2 the children may respond by saying, *They are balls.* To correct, say, Yes, **because** they are balls. Let's say "because they are balls."

EXERCISE 6 Same

1. Two of these elephants are wearing the same thing.
   - **(Point to a.)**
     What is this elephant wearing? **(Touch.)**
     A hat.
   - **(Point to c.)**
     What is this elephant wearing? **(Touch.)**
     A hat.
   - Everybody, what are they wearing that's the same? **(Touch.)** *A hat.*
     So why are these elephants the same? **(Touch.)** *Because they're wearing hats.*
   - Say the whole thing about why these elephants are the same. **(Signal.)** *These elephants are the same because they're wearing hats.*

2. Two of these elephants are holding the same thing.
   - **(Point to a and b.)**
     These animals are holding the same thing.
   - **(Point to a.)**
     What is this elephant holding? **(Touch.)**
     Flowers.
   - **(Point to b.)**
     What is this elephant holding? **(Touch.)**
     Flowers.
   - Everybody, what are they holding that's the same? **(Touch.)** *Flowers.*
     So why are these elephants the same? **(Touch.)** *Because they are holding flowers.*
   - Say the whole thing about why these elephants are the same. **(Signal.)** *These elephants are the same because they're holding flowers.*

3. Two of these elephants are doing the same thing.
   - **(Call on a child.)** Point to those elephants. Everybody, what are they doing that's the same? **(Signal.)** *Sitting.*

- **(Point to b and c.)**
  Everybody, what are they doing? **(Touch.)**
  Sitting.
  So why are these elephants the same?
  (Touch.) *Because they're sitting.*

- Say the whole thing about why these elephants are the same. **(Signal.)** *These elephants are the same because they're sitting.*

4. **(Repeat the exercise until all children's responses are firm.)**

Lesson 96: Same

In this exercise the children make observations about different ways that things are "the same."

Teaching Techniques

■ When presenting part 1, point to the hats. When presenting part 2, point to the flowers. When presenting part 3, point to the back legs of each elephant to prompt the correct responses.

■ The more quickly you move through these steps, the greater the chance that the children will see the basis for judging why each pair of elephants is the same.

⭐ **EXERCISE 5** Same—Class

I'm going to name some things that are in the same class. You're going to tell me the class.
  a. Listen. Bucket, glass, package. They're in the same class. Everybody, what class are they in? (Signal.) *Containers.*
     (Repeat until all children's responses are firm.)
  b. Listen. Tricycle, motorboat, taxi. They're in the same class. Everybody, what class? (Signal.) *Vehicles.*
     (Repeat until all children's responses are firm.)
  c. Listen. Banana, toast, potato. They're in the same class. Everybody, what class? (Signal.) *Food.*
     (Repeat until all children's responses are firm.)
  d. Listen. Monkey, pig, rabbit. They're in the same class. Everybody, what class? (Signal.) *Animals.*
     (Repeat until all children's responses are firm.)
  e. Listen. Cabinet, cup, bag. They're in the same class. Everybody, what class? (Signal.) *Containers.*
     (Repeat until all children's responses are firm.)

Lesson 99: Same—Class

This exercise is the first of a series of exercises that teaches the children about objects that are in the same class, objects that do the same thing, objects that are found in the same place, and objects that have the same parts. Treat these exercises as games. In the classification game, you say, I'm going to name some things that are in the same class. You're going to tell me the class. Name several vehicles, and then ask, What class are they in? The children operate from words only—there are no pictures.

Teaching Techniques

■ You may wish to pause after naming the objects. This pause is critical and should last at least two seconds. Some children need this thinking time. Later you can reduce the length of the pause. If you hurry the children too much, they will begin to guess.

■ It is important that you acknowledge all appropriate responses. For example, if you ask what chalk and a pencil do that is the same, a

child might say, *You draw with them.* Accept the response: Yes, you draw with them. Let's say that they write. Listen. Chalk and a pencil (pause). What do they do that's the same?

Corrections

If children have trouble with more than one step, repeat the entire exercise until they can respond correctly.

Lesson 113: Actions—Different

In this actions exercise the word **different** is introduced.

 EXERCISE 1 Actions—Different

1. Listen. If I don't do the same thing you do, I'll do something that is different.
   a. Your turn. Touch your head, and keep touching it.
   • My turn to do the same thing you are doing. Watch. (Touch your head.)
   • My turn to do something that is different. Watch. (Touch your nose.)
   b. Keep touching your head. I'll do some things. Tell me if they are the same as you are doing or something different.
   • (Touch your head.) Same or different? (Signal.) *Same.*
   • (Touch your elbow.) Same or different? (Signal.) *Different.*
   • (Touch your knees.) Same or different? (Signal.) *Different.*
   • Everybody, put your hands down.
   c. My turn to do something. (Touch your elbow, and keep touching it.)
   • Everybody, do the same thing I am doing. ✔
   • Everybody, do something different. ✔
   d. Listen. What am I doing? (Signal.) *Touching your elbow.*
     Are you doing the same thing or something different? (Signal.) *Something different.*

2. (Repeat steps c and d until all children's responses are firm.)

Teaching Techniques

Move quickly through each of the steps. Make sure the children are watching you. When you ask, Are you doing the same thing or something different? emphasize the word **different.**

Make sure the children keep touching their head from step a through step b. At the end of step b, tell them to put their hands down.

Corrections

The children may have difficulty saying *Something different.* Repeat the words with them several times. If children don't answer a question correctly, tell them the answer. Then return to the beginning of part 1.

EXERCISE 4 Same/Different—Class

1. We're going to talk about the classes things are in.
   - Everybody, what class is a hat in? (Signal.) *Clothing.*
   - Everybody, what class is a shirt in? (Signal.) *Clothing.*
   - Everybody, what class is a horse in? (Signal.) *Animals.*
   - Everybody, what class is a suitcase in? (Signal.) *Containers.*
   (Repeat until all children's responses are firm.)

2. Listen.
   a. A hat and a shirt. (Pause.)
      Are they in the same class or in different classes? (Pause. Signal.) *The same class.*
      You're right. They are in the same class.
      - What class is a hat in? (Pause. Signal.) *Clothing.*
      - Is a shirt in the same class? (Pause. Signal.) *Yes.*
      So a hat and a shirt are in the same class.
   b. A hat and a horse. (Pause.)
      Are they in the same class or in different classes? (Pause. Signal.) *Different classes.*
      You're right. They are in different classes.
      - What class is a hat in? (Pause. Signal.) *Clothing.*
      Yes, clothing.
      - Is a horse in the same class? (Pause. Signal.) *No.*
      No, it's not in the same class.
      So a hat and a horse are in different classes.
   c. A hat and a suitcase. (Pause.)
      Are they in the same class or in different classes? (Pause. Signal.) *Different classes.*
      You're right. They are in different classes.
      - What class is a hat in? (Pause. Signal.) *Clothing.*
      Yes, clothing.
      - Is a suitcase in the same class? (Pause. Signal.) *No.*
      No, it's not in the same class.
      So a hat and a suitcase are in different classes.

Individual Turns
(Repeat the exercise, calling on different children for each step.)

Lesson 116: Same/Different—Class

In this exercise the children apply the concept of **same and different** to what they have learned about classes.

Teaching Techniques

The pauses indicated in the exercise are important. Give the children ample thinking time before signaling for their response.

Corrections

If the children answer the first question in part 2 incorrectly, say, Listen. What class is a hat in? The children say *Clothing*. What class is a shirt in? The children say *Clothing*. Then say, So are a hat and a shirt in the same class? The children say *Yes*. Then return to the beginning of part 2. Adapt this correction for questions about objects in a different class.

⭐ **EXERCISE 4** **Same/Different**

1. We're going to tell why things are the same and why they are different.
A bird and an airplane. Think of them. Why are they the same? **(Call on a child. Accept reasonable responses such as** *Because they both fly.***)**

2. My turn. I'm going to name some ways that they are different.
  a. Listen. A bird is alive, but an airplane is not alive. Everybody, say that. **(Signal.)** *A bird is alive, but an airplane is not alive.*
  That's one way they are different.
  b. Listen. A bird is an animal, but an airplane is not an animal. Everybody, say that. **(Signal.)** *A bird is an animal, but an airplane is not an animal.*
  That's another way they are different.

3. Now it's your turn.
  a. Raise your hand if you can name a way that a bird and an airplane are different. **(Call on a child. If the child gives an appropriate response, say:)** Everybody, say that. **(Signal.)** ●
  b. Name another way that a bird and an airplane are different. **(Call on another child. If the child gives an appropriate response, say:)** Everybody, say that. **(Signal.)**
  c. **(Repeat step b until all children who have raised their hands have responded.)**

---CORRECTIONS---
EXERCISE 4

● **Error**
(The child cannot give an appropriate response.)
Correction
(If necessary, prompt the child with these questions.)
Is a plane a vehicle?
Does a bird have windows?
Does an airplane have feathers?
Does an airplane breathe?
Is a bird made of metal?

Lesson 118: Same/Different

In this exercise the children make observations about how two objects can be different. You give them two examples of how two objects are different, and then they make observations of their own.

Teaching Techniques

■ In part 3, the children are to name ways in which an airplane and a bird are different. Acceptable responses include any that you have provided as examples in part 2.

■ Have the children repeat acceptable responses, and then call on other children to name additional ways the two objects differ.

■ Listen carefully to all responses, and praise children who give unique responses.

Corrections

If the children do not produce any responses in part 3, repeat part 2. Then present part 3 again. Praise the children even if they repeat only the responses you specified. Then suggest another response. Keep prompting the children until they begin to give good responses.

EXERCISE 4 Same/Different

1. We're going to tell why things are the same and why they are different.
   A bird and an airplane. Think of them. Why are they the same? **(Call on different children. Accept reasonable responses such as** *Because they both fly.)*

2. My turn. I'm going to name some ways that they are **different.**
   a. Listen. A bird has feathers, but an airplane does not have feathers. Everybody, say that. **(Signal.)** *A bird has feathers, but an airplane does not have feathers.*
   b. Listen. A bird is an animal, but an airplane is not an animal. Everybody, say that. **(Signal.)** *A bird is an animal, but an airplane is not an animal.*
   • That's another way they are different.

3. Now it's your turn.
   a. Raise your hand if you can name a way that a bird and an airplane are different. **(Call on a child. If child gives an appropriate response, say:)** Everybody, say that.
   b. Name another way that a bird and an airplane are different. **(Call on another child. If child gives an appropriate response, say:)** Everybody, say that.
   c. **(Repeat step b until all children who have raised their hands have responded.)**

4. Here's a new one.
   a. Listen. A broom and a toothbrush. Think of them. See if you can name two ways they are the same. **(Call on different children. Have the group repeat each correct answer. Then say:)** You told me how a broom and a toothbrush are … (signal) *the same.*
   b. Listen. A broom and a toothbrush. Think of them. See if you can name two ways they are different. **(Call on different children. Have the group repeat each correct answer. Then say:)** You told me how a broom and a toothbrush are … (signal) *different.*

Lesson 122: Same/Different

In this exercise the children have to name ways in which two objects are the same and ways in which they are different.

Teaching Techniques

Have fun with these exercises. Accept all reasonable answers. If the children come up with many different responses, have the group repeat only two or three. But do have everyone complete the statement You told me how a bird and an airplane are . . . (Signal.).

Corrections

If all the previous same/different exercises have been well taught, the children should do well on these review exercises. If you don't get any answers after a couple of seconds, give an example. This procedure will usually get the children started.

Some, All, None
Lessons 92–105

The words **some, all,** and **none** are used in many teacher instructions and written directions. The objective of this track is that the children will learn the precise meaning of each of these words. The meaning of each word is first demonstrated in an actions exercise: **All** is introduced first, then **some** and how it differs in meaning from **all.** **None** is taught last in exercises that contrast its meaning to **all** and **some.**

In lesson 96 the children learn to use **some** and **all** in pictures exercises. Later in the program, **some, all,** and **none** appear in the concept application track.

EXERCISE 1 Actions—Some/All

1. Look at my hands.
   a. My turn. I'm going to hold up all of my fingers. What am I going to hold up? (Signal.) *All of your fingers.*
   b. Here I go. (Hold up all ten fingers.) What am I holding up? (Signal.) *You are holding up all of your fingers.*
   c. Your turn. Hold up all of your fingers. (Signal. Wait.)
      What are you holding up? (Signal.) *All of my fingers.*
      Say the whole thing. (Signal.) *I am holding up all of my fingers.*
   d. (Repeat part 1 until all children's responses are firm.)

2. Put your hands down. Watch me.
   a. (Hold up four fingers.) Am I holding up all of my fingers? (Signal.) *No.*
      (Hold up nine fingers.) Am I holding up all of my fingers? (Signal.) *No.*
      (Hold up three fingers.) Am I holding up all of my fingers? (Signal.) *No.*
   b. (Hold up ten fingers.) Am I holding up all of my fingers? (Signal.) *Yes.*
      What am I holding up? (Signal.) *All of your fingers.*
      Say the whole thing. (Signal.) *You are holding up all of your fingers.*
   c. (Repeat part 2 until all children's responses are firm.)

Individual Turns
(Repeat part 2, calling on different children for each step.)

Lesson 92: Actions—Some/All

In this first exercise the children learn the difference between **all** and **not all**.

Teaching Techniques

- Because you are sometimes holding up all your fingers, you cannot use the hand-drop signal in this exercise. You can signal by moving your hands up and down or by tapping your foot. In any case, be sure to maintain the same timing you use with the hand-drop signal.

- Keep the pacing brisk. Move from one step to another without pausing between steps. When the children are to repeat the statement, make the pause longer.

- Make sure the children correctly say the statements in the exercise, pronouncing each word and maintaining an appropriate rate.

⭐ **EXERCISE 2 Actions—Some/All**

1. Look at my hands.
   a. (Hold up four fingers.) Am I holding up **all** of my fingers? (Signal.) *No.*
   I'm not holding up **all** of my fingers. I'm holding up **some** of my fingers.
   b. (Hold up eight fingers.) Am I holding up **all** of my fingers? (Signal.) *No.*
   I'm holding up **some** of my fingers.
   c. (Hold up nine fingers.) Am I holding up **all** of my fingers? (Signal.) *No.*
   I'm holding up **some** of my fingers.
   d. (Repeat part 1 until all children's responses are firm.)

2. Watch me. Tell me if I hold up **all** of my fingers or **some** of my fingers.
   a. Watch. (Hold up ten fingers.) Is this all of my fingers or some of my fingers? (Signal.) *All of your fingers.*
   b. Watch. (Hold up nine fingers.) Is this all of my fingers or some of my fingers? (Signal.) *Some of your fingers.*
   c. Watch. (Hold up six fingers.) Is this all of my fingers or some of my fingers? (Signal.) *Some of your fingers.*
   d. Watch. (Hold up ten fingers.) Is this all of my fingers or some of my fingers? (Signal.) *All of your fingers.*
   e. (Repeat steps a through d until all children's responses are firm.)
   f. (Hold up four fingers.) Is this **all** of my fingers or **some** of my fingers? (Signal.) *Some of your fingers.*
   Say the whole thing about what I am holding up. (Signal.) *You are holding up some of your fingers.*
   g. (Repeat step f until all children's responses are firm.)

3. Now it's your turn.
   a. Hold up **all** of your fingers. (Signal.) What are you holding up? (Signal.) *All of my fingers.*
   b. Put your fingers down.
   Hold up **some** of your fingers. (Signal. Quickly point to each child who is holding up some of his/her fingers. Say:) _____ is holding up some of his/her fingers.
   Put your hands down.
   c. (Repeat steps a and b until all children's responses are firm.)
   d. Everybody, hold up some of your fingers. (Signal.)
   What are you holding up? (Signal.) *Some of my fingers.*
   Say the whole thing. (Signal.) *I am holding up some of my fingers.*
   e. (Repeat step d until all children's responses are firm.)

Lesson 93: Actions—Some/All
This exercise introduces the word **some.**

Teaching Techniques
First you demonstrate what **some** means, and then you present a series of examples. Go through these quickly. In part 3 the children must follow your instructions, holding up some or all of their fingers. If a child holds up one finger, say, Yes, that's some of your fingers. Step b demonstrates the idea that **some** is not a specific number of fingers.

In lesson 99 a similar exercise introduces the word **none.**

★ EXERCISE 4 **Some/All**

[Note: You will need an extra piece of paper for this exercise.]

1. Look at the boys. Tell me if I cover some of the boys or all of the boys.
- (Cover two boys.) Did I cover some of the boys or all of the boys? (Signal.) *Some of the boys.*
  Say the whole thing about what I did. (Signal.) *You covered some of the boys.*
- (Cover all the boys.) Did I cover some of the boys or all of the boys? (Signal.) *All of the boys.*
  Say the whole thing about what I did. (Signal.) *You covered all of the boys.*
- (Cover three boys.) Did I cover some of the boys or all of the boys? (Signal.) *Some of the boys.*
  Say the whole thing about what I did. (Signal.) *You covered some of the boys.*

2. (Repeat part 1 until all children's responses are firm. Praise children.)

Lesson 96: Some/All

The first pictures exercise appears at lesson 96, after **some** and **all** have been introduced in actions exercises. The pictures exercises should be easy if the children's responses were firm on the actions exercises.

Teaching Techniques

■ In part 1 you hold a piece of paper over the pictures of the boys. Ask the question, Did I cover up some of the boys or all of the boys? Signal the response using the hand-drop signal or a foot tap, and then quickly move to the next step.

■ You should be able to do the steps in quick succession.

Corrections

If the children make a mistake on either the **all** question or the **some** question, stop them, and lift up the paper. Say, Watch me. Then slowly cover the same number of boys as before. Ask, Did I cover **some** or

all of the boys? Repeat the entire sequence until the children are responding correctly.

> ## Actions—Or
> ## Lessons 102–118

This track has only actions exercises, although the concept **or** appears in the concept application track.

The concept **or** is one of the most important in logical reasoning. When children are able to figure out alternative possibilities, they can work a large range of logical problems. If they are to have an adequate idea of possibilities and know how to express them, they must be able to use statements containing **or.**

Young children, however, often have trouble saying the word **or** in a statement such as *She will go on the swing or the slide.* They may say **and** or **are** or omit the word. The actions exercises in this track demonstrate the meaning of the word and give children practice in using it.

The objectives of the track are that the children learn

1. how to talk about more than one possibility using **or.**
2. the relationship between **or** alternatives and the word **maybe.**
3. to give oral responses that contain the word **or.**

 EXERCISE 2 Actions—Or

1. I'm going to do something. See if you can figure out what I'm going to do.
    a. Listen. I'm going to frown or smile. What am I going to do? (Signal.) *Frown or smile.* (Repeat step a until all children's responses are firm.)
    Yes, maybe I'll frown, or maybe I'll smile.
    b. Listen. I'm going to frown or smile. Am I going to drink juice? (Signal.) *No.* Am I going to frown? (Signal.) *Maybe.* Am I going to smile? (Signal.) *Maybe.* (Repeat step b until all children's responses are firm.)
    c. I'm going to frown or smile. What am I going to do? (Signal.) *Frown or smile.* Here I go. (Smile.) Did I frown? (Signal.) *No.* Did I smile? (Signal.) *Yes.*
    d. What did I do? (Signal.) *Smiled.* Say the whole thing. (Signal.) *You smiled.* (Repeat step d until all children's responses are firm.)

2. (Repeat part 1 until all children's responses are firm.)

Lesson 102: Actions—Or

Teaching Techniques

■ In part 1 make sure that the children are actually saying **or** when they make the response *frown or smile.* (They may become confused and actually be saying **are.**) Listen carefully to their responses.

■ Pause before each question. If you rush the children, they may make mistakes.

■ Exaggerate your action at step c, and then quickly ask the questions Did I frown? Did I smile?

Corrections

To correct mistakes in pronouncing **or,** do the following:

1. Say the word. Listen. **Or.** Everybody say that. Repeat until responses are firm.

2. Present the phrase "frown or smile." Listen. Frown or smile. Everybody, say that. Make sure that the children are saying **or** and are stressing the word.

3. Repeat step a. Listen. I'm going to frown or smile. What am I going to do? Repeat this sequence until all the children's responses are firm.

If children say *Yes* to the question Am I going to frown? in step b, correct in this manner: **Maybe** I'll frown, and maybe I'll smile. My turn. I'm going to frown **or** smile. Am I going to frown? **Maybe.** Am I going to drink juice? **No.** Your turn. Am I going to frown? The children respond, *Maybe.*

Expect to repeat this correction a few times. Make sure that the children are responding *Maybe* to the questions Am I going to frown? and Am I going to smile?

If the children miss the questions in step c, ask, What did I do? Then ask either Did I frown? or Did I smile?

If the children make mistakes in steps b or c, repeat the exercise from step a.

First/Next and Before/After
Lessons 98–117

Before and **after** are used to relate events on a time scale. When a child goes down a slide, he or she first climbs the ladder, then slides down the slide, then stands up on the ground. When you ask the child questions about this series of events—what happened **before** what—you are asking him or her to remember the order of events and then to specify which event preceded another.

The concept **after** is easier for children than **before** because children are dealing with events in a normal order when using **after.** To talk about an event that occurred before, they must take one step back in time.

The objectives of the First/Next and the Before/ After tracks are

1. to relate the words **first** and **next** to the words **before** and **after.**

2. to teach the meaning of the word **after** and to demonstrate its relationship to **next.**

3. to teach **before** as the opposite of **after.**

4. to apply both **before** and **after** to comic-strip picture sequences.

⭐ **EXERCISE 2 Actions—First, Before, After**

1. It's time for some actions.
   a. Listen. **First** you're going to stamp your foot. Then you're going to touch your nose. What are you going to do **first**? (Signal.) *Stamp my foot.*
   What are you going to do **after** you stamp your foot? (Signal.) *Touch my nose.*
   b. (Repeat step a until all children's responses are firm.)
   c. Everybody, show me what you do **first**. (Signal. Children respond.)
   What are you doing? (Signal.) *Stamping my foot.*
   d. What are you going to do **after** you stamp your foot? (Signal.) *Touch my nose.*
   Do it. (Signal. Children respond.)
   What are you doing? (Signal.) *Touching my nose.*
   e. What did you do **before** you touched your nose? (Signal.) *Stamped my foot.*
   Yes, you stamped your foot.
   (Repeat step e until all children's responses are firm.)

2. (Repeat part 1 until all children's responses are firm.)

3. Let's do another one.
   a. Listen. **First** you're going to clap. Then you're going to wave. Then you're going to touch the floor.
   b. What are you going to do **first**? (Signal.) *Clap.*
   What are you going to do **after** you clap? (Signal.) *Wave.*
   What are you going to do **after** you wave? (Signal.) *Touch the floor.*
   (Repeat step b until all children's responses are firm.)
   c. Everybody, show me what you do **first**. (Signal. Each child is to clap.)
   What are you doing? (Signal.) *Clapping.*
   d. What are you going to do **after** you clap? (Signal.) *Wave.*
   Do it. (Each child is to wave.)
   What are you doing now? (Signal.) *Waving.*
   What did you do before you waved? (Signal.) *Clapped.*
   e. Listen. What are you going to do after you wave? (Signal.) *Touch the floor.*
   Do it. (Each child is to touch the floor.)
   What are you doing now? (Signal.) *Touching the floor.*

4. (Repeat part 3 until all children's responses are firm.)

Individual Turns
(Repeat the exercise, calling on different children for each step.)

Lesson 103: Actions—First, Before, After

Starting in lesson 103, children learn **before**. In this exercise, the meaning of **before** is related to **after**.
In part 1 the children do a two-part action routine, answering **before** and **after** questions. Part 3 involves a three-part exercise (clap, wave, touch the floor). The pattern of both parts of the task is the same: first the children work on **after**, then on **before**.

Teaching Techniques

Make sure the children can respond to the questions in part 1 before proceeding to part 3.

Corrections

Expect the children to have trouble with **before** questions. For example, in part 3, when they answer the question What did you do before you waved? they may say, *Touch the floor.* To correct, say, You told me what you did **after** you waved. I want to know what you did **before** you waved. Repeat the question. If children still have trouble, show the actions sequence, and point out when you clap, That's what I do **before** I wave. Then return to part 3, and repeat all of the steps.

⭐ **EXERCISE 1 Actions—Before**

1. Here's the first game.
   a. Watch me. (Clap your hands.) What am I doing? (Signal.) *Clapping.*
   (Touch your knees, and keep touching them.) What am I doing now? (Signal.) *Touching your knees.*
   b. What did I do **before** I touched my knees? (Signal.) *Clapped.*
   Yes, I clapped.
   (Repeat until all children's responses are firm.)
   c. Let's say the whole thing about what I did before I touched my knees. (Signal. Respond with children.) *You clapped before you touched your knees.*
   d. All by yourselves. Say the whole thing about what I did before I touched my knees. (Signal. Do not respond with children.) *You clapped before you touched your knees.*
   e. (Repeat steps c and d until all children can make the statement.)
   f. What am I doing now? (Signal.) *Touching your knees.*
   Say the whole thing about what I am doing. (Signal.) *You are touching your knees.*
   (Repeat until all children's responses are firm.)

2. Here's a new one.
   a. Watch me. (Touch your elbow. Keep touching it.) What am I doing? (Signal.) *Touching your elbow.*
   (Stop touching your elbow. Touch your head, and keep touching it.) What am I doing now? (Signal.) *Touching your head.*
   b. What did I do **before** I touched my head? (Signal.) *Touched your elbow.*
   Yes, I touched my elbow.
   (Repeat until all children's responses are firm.)
   c. Say the whole thing about what I did before I touched my head. (Signal. Do not respond with children.) *You touched your elbow before you touched your head.*
   (Repeat until all children's responses are firm.)
   d. What am I doing now? (Signal.) *Touching your head.*
   Say the whole thing about what I am doing. (Signal.) *You are touching your head.*
   (Repeat until all children's responses are firm.)

Individual Turns
(Repeat the exercise, calling on different children for each step.)

Lesson 108: Actions—Before

In this exercise, the children make complete statements using the word **before.** They make complete statements with **after** in later exercises.

Teaching Techniques

In steps c and d the children make the **before** statement. Be sure the children's responses are firm before going to the next steps.

Corrections

If the children have trouble making the statements, use the model-lead-and-test procedure to help them.

EXERCISE 7 After

1. These pictures tell a story about what a man did.
   a. (Point to a.)
      First the man got out of the car. What did he do? (Touch.) *Got out of the car.*
   b. (Point to b.)
      Then he changed the tire. What did he do? (Touch.) *Changed the tire.*
   c. (Point to c.)
      Then he got in the car. What did he do? (Touch.) *Got in the car.*
   d. (Point to d.)
      Then he drove away. What did he do? (Touch.) *Drove away.*

2. Let's make it a little harder. Look at the pictures. ●
   • What did the man do first? (Touch a.) *Got out of the car.*
   • What did he do after he got out of the car? (Touch b.) *Changed the tire.*
   • What did he do after he changed the tire? (Touch c.) *Got in the car.*
   • What did he do after he got in the car? (Touch d.) *Drove away.*

3. (Repeat part 2 until all children's responses are firm.)

4. Let's do it again. This time I'm not going to point to the pictures.
   • What did the man do first? (Signal.) *Got out of the car.*
   • What did he do after he got out of the car? (Signal.) *Changed the tire.*
   • What did he do after he changed the tire? (Signal.) *Got in the car.*
   • What did he do after he got in the car? (Signal.) *Drove away.*

5. (Repeat part 4 until all children's responses are firm.)

CORRECTIONS
EXERCISE 7

● **Error**
(Use the following correction for any error children make in part 2.)

Correction
1. (Touch the appropriate picture.) Here's what he did after he . . .
2. What did he do after . . . ?
3. (Return to the exercise, and repeat part 2.)

Lesson 106: After

Starting in lesson 106, the children work from picture sequences in the before/after exercises. The first exercises are only with **after**; a similar exercise in lesson 109 combines **before** and **after**.

Teaching Techniques

In part 2 you should touch the pictures in the following way to signal responses: 1) Touch picture a to signal response to the question What did the man do first? 2) Keep touching picture a as you ask the question What did he do after he got out of the car? 3) Then touch picture b, and keep touching it as you ask, What did he do after he changed the tire? 4) Touch picture c, and keep touching it as you present the next question.

Practice this touching procedure. It helps the children see how the progression from picture to picture relates to the series of **after** questions.

Note that you are not to point or touch in part 4. The children must be firm before you present the final series of questions.

Corrections

Expect the children to give responses other than those called for by the exercise. Instead of saying, *Changed the tire,* they may say, *He is pumping up that tire.* Instead of saying, *Got in the car,* they may say, *Get in the car.* Instead of saying, *Drove away,* they may say, *Droved away* or *Drived away.*

Accept these answers if they express the correct idea and are consistent with what is shown in the picture. Then tell the children the response in the book: Let's say, **drove away.** Say it. Repeat the question until the children's responses are firm. Then continue the exercise.

If–Then Rules
Lessons 125–150

This track introduces the children to deductive reasoning. An **if-then** "rule" is actually a statement with a premise and a conclusion. The initial rules that the children work with do not refer to real life *(If it rains, the flowers will grow)* but to made-up situations

(*If a door is striped, it has a lion behind it*). This tactic forces the children to focus on the information in the statement rather than on knowledge they already have or on intuition. The skill of applying specific information (deductive reasoning) is very important in working mathematical and scientific problems, where the answers are not obvious but are predictable from **if-then** rules.

The **if-then** statements, or rules, have two parts—the **if** part and the **then** part: *If a dog is fat,* (then) *he has a bone.* The key to understanding this statement is to focus on the first part. If the dog is fat, the second part of the statement will be true. The statement does not say anything about dogs that are not fat. They may or may not have a bone.

In this track the children will learn

1. the meaning of **if-then** by means of a game in which the children respond to a command **only if** a specified condition is fulfilled (*If the teacher says "Go," touch your head*).

2. to apply an **if-then** rule by selecting from a group of pictures the picture or pictures that fulfill the condition in the **if** part of the rule.

3. to make up **if-then** rules based on features of illustrated objects.

1. Get ready to learn a rule and play a game.
  a. Listen to this rule: If the teacher says "Go," touch your head.
  b. Listen again. If the teacher says "Go," touch your head.
  c. Everybody, say the rule with me. (Signal.) *If the teacher says "Go," touch your head.*
  d. All by yourselves. Say the rule. (Signal.) *If the teacher says "Go," touch your head.*
  e. (Repeat steps a through d until all children can say the rule.)

2. Tell me.
  a. What are you going to do if the teacher says "Go"? (Signal.) *Touch my head.* ● ◆
  b. Are you going to touch your head if the teacher says "Go"? (Signal.) *Yes.*
  c. Are you going to touch your head if the teacher says "Touch your head"? (Signal.) *No.*
  d. Are you going to touch your head if the teacher says "Stand up"? (Signal.) *No.*

3. Now we're going to play a game. Remember—If the teacher says "Go," touch your head. Wait for my signal.
  a. Let's see if I can fool you. Get ready. (Pause.) Go. (Signal. Children touch their head.) ▲
  b. Let's see if I can fool you. Get ready. (Pause.) Clap. (Signal. Children should not do anything.) ■
  c. Let's see if I can fool you. Get ready. (Pause.) Stand up. (Signal. Children should not do anything.)
  d. (Repeat steps a through c until all children correctly perform the action.)

CORRECTIONS
EXERCISE 1

● **Error**
(Children don't say *Touch my head.*)
Correction
1. What's the rule? (Signal.) *If the teacher says "Go," touch your head.*
2. So, what are you going to do if the teacher says "Go"? You're going to touch your head.
3. (Repeat part 2 of the exercise.)

◆ **Error**
(Children perform the action.)
Correction
1. I said tell me what you're going to do if I say "Go."
2. Tell me what you're going to do if I say "Go." (Signal.) *Touch my head.*

3. Yes, you have to wait until I say "Go" to do it.
4. (Repeat part 2 of the exercise.)

▲ **Error**
(Children don't perform the action.)
Correction
1. Everybody, what did I just say? (Signal.) *Go.*
2. And what's the rule? (Signal.) *If the teacher says "Go," touch your head.*
3. So, what do you do when I say "Go"? (Signal.) *Touch my head.*
4. Let's try the game again. (Repeat part 3 of the exercise.)

■ **Error**
(Children perform the action.)
Correction
1. Everybody, what's the rule? (Signal.) *If the teacher says "Go," touch your head.*
2. Did I say "Go"? (Signal.) *No.*
3. So, should you touch your head? (Signal.) *No.*
4. Let's try the game again. (Repeat part 3 of the exercise.)

Lesson 125: Actions—Rules

In this exercise the children play a game. They are to respond to a command **if** the teacher does the action specified in the first part of the rule. If the teacher does anything else, they are to do nothing.

Teaching Techniques

■ In part 1, present the rule as follows: If the teacher says "go" (pause) touch your head.

■ Make sure that all the children can say the rule before you move to part 2.

■ Present part 3 of the exercise as a game—challenge the children. Let them know you would **like** to fool them.

Corrections

If the children have trouble saying the rule, repeat the model-lead-and-test procedure specified in part 1.

If the children make errors, follow the corrections specified in the box. You will need to practice these corrections, as you will probably have occasion to use all of them.

EXERCISE 9 **Rules—If, Then**

1. Here's the rule for these dogs. Listen. If the dog is fat, it has a bone.
   a. Everybody, say the rule. (Signal.) *If the dog is fat, it has a bone.*
   • (Repeat step a until all children can say the rule.)
   b. What do you know about the fat dog? (Signal.) *It has a bone.*
      Yes, the rule tells you about the fat dog.

2. Now answer these questions.
   a. (Point to a.)
      Is this dog fat? (Touch.) *No.*
      So does the rule tell you about this dog? (Touch.) *No.*
      The rule tells you about only the fat dog.
   • (Repeat step a until all children's responses are firm.)
   b. (Point to b.)
      Is this dog fat? (Touch.) *Yes.*
      So does the rule tell you about this dog? (Touch.) *Yes.*
      What does the rule tell you about this dog? (Touch.) *It has a bone.*
   • (Repeat step b until all children's responses are firm.)
   c. (Point to c.)
      Is this dog fat? (Touch.) *No.*
      So does the rule tell you about this dog? (Touch.) *No.*
      The rule tells you about only the fat dog.
   • (Repeat step c until all children's responses are firm.)

3. (Point to the dogs.)
   Tell me, which dog has a bone?
   (Signal.) *The fat dog.*

4. Let's turn the page and see if you are right.
   (Turn the page quickly.)

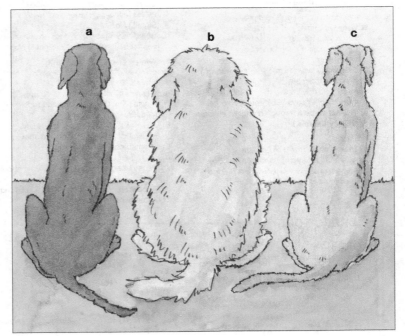

Lesson 126: Rules

This is a two-page exercise. The first page appears above, the second at the top of the next page. In this exercise the children must apply the arbitrary rule *If the dog is fat, it has a bone.*

Teaching Techniques

Make sure that the children can say the rule correctly in part 1. If they are firm on the rule, they should have no trouble with the exercise.

Present part 2 quickly. Practice the steps so that you can move through this exercise rapidly. After the children answer the question in part 3, turn the page quickly.

5. Were you right? (Signal.) *Yes.*
Everybody, what's the rule about the fat dog?
(Signal.) *If the dog is fat, it has a bone.*

6. Now let's talk about each dog.
   a. (Point to a.)
   Is this dog fat? (Touch.) *No.*
   So does the rule tell you about this dog?
   (Touch.) *No.*
   b. (Point to b.)
   Is this dog fat? (Touch.) *Yes.*
   So does the rule tell you about this dog?
   (Touch.) *Yes.*
   c. (Point to c.)
   Is this dog fat? (Touch.) *No.*
   So does the rule tell you about this dog?
   (Touch.) *No.*

7. Everybody, what's the rule? (Signal.) *If the
dog is fat, it has a bone.*
Look at the picture. Tell me which dog has a
bone. (Touch.) *The fat dog.*
That's just what the rule told us. The fat dog
has a bone.

Individual Turns
(Repeat parts 6 and 7, calling on different
children for each step.)

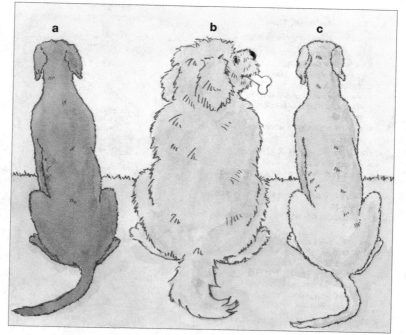

Lesson 126: Rules (second page)

Ask the questions in part 5 as if they were very
important. Praise the children for answering them
correctly. Then do the questions in part 6 very quickly.
After presenting part 7, let the children know they have
solved a problem.

Corrections

If the children make mistakes in parts 5 and 6,
return to the first page of the exercise, and repeat it.
Emphasize the questions, and watch to make sure the
children who made mistakes are looking at the pictures
as they respond.

EXERCISE 6 Rules—If, Then

Let's make up rules for these painters.

1. Look at the painters who are tall.
   a. Listen. If a painter is tall, what part of the room is he painting? (Signal.) *The ceiling.*
   b. You're going to say the rule. Start with "If a painter is tall," and tell what he is painting. (Signal.) *If a painter is tall, he is painting the ceiling.*
   c. (Repeat step b until all children can say the rule.)

2. Look at the painters who are short.
   a. Listen. If a painter is short, what part of the room is he painting? (Signal.) *The wall.*
   b. So what's the rule if a painter is short? (Signal.) *If a painter is short, he is painting the wall.*
   c. (Repeat step b until all children can say the rule.)

3. Let's say those rules again.
   a. What's the rule about a painter who is short? (Signal.) *If a painter is short, he is painting the wall.*
   b. What's the rule about a painter who is tall? (Signal.) *If a painter is tall, he is painting the ceiling.*

4. (Repeat part 3 until all children can say the rules.)

Individual Turns
(Repeat part 3, calling on different children for each step.)

Lesson 137: Rules

In this exercise the children help make up the "rule" by observing features of the picture.

Teaching Techniques

Pause after the questions so that the children can consider their responses. When you ask what the rule is, emphasize the words **tall** and **short.**

Corrections

If the children do not respond to the first question If a painter is tall, what part of the room is he painting? correct as follows:

1. Show me a painter who is tall.
Show me another painter who is tall.
2. Point to the first tall painter. What part of the room is this painter painting? *The ceiling.*
3. So, if a painter is tall, what part of the room is he painting? *The ceiling.*
Repeat this step with the second tall painter.
If necessary, use the same procedure for the next questions. Then repeat the entire exercise.

When this track begins, the children have already had experience with **where** questions (in the prepositions track) and with a variety of **what** questions and **who** questions (in the actions track). **When** questions are introduced in this track. Primary-grade teachers ask these types of questions when they ask children questions about their reading. Children who can accurately answer **where, what, who,** and **when** questions about pictures, spoken sentences, and paragraphs will be ready to deal with questions when they are asked about stories they read.

The objective of the track is to help the children learn to listen to and discriminate between questions that start with **who, what, where,** and **when,** and to respond to them.

 EXERCISE 6 When

1. Listen.
   a. First a boy ran. Then the boy sat. Once more. First the boy ran. Then the boy sat.
   b. What did the boy do first? (Signal.) *Ran.* Then what did the boy do? (Signal.) *Sat.*

2. Listen.
   a. The boy sat after he ran. Say that. (Signal.) *The boy sat after he ran.*
   b. My turn. When did the boy sit? After he ran.
   • Your turn. When did the boy sit? (Signal.) *After he ran.*

3. Listen.
   a. The boy ran before he sat. Say that. (Signal.) *The boy ran before he sat.*
   b. When did the boy run? (Signal.) *Before he sat.*

4. (Repeat parts 1 through 3 until all children's responses are firm.)

Individual Turns
(Repeat the exercise, calling on different children for each step.)

EXERCISE 9 Where, Who, When, What

1. These pictures tell a story about what an owl did.
  a. (Point to the ladder in picture a.)
    This ladder is next to the tree. Where is this ladder? (Touch.) *Next to the tree.*
  • (Point to a.)
    First the owl climbed the ladder. Who climbed the ladder? (Touch.) *The owl.*
  b. (Point to b.)
    What is the owl doing in this picture? (Touch.) *Eating an apple.*
  • (Repeat part 1 until all children's responses are firm.)

2. Now I'm not going to touch the pictures.
  • Everybody, what did the owl do first? (Signal.) *Climbed the ladder.*
    Yes.
  • My turn. When did it climb the ladder? Before it ate the apple.
    Your turn. When did it climb the ladder? (Signal.) *Before it ate the apple.*
  • (Repeat part 2 until all children's responses are firm.)

3. Now answer these questions.
  • What did the owl eat? (Signal.) *An apple.*
  • Where was the ladder? (Signal.) *Next to the tree.*
  • Who climbed the ladder? (Signal.) *The owl.*
  • (Repeat part 3 until all children's responses are firm.)

4. Let's do those questions again.
  • Who climbed the ladder? (Signal.) *The owl.*
  • Where is the ladder? (Signal.) *Next to the tree.*
  • When did the owl climb the ladder? (Signal.) *Before it ate the apple.*

  • (Repeat part 4 until all children's responses are firm.)

5. (Repeat parts 1 through 4 until all children's responses are firm.)

Individual Turns
(Repeat the exercise, calling on different children for each step.)

Lesson 121: Where, Who, When, What

This exercise and the exercise on page 101 are the first two exercises in the **where, who, when,** and **what** track. In exercise 6 the children focus on **when** by responding to your questions about what a boy did and when he did what he did. In exercise 9, the children respond to a group of **who, what, where,** and **when** questions. The concepts **before** and **after** are also incorporated into these exercises.

Teaching Techniques

Starting in part 2 in exercise 9, you do not touch the pictures. You want the children to respond to the words in the questions. You also need to pause after each response before presenting the next question. Give the children time to think. If you rush them, they will make errors.

Corrections

To correct any mistake, tell the children the right answer. Then repeat the question. If they make more than one mistake in part 4, repeat the entire exercise. If the children start making mistakes, you should pause before signaling their response.

Classification

Classification
Lessons 51–136

Children who are able to identify an object such as a car may not understand the relationship between a car and the broader class **vehicles,** which includes not only cars but also other objects that have a particular set of features. For example, when we say that a car is a vehicle, we indicate that it shares some features with trucks, boats, and other members of the class **vehicles.**

Classification concepts are important in logical reasoning for these reasons:

1. They prepare children to group objects in different ways (for example, as cars, as vehicles, as things made of metal).
2. They support the idea that there are many things we can say about a given object—including a statement of classification.
3. Finally, the understanding of classification is essential to reasoning from analogy and other higher-order thinking skills.

In this track, the children learn

1. common classification words.
2. the names of objects that are found in each class.
3. statements for describing objects and the classes they are in.

4. classification rules for some classes and the use of these rules to determine whether or not an object is in a given class.

Following is a list of the classification concepts taught in the program and the lesson where each word first appears:

vehicles	51	clothing	74	plants	111
food	61	animals	83	tools	122
containers	71	buildings	110	furniture	133

A similar sequence of exercises is used for each class. First the children are introduced to the class name (**vehicles,** for example) used to describe a group of objects (a car, a boat, an airplane, for example). They are then shown that different members of the class have different names. Often these names are already familiar to the children; others may be new. For some of the classes, a rule (a vehicle is made to take you places, for example) is then introduced, and the children practice applying the rule. They also practice statements that express the relationship between the class name and the names of members of the class. Finally, they play a classification game.

Classes are reviewed and integrated with other tracks. They appear in concept application as well as in location and same/different exercises.

☆ EXERCISE 6 **Classification—Vehicles**

1. We're going to talk about vehicles.
   (Point to a.) This is a vehicle.
   (Point to b.) This is not a vehicle.
   (Point to c.) This is not a vehicle.
   (Point to d.) This is a vehicle.
   (Point to e.) This is a vehicle.
   (Point to f.) This is a vehicle.

2. Get ready to tell me which objects are vehicles.
   (Point to each object, and ask:) Is this a vehicle?
   (Touch. Children answer *yes* or *no*.) ●

3. Now let's look at some more vehicles.
   (Turn the page quickly.)

┌─ **CORRECTIONS** ──────────
│ **EXERCISE 6**
│
│ ● **Error**
│   (Children name the object.)
│   **Correction**
│   **1.** You're right. It is a (name of object).
│   But it is also a vehicle or
│   But it is not a vehicle.
│   **2.** (Repeat parts 1 and 2 of the exercise.)
└──────────────────────────

EXERCISE 6 **Classification (cont.)**

4. Let's talk about these pictures.
   a. (Point to a.) Is this a vehicle? (Touch.) *Yes.*
      Say the whole thing. (Touch.) *This is a vehicle.*
      • What kind of vehicle is this? (Touch.) *A car.*
      Yes, this vehicle is a car.
      Say the whole thing about this vehicle. (Touch.) *This vehicle is a car.*
      • (Repeat step a until all children's responses are firm.)
   b. (Point to b.) Is this a vehicle? (Touch.) *Yes.*
      Say the whole thing. (Touch.) *This is a vehicle.*
      • What kind of vehicle is this? (Touch.) *A bike.*
      Yes, this vehicle is a bike.
      Say the whole thing about this vehicle. (Touch.) *This vehicle is a bike.*
      • (Repeat step b until all children's responses are firm.)
   c. (Point to c.) Is this a vehicle? (Touch.) *Yes.*
      Say the whole thing. (Touch.) *This is a vehicle.*
      • What kind of vehicle is this? (Touch.) *A truck.*
      Yes, this vehicle is a truck.
      Say the whole thing about this vehicle. (Touch.) *This vehicle is a truck.*
      • (Repeat step c until all children's responses are firm.)
   d. (Point to d.) Is this a vehicle? (Touch.) *Yes.*
      Say the whole thing. (Touch.) *This is a vehicle.*
      • What kind of vehicle is this? (Touch.) *An airplane.*
      Yes, this vehicle is an airplane.
      Say the whole thing about this vehicle. (Touch.) *This vehicle is an airplane.*

   • (Repeat step d until all children's responses are firm.)

5. (Call on different children to answer this question.)
   • These are all vehicles. Which vehicle would you like to be in?

Individual Turns
(Repeat part 4, calling on different children for each step.)

Lesson 51: Classification

Vehicles, the first classification concept taught, is presented in a two-page exercise (see facing page). The first page shows pictures of objects that can be classified as vehicles and objects that cannot. The second-page pictures are all of vehicles.

Teaching Techniques

■ Identify each object on the first page of the exercise as a vehicle or not a vehicle, so that the information sounds very important. Emphasize the word **not** when you talk about objects that are **not** vehicles.

■ You are testing the children's understanding with the question Is this a vehicle? Ask these questions quickly.

■ In part 4 the children establish the relationship between the word **vehicle** and the objects on the page. Stress the words **this vehicle.** If you don't, the children may produce the statement *This is a vehicle* instead of *This vehicle is a car.*

Corrections

On the first page, some children will answer the question Is this a vehicle? with *No, it's a car.* Follow the correction specified in the corrections box. Let the children know that what they are saying is reasonable, but do not labor the correction or get into lengthy explanations.

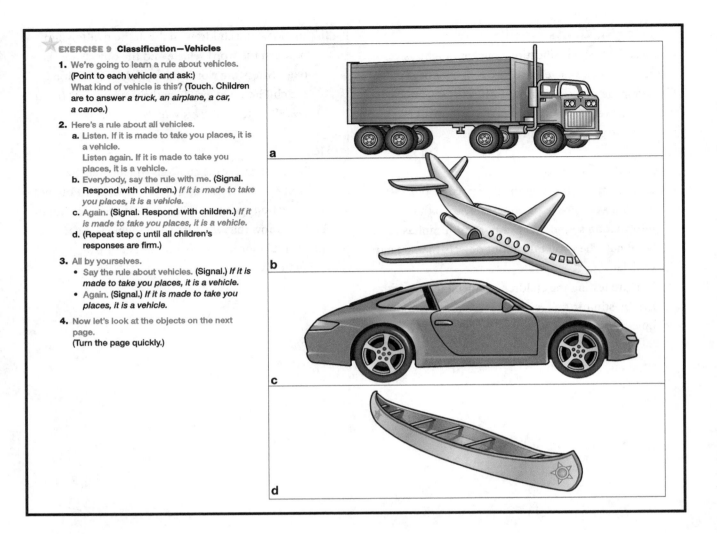

★ **EXERCISE 9 Classification—Vehicles**

1. We're going to learn a rule about vehicles.
(Point to each vehicle and ask:)
What kind of vehicle is this? (Touch. Children are to answer *a truck, an airplane, a car, a canoe.*)

2. Here's a rule about all vehicles.
  a. Listen. If it is made to take you places, it is a vehicle.
  Listen again. If it is made to take you places, it is a vehicle.
  b. Everybody, say the rule with me. (Signal. Respond with children.) *If it is made to take you places, it is a vehicle.*
  c. Again. (Signal. Respond with children.) *If it is made to take you places, it is a vehicle.*
  d. (Repeat step c until all children's responses are firm.)

3. All by yourselves.
  • Say the rule about vehicles. (Signal.) *If it is made to take you places, it is a vehicle.*
  • Again. (Signal.) *If it is made to take you places, it is a vehicle.*

4. Now let's look at the objects on the next page.
(Turn the page quickly.)

Lesson 56: Classification

The word **rule** as used in the classification exercises refers to a statement that is true of all the examples covered by the rule. Rules are taught for these classifications: vehicles, food, plants, containers, clothing, buildings, and tools. The rule for vehicles is *If it is made to take you places, it is a vehicle.*

The first page of the exercise in which the rule is introduced appears above.

Teaching Techniques

To make the rule easier for the children to hear and repeat, present it this way: **If** (pause) it is made to **take** you places, (pause) it is a **vehicle.** You stress **if** when they try to say the statement. The pause helps them hear if it, which may be a tongue-twister for some children.

Stressing **-es** in **places** calls the children's attention to the last word in the phrase and to the ending (which some children omit). The pause after **places** allows the children to say the second part of the sentence more easily: *it is a vehicle.*

Corrections

If the children have trouble saying the statement, break the statement into two parts as described above. First have them say *If* (pause) *it is made to take you places;* then have them say, *It is a vehicle.* Finally, have them say the whole statement without pausing.

Some children will not need this help; they will say the statement after a few trials. Others, however, may require many corrected repetitions before producing the statement correctly.

5. We'll talk about these pictures.
   a. (Point to a.)
      Can this take you places? (Touch.) *No.*
   • A tree can not take you places. So what do
      you know about a tree? (Touch.) *It's not a
      vehicle.*
      Again. What do you know about a tree?
      (Touch.) *It's not a vehicle.*
   • (Repeat step a until all children's
      responses are firm.)
   b. (Point to b.)
      Can this take you places? (Touch.) *Yes.*
      If it is made to take you places, it's a . . .
      (touch) *vehicle.*
   • A boat can take you places. So what do
      you know about a boat? (Touch.) *It's a
      vehicle.*
      Again. What do you know about a boat?
      (Touch.) *It's a vehicle.*
   • (Repeat step b until all children's
      responses are firm.)
   c. (Point to c.)
      Can this take you places? (Touch.) *Yes.*
      If it is made to take you places, it's a . . .
      (touch) *vehicle.*
   • A taxi can take you places. So what do you
      know about a taxi? (Touch.) *It's a vehicle.*
      Again. What do you know about a taxi?
      (Touch.) *It's a vehicle.*
   • (Repeat step c until all children's
      responses are firm.)

6. (Repeat part 5 until all children's responses
   are firm.)

Individual Turns
(Repeat part 5, calling on different children for
each step.)

a

b

c

Lesson 56: Classification (second page)

Teaching Techniques

Your presentation of the steps in part 5 should
indicate that they go together. As soon as the children
answer *No* to the first question, present the next line
immediately. Pause a second before you touch the
picture. After the children say, *It's not a vehicle*, ask the
final question.

Corrections

In step b some of the children may respond to the
question So what do you know about a boat? by saying,
Vehicle or *Vehicles.* Correct by saying, **It is** a vehicle.
Then return to the beginning of step b. The reason for
holding the children to the responses *It is a vehicle* (or
it's a vehicle) is that the wording appears in the rule *If
it is made to take you places, it is a vehicle.* The wording
it is makes the relationship of the rule to the response
more obvious.

If children have trouble answering any of the
questions in part 5, repeat all the steps on the page until
their responses are firm.

1. Let's see if you remember the different rules we've learned.
   a. What's the rule about food? (Signal.) *If you can eat it, it's food.*
   • What's the rule about clothing? (Signal.) *If you can wear it, it's clothing.*
   • What's the rule about vehicles? (Signal.) *If it's made to take you places, it's a vehicle.*
   • What's the rule about containers? (Signal.) *If you put things in it, it's a container.*
   b. (Repeat step a until all children's responses are firm.)

2. Listen. We're going to play a game about foods. I'm going to name some foods, but don't let me fool you.
   a. If I name something that is a food, you say **yes**.
   If I name something that is not a food, you say **not a food**.
   b. What are you going to say if it is a food? (Signal.) *Yes.*
   What are you going to say if it is not a food? (Signal.) *Not a food.*

3. Remember, I'm going to name some foods, but I may fool you.
   a. Listen. (Pause.) Peanut. (Signal.) *Yes.*
   Cheese. (Signal.) *Yes.*
   Boy. (Signal.) *Not a food.*
   Why did you say not a food? (Signal.) *Because a boy is not food.*
   b. Listen. (Pause.) Egg. (Signal.) *Yes.*
   Lettuce. (Signal.) *Yes.*
   Popcorn. (Signal.) *Yes.*
   Hammer. (Signal.) *Not a food.*
   Why did you say not a food? (Signal.) *Because a hammer is not a food.*
   c. Listen. (Pause.) Pie. (Signal.) *Yes.*
   Orange. (Signal.) *Yes.*
   Meat. (Signal.) *Yes.*
   Banana. (Signal.) *Yes.*
   Cup. (Signal.) *Not a food.*
   Why did you say not a food? (Signal.) *Because a cup is not a food.*
   d. Listen. (Pause.) Potato. (Signal.) *Yes.*
   Salad. (Signal.) *Yes.*
   Hamburger. (Signal.) *Yes.*
   Umbrella. (Signal.) *Not a food.*
   Why did you say not a food? (Signal.) *Because an umbrella is not a food.*

Lesson 79: Classification

This exercise is a word game that is used with different classes throughout the rest of the program.

To perform successfully in this exercise, the children must be able to keep in mind the class term being used, relate the objects you name to the term, and decide whether or not each object belongs in the class. Children like playing this game.

Teaching Techniques

Present this activity as a game—it's played according to rules and with the goal of winning. Act as if you enjoy the idea of being able to fool the children. When they respond correctly, act a little disappointed, saying, for example, You children are too smart for me.

Don't give away the correct response with your expression—don't smile when you name a food and frown when you name something else. If you want to make the game more fun for the children, smile for one food and frown for the next, or maintain the same expression as you read each word on the list. Pause very briefly before you give the signal. The children must have a moment to relate the object you named to the class term—in this case, food.

Corrections

If the children don't say, *Not a food* for the nonfood in the list, preface your correction by saying, I fooled you that time. Then say, A hammer is **not** food.

Problem-Solving Strategies and Applications

The tracks in this group are

Review	38–52
Concept Application	43–150
Absurdities	125–149

The purpose of these exercises is not to teach new concepts but to provide new contexts, new uses, and new statements for the concepts taught in the other tracks of the program.

The review exercises prepare children for the concept-application exercises. The primary activity of the Concept Application track provides children with a rule for a picture. In the concept-application exercises, a rule is a statement that is used to solve a problem. Children predict the outcome that is based on the rule. Then they receive confirmation in the form of a picture that shows the outcome.

Absurdities exercises provide an opportunity for children to use what they have learned to tell what is wrong with a picture and why it is wrong.

⭐ **EXERCISE 6 Review**

1. Let's look at this picture.
   - (Point to the fence.) This is a fence. What is it? (Touch.) *A fence.*
   - (Point to the ducks.) These are ducks. What are these? (Touch.) *Ducks.*
   - (Point to the cow.) This is a cow. What is it? (Touch.) *A cow.*

   [Note: Do not point to the pictures for the rest of the exercise.]

2. Look at the picture again.
   a. Someone is jumping over the fence. Who is jumping over the fence? (Signal.) *The boy.*
      Yes, the boy.
      (Call on a child.) Why is the boy doing that? (Signal. Idea: *The cow is chasing him.*)
   b. Someone is feeding the ducks. Everybody, who is feeding the ducks? (Signal.) *The woman.*
      Yes, the woman.
   c. Something is sitting on the fence. What is sitting on the fence? (Signal.) *A cat.*
      Yes, a cat.
   d. Look at the boy again. What is the boy doing? (Signal.) *Jumping over the fence.*
      Say the whole thing about what the boy is doing. (Signal.) *The boy is jumping over the fence.*
   e. Look at the woman again. What is the woman feeding? (Signal.) *The ducks.*
      Say the whole thing about what the woman is doing. (Signal.) *The woman is feeding the ducks.*
   f. Look at the cat again. What is the cat sitting on? (Signal.) *The fence.*
      Say the whole thing about what the cat is sitting on. (Signal.) *The cat is sitting on the fence.*

3. Let's do it again.
   (Repeat part 2 until all children's responses are firm.)

4. (Call on different children to answer these questions.)
   What would you do if a cow chased you?
   What would you feed the ducks?
   (Praise reasonable responses.)

Individual Turns
(Repeat part 2, calling on different children for each step.)

Review
Lessons 38–52

A primary focus of these exercises is the review of the concepts that will be used in the rules that follow in the concept-application exercises. As the exercise from lesson 38 shows, the children talk about the picture.

Teaching Techniques

■ Do not point to the picture in part 2. The children must respond to your questions without any extra prompting.

■ These exercises provide the children with a relatively easy context for practicing phrases and statements. Children may require some repetition on the phrases and the statements. Make sure that they are firm before proceeding to the next exercise, as statements of this type will occur later.

⭐ **EXERCISE 7** **Concept Application**

Look at the picture. The rabbit will eat only one of these apples.

1. Listen. The rabbit will eat the big apple that has leaves. Which apple will it eat? (Signal. **Respond with children.)** *The big apple that has leaves.*

Say the whole thing about the apple the rabbit will eat. (Signal.) *The rabbit will eat the big apple that has leaves.*

2. We'll talk about each apple.
a. (Point to a.)
Is this apple big? (Touch.) *Yes.*
Does this apple have leaves? (Touch.) *No.*
- So will the rabbit eat this apple? (Touch.) *No.*
Why won't the rabbit eat this apple? (Call on a child. Idea: *It doesn't have leaves.*)
You're right. This apple doesn't have leaves.
b. (Point to b.)
Is this apple big? (Touch.) *Yes.*
Does this apple have leaves? (Touch.) *Yes.*
- So will the rabbit eat this apple? (Touch.) *Yes.*
How do you know the rabbit will eat this apple? (Call on a child. Idea: *It's big, and it has leaves.*)
You're right. This apple is big, and it has leaves.
c. (Point to c.)
Is this apple big? (Touch.) *No.*
Does this apple have leaves? (Touch.) *Yes.*
- So will the rabbit eat this apple? (Touch.) *No.*
Why won't the rabbit eat this apple? (Call on a child. Idea: *It isn't big.*)
You're right. This apple isn't big.

d. (Point to d.)
Is this apple big? (Touch.) *No.*
Does this apple have leaves? (Touch.) *No.*
- So will the rabbit eat this apple? (Touch.) *No.*
Why won't the rabbit eat this apple? (Call on a child. Idea: *It isn't big, and it doesn't have leaves.*)
You're right. This apple isn't big, and it doesn't have leaves.

3. (Repeat part 2 until all children's responses are firm.)

4. Everybody, say the whole thing about the apple the rabbit will eat. (Signal.) *The rabbit will eat the big apple that has leaves.*
Let's see if you are right.
(Turn the page quickly.)

Concept Applications
Lessons 43–150

The rabbit will eat the big apple that has leaves is the rule for the concept-application exercise from lesson 84 that is at the top of this page. Children say the rule, observe each apple to determine whether it is big and has leaves, and then make a prediction about the apple the rabbit will eat. The illustration on the next page confirms the prediction. It shows the rabbit eating the big apple that has leaves. The rule says nothing about the other animals and what they will do, but the second page of the exercise shows what they are doing.

The concepts the children must use to solve the problem are taught in different tracks—future tense, actions, opposites, and parts. What is new is the process of combining two descriptive attributes. The problem is "Which apple will the rabbit eat?" The rule is, *The rabbit will eat the big apple that has leaves.*

To apply the rule about the apple the rabbit will eat, the children must look at each apple and answer the two questions Is this apple big? and Does this apple have leaves? The apple for which each question is answered *Yes* satisfies the conditions laid down by the rule, and the children can predict which apple the rabbit will eat. The teacher then turns the page, and the children see a picture of the rabbit eating the apple that is big and has leaves. This picture confirms their prediction. They have used the rule to come up with the correct solution to the problem.

EXERCISE 7 Concept Application (cont.)

5. Look at the picture. (Point.)
   - Which apple is the rabbit eating? (Call on a child. Idea: *The big apple that has leaves.*)
   - (Point to a.)
     Why isn't the rabbit eating this apple? (Call on a child. Idea: *It doesn't have leaves.*)
   - (Point to c.)
     Why isn't the rabbit eating this apple? (Call on a child. Idea: *It isn't big.*)
   - (Point to d.)
     Why isn't the rabbit eating this apple? (Call on a child. Idea: *It isn't big, and it doesn't have leaves.*)
   - (Repeat part 5 until all children's responses are firm.)

6. Let's talk about the other animals.
   - (Point to a.) What is this deer doing? (Touch.) *Eating an apple.*
     Say the whole thing about what this deer is doing. (Touch.) *This deer is eating an apple.*
   - (Point to c.) What is this bear doing? (Touch.) *Eating an apple.*
     Say the whole thing about what this bear is doing. (Touch.) *This bear is eating an apple.*
   - (Point to d.) What is this dog doing? (Touch.) *Eating an apple.*
     Say the whole thing about what this dog is doing. (Touch.) *This dog is eating an apple.*

7. (Ask different children to answer the following questions.)
   Which animal do you think has the best apple? Tell why.
   Do you think the deer likes its apple?
   Do dogs really like apples?
   Do you like to eat apple leaves? Tell why.

Individual Turns
(Repeat parts 5 and 6, calling on different children for each step.)

Concept-application exercises are a central feature in the program for the following reasons:

1. Each exercise provides children with a new problem and shows that the concepts learned earlier can be used in problem-solving situations.

2. Each of the exercises presents different sentence structures, which ensures that the children will develop a facility for using two concepts in different contexts. Children won't be locked into one sentence structure for handling a particular concept. Rather, they will have a more flexible understanding of each concept and how it can be used.

3. The exercises provide a continuous review of the concepts taught in the program. After plurals have been taught, for example, they are reviewed in the concept-application track. This review is helpful to all the children but particularly valuable for lower-performing children because it provides them with extra practice with the concepts they have been learning.

4. Each exercise provides practice both in repeating new statements that involve familiar concepts and in applying problem-solving skills.

5. The exercises contain questions that allow children to express their feelings and observations about the situations depicted in the pictures.

6. The exercises are enjoyable. The children enjoy being challenged to solve the problems and the sense of accomplishment that comes from doing them correctly.

After a concept has been taught in some other track, it often appears in a concept-application exercise. At least one concept-application exercise appears in almost every lesson, starting with lesson 43. This means that children receive substantial practice in applying concepts to different types of problems.

Here is a list of the different concept-application exercise types. It shows the beginning lesson number for each of these exercise types and the concepts the children use in working the problems.

Sample Rule	Principal Concepts
The black dog will run.	Color Actions
The boy wearing a hat is big.	Opposites Actions
The small monkey will climb up a table leg.	Opposites Actions Parts
The goats with spots will eat the grass.	Descriptive Terms Future Tense Actions
The vehicle with wheels will get stuck.	Classification Parts Future Tense Plurals
The rabbit will eat the big apple that has leaves.	Future Tense Actions Multiple Descriptive Terms Opposites Parts
The man will push the vehicle with four wheels.	Classification Multiple Descriptive Terms Parts Future Tense
Only the boys wearing hats will do the same thing.	Same Only Future Tense Descriptive Terms
The boys who will go swimming are wearing hats.	Future Tense Plurals Actions
Every boy is smiling.	Every Actions Descriptive Terms
The rabbit will eat a potato or eat a carrot.	Or Classification Future Tense Actions
A rabbit will jump into the can or the bowl.	Future Tens Actions Prepositions Or
All of the petals are on the flower.	All Part/Whole Prepositions
The rabbit will sit next to the plant that is smaller.	Prepositions Classification Comparatives
The man chopped down (all, some, none) of the trees.	All, Some, None Tense Plurals

The exercise type changes from day to day. In lesson 84, for example, the children do one type of exercise; in lesson 85 they do another.

Teaching Concept-Application Exercises

Only three of the concept-application exercises appear in this teacher's guide. The teaching techniques and corrections that are described for these three exercises can be applied to any of the other concept-application exercises.

Study the exercises before you present them. Anticipate the errors the children will make. They may have trouble repeating the rules. The children must be able to state the rules in order to work the problems; they must know the meaning of any new words to understand what the problems are about.

Present these exercises as "tough problems." When the children solve them, praise them for "good thinking."

Precise pointing and touching signals are important to the proper pacing of concept-application exercises. Be sure to keep touching the picture as long as the children are responding. Proceed quickly through each page of the exercise. Good pacing will not only help the children solve the problems, it will also make the exercises a lot more fun.

Lesson 43: Concept Application

Here is the first concept-application exercise in the program. In some of the early concept-application exercises, the children practice saying the rule before they see the picture. The color **black** and the action **run** are used in this exercise. Here is what appears on the first page of exercise 3.

★EXERCISE 3 **Concept Application**

1. We're going to solve a problem about dogs. Only one dog will run. You're going to figure out which dog will run.
   a. Listen. The black dog will run. Listen again. The black dog will run. Everybody, say the rule about the black dog. (Signal.) *The black dog will run.*
   b. Again. (Signal.) *The black dog will run.* (Repeat step b until all children can say the sentence.)
   c. Let's use the rule. Remember, only one of these dogs will run. Which dog will run? (Signal.) *The black dog.* Yes, the black dog will run. (Turn the page quickly.)

EXERCISE 3 Concept Application
(cont.)

2. Remember, only one dog will run. Which dog
   will run? (Signal.) *The black dog.*
   Yes, the black dog.
   a. (Point to a.) Is this dog black? (Touch.) *No.*
      So will this dog run? (Touch.) *No.* ●
   b. (Point to b.) Is this dog black? (Touch.) *Yes.*
      So will this dog run? (Touch.) *Yes.*
      This dog is black, so it will run.
   c. (Point to c.) Is this dog black? (Touch.) *No.*
      So will this dog run? (Touch.) *No.*

3. Let's talk some more about these dogs.
   • (Point to dog b.) This dog is black. So,
     what else do you know about this dog?
     (Touch.) *This dog will run.*
     Yes, this dog will run.
   • (Point to dog a.) This dog is not black. So,
     what else do you know about this dog?
     (Touch.) *This dog will not run.*
     Yes, this dog will not run.
   • (Point to dog c.) This dog is not black. So,
     what else do you know about this dog?
     (Touch.) *This dog will not run.*
     Yes, this dog will not run.

4. We'll do some more.
   a. (Call on a child.) Show me the dog that will
      run. (The child should point to the black
      dog.)
   b. Let's see if you are right.
      (Turn the page quickly.)

CORRECTIONS
EXERCISE 3

● **Error**
  (Children say *Yes.*)

Correction
Remember the rule: The black dog will run.
(Point to dog a.) Is this a black dog? (Touch.)
No.
This dog is not black, so it won't run.
(Repeat part 2 of the exercise.)

Teaching Techniques

Make sure the children can say the rule before you turn
the page.

Corrections

If the children have trouble saying the rule in part 1, do
the following,

1. Model the statement.
2. Lead the children: Say it with me. *The black dog*
   (pause) *will run.* Repeat until their responses are
   firm.
3. Test the children: All by yourselves. Say the rule.
Here is the second page of the exercise.

Teaching Techniques

Present each part as a unit. Present the steps in each
of these parts so that they go together. In this way
the children will more easily understand how the rule
relates to the questions. In part 4, you call on a child
to show you the dog that will run. If the child points
to the right dog, say, Let's see if that dog will run, and
turn the page.

Corrections

If the children make mistakes with any question that
follows the rule, use a correction that relates the rule to
the problem:

1. Remember, only one of these dogs will run.
2. Which dog is that?
3. Repeat the question that was missed.
Here is the third page of the exercise.

EXERCISE 3   Concept Application (cont.)

5. (Do not point to the picture.)
- Everybody, look at the picture. Tell me which dog is running. (Signal.) *The black dog.*
- Say the whole thing. (Signal.) *The black dog is running.*

6. Listen.
- **a.** (Point to a.) Is this dog running? (Touch.) *No.*
- **b.** (Point to b.) Is this dog running? (Touch.) *Yes.*
- **c.** (Point to c.) Is this dog running? (Touch.) *No.*

7. Listen again.
- (Point to dog a.) What is this dog doing? (Touch.) *Sleeping.*
  Say the whole thing. (Touch.) *This dog is sleeping.*
- (Point to c.) What is this dog doing? (Touch.) *Eating.*
  Say the whole thing. (Touch.) *This dog is eating.*

8. (Call on different children.)
- Do you like dogs?
- What kind of trick would you teach a dog? (Praise reasonable responses.)

Individual Turns
(Repeat parts 5 through 7, calling on different children for each question.)

Teaching Techniques

The answers to the questions in part 6 show the children that the color of the other dogs did not satisfy the rule. Ask the questions in part 7 as you point to and touch each dog. Be sure to lift your finger after each answer; then point to the next dog while you ask the next question. Keep touching the picture until the children finish responding.

Corrections

If the children respond with the wrong dog in part 5, repeat the entire exercise, saying, I think we'd better try this again.

If the children are weak on any step within a part, correct that step, and repeat the part until the children's responses are firm.

If the children make more than one mistake on any page of the exercise, repeat the entire page. Remind them again about the rule.

The questions at the end of the exercise are very important. They encourage the children to use language in a freer and more personal way. Have fun with these questions. If you wish, you can add one or two more. Praise good answers, and especially encourage children who give original responses.

⭐ **EXERCISE 6** **Concept Application**

1. We're going to solve a problem.
- (Point to the containers.) These objects are all in the same class. Think carefully. What class are they in? (Signal.) *Containers.*
- (Point to each container, and ask:) What kind of container is this? (Touch. Children are to answer *a bowl, a glass, a can.*)

2. Listen. The rabbit will jump into the can or the bowl.
- Say that. (Signal.) *The rabbit will jump into the can or the bowl.*
- (Have children repeat the statement until they can say it.)

3. Now answer these questions.
- Will it jump into the bowl? (Signal.) *Maybe.*
- Will it jump into the can? (Signal.) *Maybe.*
- Will it jump into the glass? (Signal.) *No.*
- (Repeat until all children's responses are firm.)

4. Remember—the rabbit will jump into the can or the bowl.
- **a.** (Point to a.) Will it jump into this container? (Touch.) *Maybe.*
- **b.** (Point to b.) Will it jump into this container? (Touch.) *No.*
- **c.** (Point to c.) Will it jump into this container? (Touch.) *Maybe.*

5. (Point to the can and the bowl.) We know the rabbit will jump into the can or the bowl. What do we know? (Call on a child. Idea: *The rabbit will jump into the can or the bowl.*)

6. I'll tell you something about the container it will jump into. Listen. The rabbit will jump into the container that has a lid. Everybody, tell me which container it will jump into. (Signal.) *The can.*

7. Let's see if you are right. (Turn the page quickly.)

Lesson 112: Concept Application

This concept-application exercise uses more advanced concepts. The children no longer say the rule before they see the picture. Instead they see the picture and hear the rule at the same time. The class word **container** and the concept **or** are used in this exercise.

Teaching Techniques

Make sure that the children are secure on the information in part 1, that they know the class name for the objects—containers—and the name of each kind of container.

In part 2 use a hand-drop signal, not a point-and-touch. If you point to the correct picture, you will be giving away the answer; if you point to another picture, you will confuse the children.

As the children say the rule, check to see they are saying **or** and not **are.**

Continue to use the hand signal in part 3. Ask these questions quickly.

In part 4 present the questions quickly.

Part 6 is the most important part in the exercise. The children must remember the information and then process the new piece of information you give them. Do not point to the correct picture to signal the response. Do use the hand-drop signal. Do give the children enough time to think before you signal for the answer.

Turn the page, and ask the question in part 8. Praise the children for figuring out the right answer.

Finish the questions on the second page of the exercise quickly.

8. Listen.
- Which container did the rabbit jump into? (Signal.) *The can.*
- Say the whole thing about what the rabbit did. (Signal.) *The rabbit jumped into the can.*
- Again. Say what the rabbit did. (Signal.) *The rabbit jumped into the can.*

9. (Point to the bowl.)
Did anything jump into the bowl? (Touch.) *No.*
- (Point to the glass.)
Did the mouse jump into the glass? (Touch.) *No.*

10. No one jumped into the bowl or the glass.
- Say that. (Signal.) *No one jumped into the bowl or the glass.*
- Again. (Signal.) *No one jumped into the bowl or the glass.*

Individual Turns
(Repeat parts 8 through 10, calling on different children for each task.)

Corrections

If the children have trouble with the rule, use the model-lead-and-test procedure. You may have to practice saying the rule with children who slur the word **or** or say **are** instead of **or.** (You can make the statement easier to repeat if you pause before saying **or** and also stress **or.**)

If the children say *Yes* to the second question in part 3, correct them immediately. Say, You don't know. **Maybe** it will jump into the can, or **maybe** it will jump into the bowl. Then present a model for the children: Listen. Will the rabbit jump into the can? Maybe. Will the rabbit jump into the bowl? Maybe.

The exercises in this track give the children an opportunity to apply what they have learned in another context. They decide, on the basis of what they have learned about objects and events, that certain situations are absurd, and they figure out why they are absurd.

An understanding of absurdity is useful not only in situations that call for logical analysis but also in everyday life. Humor is often based on appeals to our understanding of the absurd.

Three kinds of absurdities are introduced in the program:

1. Absurdities of function: an object is put to an absurd use.
2. Absurdities of parts: an object has absurd parts.
3. Absurdities of location: something is in an absurd location.

All the parts, locations, and objects that appear in the absurdities exercises have been taught in other tracks. These exercises, therefore, provide the children with a good review of these concepts.

 EXERCISE 5 Absurdity—Function

1. It's time for an absurdity.
   a. Listen. If something is absurd, it is very silly. What do we call something that is very silly? (Signal.) *Absurd.*
   b. (Repeat step a until all children's responses are firm.)

2. Now answer these questions.
   a. Everybody, why do we need pencils? (Praise appropriate responses such as *To write with; to do our lessons with.*)
   b. Why do we need forks? (Praise appropriate responses such as *To eat with; to pick up our food.*)
   c. Would you use a pencil to brush your teeth? (Signal.) *No.*
      That would be absurd.
   d. Would you use a pencil to write your name? (Signal.) *Yes.*
   e. Would you use a pencil to put things in? (Signal.) *No.*
      That would be absurd.

3. On the next page we're going to see a picture with a pencil in it. See if you can find something in the picture that is absurd. (Turn the page quickly.)

The first page of this exercise is followed by a second page with a picture.

Teaching Techniques

In part 2 ask one or two children the questions. Accept and praise any reasonable responses.

Ask the remaining questions quickly, but before signaling the response, pause long enough for the children to consider the question.

Turn the page. Why is it absurd to eat with a pencil? is the critical question. The child's response must indicate a problem that would result if you tried to eat with a pencil *(the pencil might not pick up the food, it would hurt your mouth, it would taste funny)*. If the response does not describe a problem, the child has not answered the question. Do not leave the questions until the children have given at least three reasons why eating with a pencil is absurd.

Call on different children for the questions in part 5. Have fun with these questions. The children enjoy these exercises. You will find them using the concept **absurdity** in their conversations outside of the language lessons.

Corrections

If the children don't come up with good answers to the questions in part 2, help them, and then repeat the questions. The children must be firm on these questions before you proceed.

If the children give wrong answers in step b, tell them right away they are wrong and why they are wrong. For example, if the children say *Yes* in response to the last question, say, No, you can't put things in a pencil. It's too small. Then repeat the series. The children should correctly answer all the questions in part 2 before you turn the page.

If the children don't produce acceptable answers in part 4, say, My turn. Here's why it's absurd. The pencil wouldn't pick up the food. Here's another one. The point would hurt your mouth. Your turn. Tell me why it's absurd to eat with a pencil. Praise children who repeat any of the reasons you gave. Provide lavish praise for any children who give additional reasons. Do not accept responses that have been given by other children. That one has been said, Tom. Think of another one.

4. Look at the picture.
   a. The boy is doing something absurd with
      the pencil. What is he doing that is absurd?
      (Call on a child. Idea: *Eating with it.*)
      Yes, he is eating with it.
   b. Why is it absurd to eat with a pencil? (Call
      on different children. Praise acceptable
      observations such as *The pencil wouldn't
      pick up the food; the point would hurt your
      mouth; the pencil would write on you.*)
   c. What should the boy do with the pencil?
      (Praise acceptable answers.)
      What should the boy use to eat?
      (Praise acceptable answers.)

5. (Ask different children the following
   questions.)
   Would you eat with a pencil?
   What do you really use to eat with?
   Would you write your name with a fork?
   What would you use to write your name?

EXERCISE 5 Absurdity—Location

1. We're going to talk about a grocery store.
   a. Name some things you would find in a grocery store. (Call on different children. Praise appropriate observations. Have the group repeat each good observation. For example:) Right. We find shelves in a grocery store. Let's all say that. (Signal.) *We find shelves in a grocery store.*
   b. Would you find an elephant in a grocery store? (Signal.) *No.*
      It would be absurd to see an elephant in a grocery store.
   c. Would you find a checker in a grocery store? (Signal.) *Yes.*
      Yes, you find a checker in a grocery store.
   d. Would you find a swimming pool in a grocery store? (Signal.) *No.*
      That would be absurd.
   e. Would you find an airplane in a grocery store? (Signal.) *No.*
      That would be absurd.

2. We're going to look at a picture of a grocery store on the next page. See if you can find something absurd in the picture.
   (Turn the page quickly.)

This exercise is similar to the absurdity—function exercises. The children first review the information about what would be and what would not be absurd to find in a grocery store. Then the children look at the picture on the next page and tell what is absurd in the picture and why it is absurd.

Below is the picture they see.

EXERCISE 5 Absurdity—Location (cont.)

3. There is something absurd in this picture.
   • Everybody, what do you see that is absurd? (Signal.) *A tree.*
   • What's absurd about that tree in the grocery store? (Praise appropriate observations such as *The tree takes up too much room; the leaves make a mess; the tree needs sunlight.*)
   • Where do you find trees? (Praise reasonable answers such as *Outside; in the park; in the yard; in a forest.*)
   • (Call on a child.) Point to something that you would find in a grocery store. (Child is to point to something in the picture.)
     Now tell us what it is.
   • (Call on different children to find and name different things.)

4. (Call on different children to answer the following questions.)
   What would you do if you saw a tree in a grocery store?
   Can you think of something else that would be absurd in a grocery store?
   Have you ever seen anything absurd in a grocery store?

Workbook activities are a part of each lesson, starting with lesson 1. The workbook activities of *Language for Learning* have the following objectives:

1. **To expand upon what the children learn in other parts of the lessons** For example, after children learn prepositions, they do workbook activities that require them to apply their knowledge of prepositions in another context. After children learn about different classes, they do workbook activities that require them to identify objects in one or more of these classes. Nearly every concept the children learn in the exercises, from plurals to locations, also appears as a workbook activity.

2. **To introduce new concepts** The children learn colors and shapes through the workbook activities. In addition, they learn to do a variety of matching and picture-completion activities that involve skills that are particularly suited to a workbook format. For example, they learn to complete and draw shapes, to draw lines that show where pictured objects belong, and to arrange things in sequence. In the temporal first-next activities, the children learn to follow an arrow and to sequence events that are illustrated on the shaft of the arrow.

3. **To provide practice in following directions** The workbook activities provide children with a good foundation for following directions. Much of what children will do in school involves their knowing how to follow directions. Knowing how to follow directions is important to school learning.
   As the children do their workbook activities, you will get valuable feedback regarding how individual children are progressing. In a sense, workbook activities are like individual turns that are presented at the same time to different children. You can watch what individual children are doing and can readily identify any problems they may be having. You can repeat directions that give them problems, and you can let them know when they are doing well.

4. **To provide the children with practice in performing the motor skills associated with many classroom activities (coloring, marking, matching, circling, and drawing)** The workbook activities give children practice in staying within the lines of what they are coloring, following the dots, and drawing shapes and pictures. The children also learn to keep track of their crayons and papers. These motor and organizational skills are also important to success in school.

The Content of the Workbook Activities

The major workbook activities of the program are discussed in this section. The workbook Scope and Sequence Chart on the next page displays the workbook tracks in the program as well as the starting and ending lessons for each track.

As the chart shows, three activities appear in lesson 1. These are simple activities that introduce the children to the kind of work they will do in their workbooks and the kind of directions they will follow. Children do three workbook activities in each lesson through lesson 35. In most of the remaining lessons, they do four or more workbook activities.

Presenting the Workbook Activities

The directions for presenting the workbook activities appear on the final pages of each lesson. The title Workbook Lesson appears in the upper left-hand corner of these pages. A sentence under the title indicates what crayons and other materials the children will need for that day's set of activities. The directions follow the same conventions as the exercises in the main part of the lesson.

Each child will need Workbooks A/B and C/D. The children can work on single pages that you have previously removed from a workbook or in the workbook itself.

The first few times a new workbook activity appears, it is teacher-directed. Only when the children know how to do the activity on their own should they be allowed to do so. If the children have trouble with a particular activity, show them what they should have done. Then reproduce the activity, and have the children do it again under your direction. Do not permit the children to make the same mistakes from lesson to lesson. If individual children tend to make the same type of mistakes in a certain part of an activity, alert them to what they should do, and provide lots of praise when they do it correctly.

Workbook Scope and Sequence

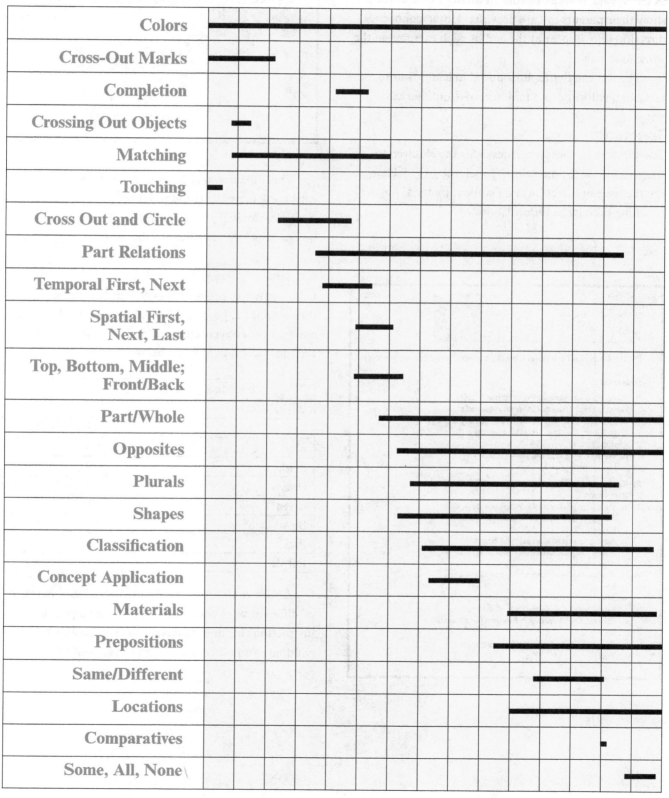

Lessons	0	10	20	30	40	50	60	70	80	90	100	110	120	130	140	150
Colors	██
Cross-Out Marks	███████
Completion					███
Crossing Out Objects	█
Matching	██████████████
Touching	▌
Cross Out and Circle		██████
Part Relations				████████████████████████████████
Temporal First, Next				███
Spatial First, Next, Last					██
Top, Bottom, Middle; Front/Back					██
Part/Whole						██████████████████████████
Opposites						████████████████████████
Plurals							████████████████
Shapes							██████████████
Classification							██████████████████
Concept Application							████
Materials										██████████
Prepositions										███████████
Same/Different											██████
Locations										███████████
Comparatives													▪
Some, All, None													████

Children take home their completed workbook pages. This can be a daily event or, preferably, one that occurs after the children have completed the activities in five or ten lessons. The pages can be stapled together as a language booklet for the children to take home and show their parents or care provider. Home-connection direction lines appear at the end of each exercise on the workbook page.

The three activities introduced in lesson 1 are touching, coloring, and making cross-out marks.

Touching

The purpose of these activities is for the children to learn to follow the direction "Touch the _____." Here are the teacher directions and student material for the touching exercise in lesson 1.

This direction will be used in a variety of other workbook activities throughout the program. For example, you will give directions such as Touch the tall boy or Touch the box next to the suitcase.

Colors

Color activities begin on lesson 1 and continue throughout the program. The activities introduce the children to seven common colors. The schedule for their introduction appears below:

Color Introduced	Lesson
Yellow	14
Red	18
Blue	23
Black	39
Orange	47
Green	51
Brown	62
Pink	113
Purple	119

Children also follow coloring "rules" in a number of different workbook activities. For example, the instructions for one classification exercise direct the children to Make each building yellow and Make each plant green.

[**Note:** Each child will need a black, a green, and a brown crayon.]

Touching

1. (Hold up a workbook. Point to each object.)
   What is this? (Touch. Children respond.)
   a. I'll show you how to touch things. My turn to touch the dog. (Touch.) I touched the dog.
   b. My turn to touch the tree. (Touch.) I touched the tree.

2. (Open workbooks to lesson 1, and distribute to children.)
   a. Your turn. Everybody, touch the dog. Get ready. (Signal. Children touch the dog.) ✔ Fingers up.
   b. Again, everybody touch the dog. Get ready. (Signal. Children touch the dog.) ✔ Fingers up.
      (Repeat until all children's responses are firm.)
   c. This time you're going to touch the tree. Everybody, touch the tree. Get ready. (Signal. Children touch the tree.) ✔ Fingers up.
      (Repeat until all children's responses are firm.)

Cross-Out Marks

Children learn to make cross-out marks (**X**s) so that they can follow a variety of directions that require them to cross out particular pictures of groups. In lesson 46, for example, the children apply what they learned to this direction: Cross out each box that does not have a car and a ball.

In the first 14 lessons, the children learn to make cross-out marks. The workbook pages present rows of cross-out marks that are dotted or partially dotted. Here is the student material from lesson 9.

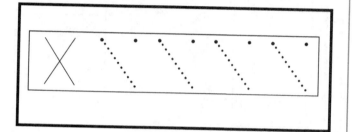

The children trace the cross-out marks and then complete them with a crayon.

A cross-out and circle activity is introduced in lesson 23 after the children have learned to make both cross-out marks and circles. Here are the teacher directions and student material from lesson 34.

The children follow the "rule." The crossed-out object shows what should be crossed out. The circled object shows what should be circled.

Cross-Out/Circle

1. Everybody, touch the tree that is crossed out. ✔
   The boxes show what you'll circle and what you'll cross out.
   What are you going to circle? **(Signal.)**
   The hats.
   What are you going to cross out? **(Signal.)**
   The trees.

2. Cross out each tree and circle each hat.
   Put your crayon down when you've finished.
   (Observe children and give feedback.)

Matching

Matching activities begin in lesson 6. In the early lessons, the children draw a line from an object in the first column to an identical object in the second column. Here is the student material from lesson 9.

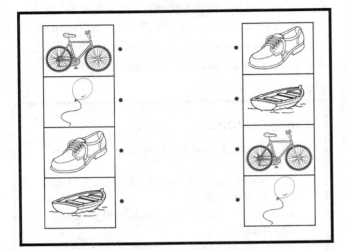

In a later variation of this activity, the children learn to match, for example, animals that are not identical. They match a horse with a horse, but one of the horses is standing and the other is sleeping. Here is the student material from lesson 28.

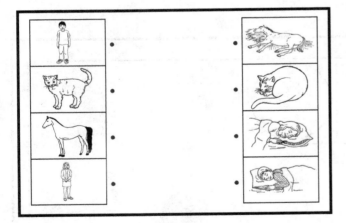

In another variation, not all of the objects are shown. Children first draw lines between the objects that are the same. Then they draw a line from the remaining object to an empty box. Finally, they draw the missing object in the empty box. Here is the student material from lesson 56.

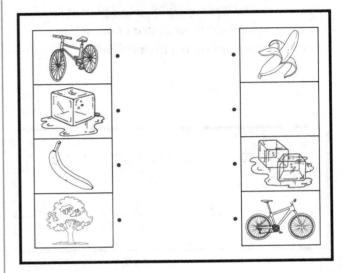

Pair Relations

In the pair relations activities, the children learn to match pairs of objects that are ordered in a particular way. This is an important reading skill because it requires the children to analyze the left-to-right relationship of the elements in the pair. Relations activities begin in lesson 36 and continue in activities of increasing difficulty to the end of the program.

In the first pair relations activity, children learn to circle each box that follows a rule and to cross out each box that does not follow the rule. Here are the teacher directions and student material from lesson 39.

WORKBOOK
LESSON 39 CONTINUED

Pair Relations

1. Find the bottle. ✔
   You're going to circle and cross out boxes.
   a. Here's the rule about the boxes: Each box should have a bottle and a glass.
      What should each box have? (Signal.)
      A bottle and a glass.
   b. Touch the first box. ✔
      Does that box have a bottle? (Signal.) *Yes.*
      Does that box have a glass? (Signal.) *Yes.*
      Listen. Does that box have a bottle and a glass? (Signal.) *Yes.*
      That's what the box should have.
   c. The next box has a bottle and a fish. Touch that box. ✔
      That box should have a bottle and a glass.
      Does that box have a bottle? (Signal.) *Yes.*
      Does that box have a glass? (Signal.) *No.*
      That box does not have a bottle and a glass, so that box is wrong.

   d. The next box has a bottle and a glass. Touch that box. ✔
      Does that box have a bottle? (Signal.) *Yes.*
      Does that box have a glass? (Signal.) *Yes.*
      So that box has a bottle and a glass.
   e. The next box has a hat and a glass. Touch that box. ✔
      That box should have a bottle and a glass.
      Does that box have a bottle? (Signal.) *No.*
      Does that box have a glass? (Signal.) *Yes.*
      Listen. Does that box have a bottle and a glass? (Signal.) *No.*
      That box does not have a bottle and a glass, so that box is wrong.
   f. The last box has a bottle and a glass. Touch that box. ✔
      Does that box have a bottle? (Signal.) *Yes.*
      Does that box have a glass? (Signal.) *Yes.*
      Listen. Does that box have a bottle and a glass? (Signal.) *Yes.*

2. Here's the circling rule: Circle each box that has a bottle and a glass.
   a. What are you going to do to each box that has a bottle and a glass? (Signal.) *Circle it.*
   b. Circle each box with a bottle and a glass. Do it. ✔

3. Here's the cross-out rule: Cross out each box that does not have a bottle and a glass.
   a. What are you going to do to each box that does not have a bottle and a glass? (Signal.) *Cross it out.*
   b. Cross out each box that does not have a bottle and a glass. Do it. ✔

A later variation presents two boxes at the top of the student material. The children cross out any box that is not like one of the boxes at the top. Here is the student material from lesson 74.

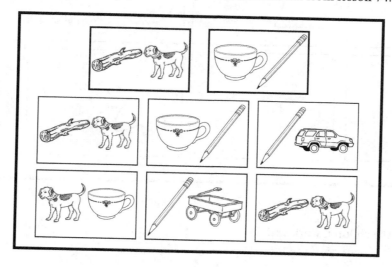

The next variation has two boxes at the top. All the other boxes have something missing. The children first circle the boxes that can be fixed up like one of the boxes at the top. The children cross out the boxes that cannot be fixed up. The children then fix up the circled boxes. Here are the teacher directions and student material from lesson 80.

WORKBOOK
LESSON 80 CONTINUED

Pair Relations

1. Find the box with the cake and the moon. ✔
   The boxes at the top show what the other boxes should look like.
   a. Touch the first box at the top. ✔
      What are the objects in that box? (Signal.)
      A cake and a moon.
   b. Touch the next box at the top. ✔
      What are the objects in that box? (Signal.)
      A bike and a triangle.

2. Listen: All the other boxes have something missing. You can fix a box if the first object is either a cake or a bike.
   a. What does the first object have to be?
      (Signal.) *A cake or a bike.*
   b. Circle every box that has a cake or a bike as the first object. ✔
   c. Cross out every box that does not have a cake or a bike as the first object. ✔

3. Later you'll fix all the boxes you circled so they are like one of the boxes at the top.

In later variations the children work with boxes that have three objects.

Temporal First

Temporal first activities begin in lesson 39. These activities provide children with information that will be useful when they start reading, when they must sequence the spoken sounds of words in time. For this activity, the pictures are on an arrow. They show what the children are to do first and next.

The children start at the ball of the arrow and follow the arrow. When they come to the first picture, they do what this picture shows. Then they come to the next picture and do what that picture shows. They then do both actions without looking at the pictures. Here are the teacher directions and student material from lesson 39.

WORKBOOK LESSON 39

[**Note:** Each child will need a yellow, a red, a blue, and a black crayon.]

Temporal First, Next

(Pass out crayons to each child.)

1. (Hold up a workbook.) These pictures show what you do first and what you do next. I'll follow the arrow. When I stop, show me what to do. Get ready.
(Quickly move and stop at the mark under picture 1. Children respond.) ✔
(Quickly move and stop at the mark under picture 2. Children respond.) ✔

2. Find the arrow in your workbook. ✔
 a. You're going to follow the arrow and stop at the marks for the pictures.
 b. Everybody, touch the ball on the arrow. Get ready. ✔
 c. Let's do that again. Fingers up. Touch the ball on the arrow. Get ready. ✔
 (Repeat until all children's responses are firm.)
 d. Keep your finger on the ball.
 Listen. When I tap, you're going to move your finger to the mark for the first picture. Get ready. (Tap.) ✔
 Let's do that again. Everybody, touch the ball on the arrow. Get ready. (Tap.) ✔
 e. Keep your finger on that mark.
 Listen. When I tap, move your finger to the next mark. Get ready. (Tap.) ✔

3. This time, you'll follow the arrow and I'll do what the pictures show.
 a. Everybody, touch the ball on the arrow. Get ready. (Tap.) ✔
 b. Move your finger to the mark for the first picture. Get ready. (Tap.) ✔
 (Children follow the arrow and stop at the mark under picture 1.)
 My turn. (Touch your nose.)
 c. Move your finger to the mark for the next picture. Get ready. (Tap.) ✔
 (Children continue and stop at the mark under picture 2.)
 My turn. (Touch your head.)
 I did what the pictures show.

4. See if you can do what the pictures show without looking.
 Everybody, show me what you do first. Get ready. (Signal.) ✔
 Show me what you do next. Get ready. (Signal.) ✔

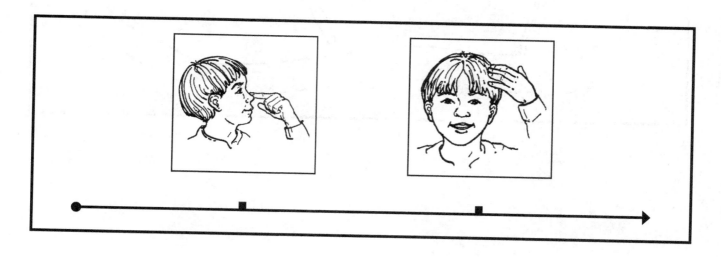

Another variation requires children to complete pictures and then follow the arrow. You demonstrate a pair of actions such as "open your mouth" and "smile."

The children then fix a pair of pictures so that they show what you did first and what you did next. Here is the student material from lesson 46.

Picture Completion

Picture completion activities begin in lesson 42. The children follow the dots to complete a picture. Here is the student material from lesson 42.

Spatial First

Spatial first activities are different from temporal first activities. In temporal first, something happens in time before something else happens. In spatial first, things are spatially arranged so that something is first if you follow a rule. For example, the first letter in the word **bug** is **b**. The letter is first only if you know the rule of reading the letters from left to right.

Spatial first activities begin in lesson 49. Here is part of the teacher directions from lesson 49.

> **b.** The car that is first in line will get to the stop sign first. Touch the car that is first in line. ✔
> Touch the car that is next in line. ✔
> Touch the car that is last in line. ✔
> **c.** (Repeat until all children's responses are firm.)
> **d.** Here is the first coloring rule: Make the first car yellow.
> Say the rule. (Signal.) *Make the first car yellow.*
> Make a little yellow mark on the first car. ✔
> **e.** Here's the next coloring rule: Make the next car blue.
> Say the rule. (Signal.) *Make the next car blue.*
> Make a little blue mark on the next car. ✔
> **f.** Here's the last rule: Make the last car red.
> Say the rule. (Signal.) *Make the last car red.*
> Make a little red mark on the last car. ✔
> **g.** Later you'll color the cars.

Notice that the children use coloring rules to identify the car that is first in line, the car that is next in line, and the car that is last in line.

The first spatial-first workbook activity is preceded by a teacher demonstration. Three children line up in front of the group. You identify which child is first in line, next in line, and last in line. Then the children use these same first, next, and last concepts in their workbook activities.

Top/Bottom

Another set of workbook activities that involves teaching demonstrations is top/bottom, which begins in lesson 49. In the first demonstration, you show a cross-out mark at the top of a piece of paper. You then reorient the paper so that the mark is not at the top. Next, the children find the cross-out mark at the top of

their workbook page. In the later exercises, the children follow directions to cross out or circle the picture that is at the top of the workbook page.

Later in the program the children learn **middle** and **bottom**. They follow directions for circling or crossing out pictures that are at the middle or the bottom of the page. Here are the teacher directions and student material from lesson 60.

WORKBOOK LESSON 60 CONTINUED

Top/Bottom/Middle

1. Everybody, turn your workbook page over. Find the turtle. ✔
  a. One of the animals is at the top. One is at the bottom. One is in the middle.
  b. Listen. Touch the animal that is in the middle of the box. ✔
  Everybody, what animal is in the middle? (Signal.) *The dog.*
  c. Listen. Touch the animal at the top. ✔
  Everybody, what animal is at the top? (Signal.) *A turtle.*
  d. Listen. Touch the animal that is at the bottom. ✔
  Everybody, what animal is at the bottom of the box? (Signal.) *A rabbit.*

2. Here is what you're going to do:
  a. You're going to circle the animal in the middle.
  What are you going to do to the animal in the middle of the box? (Signal.) *Circle it.*
  Do it. ✔
  b. Listen. You're going to cross out the animal at the top and the animal at the bottom.
  What are you going to do to the animal at the top? (Signal.) *Cross it out.*
  What are you going to do to the animal at the bottom? (Signal.) *Cross it out.*
  Do it. ✔

Part/Whole

Part/whole activities begin in lesson 56. In one variation, children draw lines to connect parts of objects to pictures of objects lacking these parts. Here is the student material from lesson 69.

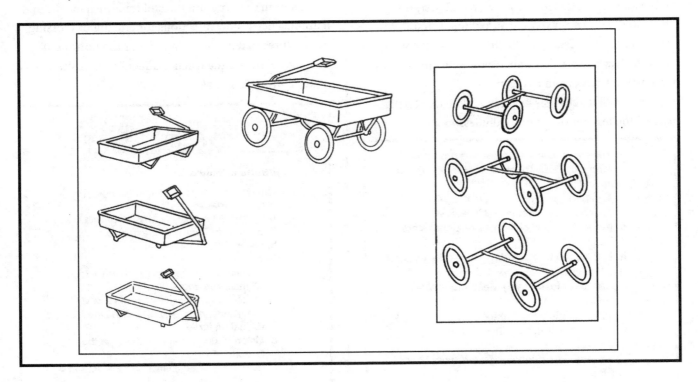

The children identify which wagons do not have wheels. They then draw lines from each set of wheels to a wagon that does not have wheels.

Another variation involves parts of objects that are the same. This variation is introduced after children learn the concept **same.** Here is the student material from lesson 113.

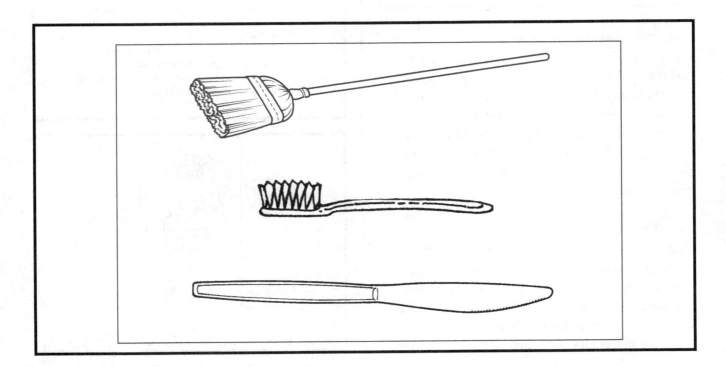

The children are told that all of these objects have a part that is the same. They follow a coloring rule to color the part of each object that is the same. They then follow a second coloring rule for the two objects that have bristles.

In a later variation, the children identify the missing parts of three illustrated objects. They then draw the missing parts and color the objects. Here is the student material from lesson 139.

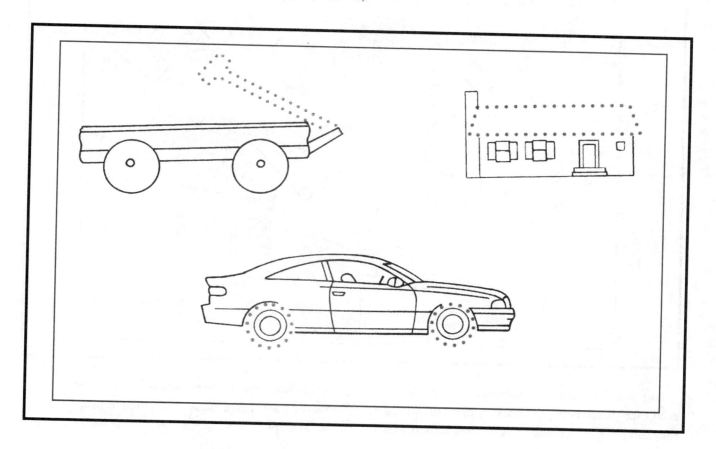

Shapes

Shapes are introduced in lesson 62. The schedule shows when different shapes are introduced.

.

Shape	Lesson
triangle	62
circle	65
rectangle	83
square	90

In addition to learning the names of shapes, the children engage in a variety of activities involving shapes. Some of these direct the children to color specific shapes; others are similar to the pair relations activities. Here is an example from lesson 74.

In some lessons the children are told that part of each triangle is missing. Before they color the triangles, they complete the missing parts. In later activities they draw shapes.

Opposites

Opposites begin in lesson 63. In the first opposite activities, the children are given coloring rules for opposites. For example, Color all of the big bikes green. Color all of the small bikes yellow. Here is the student material from lesson 63.

In later lessons the workbook activities are similar, but the teacher directions contain the term *opposite*. For example, All of the dogs that are the opposite of wet should be brown.

Plurals

Plurals appear as workbook activities in lesson 67. Here are the teacher directions and student material from lesson 67.

WORKBOOK LESSON 67 CONTINUED

Plurals

1. Listen. One picture on your workbook shows hands. Hands.
  a. Touch the picture that shows hands. ✔
  (Hold up the workbook. Point to the picture of hands.) Here's the picture that shows hands.
  b. Listen. One picture shows a hand. Touch the picture that shows a hand. ✔
  (Hold up the workbook. Point to picture of a hand.) Here's the picture that shows a hand.
  c. Listen. One picture shows cats. Touch the picture that shows cats. ✔
  (Hold up the workbook. Point to the picture of cats.) Here's the picture that shows cats.

2. Here's the coloring rule for the picture that shows hands.
  Listen. The hands in that picture should be brown.
  Make a brown mark in the picture that shows hands. ✔

3. Here's the coloring rule for the picture that shows cats.
  Listen. The cats in that picture should be yellow.
  Make a yellow mark in the picture that shows cats. ✔

4. Here's the last rule.
  a. Cross out any picture that does not show cats or hands. Listen again: Cross out any picture that does not show cats or hands.
  b. Do it. ✔

5. Later you'll color the pictures of hands and cats.

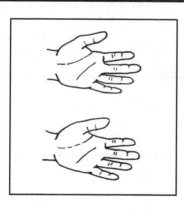

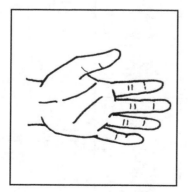

Notice that the activity involves crossing out and coloring. To do this activity, the children must listen carefully to the directions.

In a later variation, the children fix pictures. For example, the picture shows a cup on a table. You tell the children, Some objects are missing from the table. The picture should show **cups on the table.** Fix the picture so there are cups on the table. Then make all the cups red.

Classification

A variety of classification activities are presented in the program, starting in lesson 71. In the first variation, children mark the objects that are in a class you specify. For example, Make a line over every vehicle. In a later variation, the children draw lines from objects of a particular class to a particular location. Here are the teacher directions and student material from lesson 83.

WORKBOOK LESSON 83

Classification

1. Find the boat. ✔
   a. Some of these objects are food. (Point to each object, and ask:) Is this food? (Children are to respond *yes* or *no.*)
   b. Some of these objects are vehicles. (Point to each object, and ask:) Is this a vehicle? (Children are to respond *yes* or *no.*)

2. (Point to the house.) Listen: The objects that are food should be in the house.
   a. Where should the food be? (Signal.) *In the house.*
   b. Draw a black line from each object that is food to the house. ✔ Raise your hand when you have all the food in the house. ✔

3. Listen: All the vehicles should be in the bus.
   a. Where should the vehicles be? (Signal.) *In the bus.*
   b. Draw red lines from each vehicle to the bus. ✔

4. Be careful because some objects are not foods and not vehicles.

In another variation, you tell the children the coloring rules for classes. The children mark one object from each class, and then they tell you the coloring rules based on what they have marked. Here are the teacher directions and student material from lesson 107.

Classification

1. Everybody, turn your workbook page over. Find the barn. ✔

   a. Here's one of the coloring rules for this picture: Make all the animals yellow. What's the rule? (Signal.) *Make all the animals yellow.*
   Yes, so mark one animal yellow. ✔

   b. Here's another coloring rule for this picture: Make all the buildings green. What's the rule? (Signal.) *Make all the buildings green.*
   Yes, so mark one building green. ✔

2. Everybody, look at the workbook.

   a. What's the rule for all the animals? (Signal.) *Make all the animals yellow.*

   b. What's the rule for all the buildings? (Signal.) *Make all the buildings green.*

3. Remember, the marks show you what colors to make the animals and the buildings. You'll color the other objects any color you want.

Concept Applications

Concept applications are introduced as workbook activities in lesson 73. These activities involve rules that tell what will happen with the character of objects in a picture. In the earliest concept-application activities, you tell the children a rule, and the children circle any object that complies with (or matches) the rule. Here are the teacher directions and student material from lesson 80.

Concept Application

1. Find the dogs. ✔

2. Here is the rule for this picture: The big dog will run.
   Which dog will run? (Signal.) *The big dog.*

3. Circle the dog that will run. ✔

4. Cross out the dogs that will not run. ✔

In later variations, the directions are more complicated. Here are the teacher directions and student material from lesson 148.

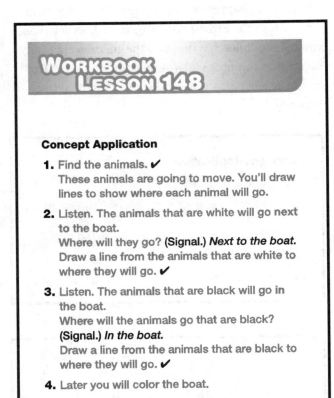

WORKBOOK LESSON 148

Concept Application

1. Find the animals. ✔
   These animals are going to move. You'll draw lines to show where each animal will go.

2. Listen. The animals that are white will go next to the boat.
   Where will they go? (Signal.) *Next to the boat.*
   Draw a line from the animals that are white to where they will go. ✔

3. Listen. The animals that are black will go in the boat.
   Where will the animals go that are black? (Signal.) *In the boat.*
   Draw a line from the animals that are black to where they will go. ✔

4. Later you will color the boat.

Draw Figures

Children draw figures starting in lesson 83. The figures have dotted outlines. The children connect the dots to complete the figures. Here is the student material from lesson 101.

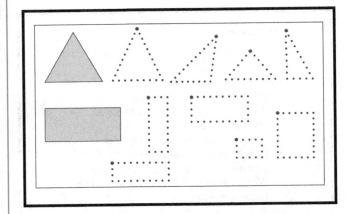

Prepositions

Preposition activities begin in lesson 95. The children follow coloring rules to identify objects that are in different places. For example, The rabbit is in the shoe. Here are the teacher directions and student material from lesson 95.

Prepositions

1. Find the boot. ✔
   a. Here's one of the coloring rules: Make the rabbit on the boot yellow.
      What's the rule? (Signal.) *Make the rabbit on the boot yellow.*
   b. So put a yellow mark on the rabbit that is on the boot. That will tell you about the rule. ✔
   c. Here's another coloring rule for this picture: Make the rabbit in the boot black.
      What's the rule? (Signal.) *Make the rabbit in the boot black.*
   d. So put a black mark on the rabbit in the boot. That will tell you about the rule. ✔

2. Everybody, look at your workbook.
   a. What's the rule for the rabbit on the boot? (Signal.) *Make the rabbit on the boot yellow.*
   b. What's the rule for the rabbit in the boot? (Signal.) *Make the rabbit in the boot black.*

3. Remember—the marks show you what color to make the rabbits. Later you'll color all the objects.

Another variation requires the children to draw lines to where, for example, animals will go. Here are the teacher directions and student material from lesson 150.

WORKBOOK LESSON 150

Prepositions

1. Find the truck. ✔
   These animals are going to move. You'll draw lines to show where each animal will go.

2. Listen. The elephant and the tiger will go in back of the truck.
   Where will the elephant and the tiger go? (Signal.) *In back of the truck.*
   Draw lines to show where the animals will go. ✔

3. Listen. The cow and the horse will go on top of the truck.
   Where will the cow and the horse go? (Signal.) *On top of the truck.*
   Draw lines to show where those animals will go. ✔

4. Listen. The animals that are not in back of the truck or on top of the truck will go next to the truck.
   Draw lines to show where these animals will go. ✔

Children choose the animals that go in back of and on top of the truck and then draw the lines. In part 4 the children draw lines for the animals that have not been used in the preceding steps—all of these animals go next to the truck.

Locations

Locations first appear in lesson 99. The children learn a number of locations in the main part of the lesson and review them in workbook activities. In one workbook activity, the children show which objects do not belong in a location by crossing them out. They then show which objects belong in the location by drawing lines from each object that belongs there. Here are the teacher directions and student material from lesson 99.

Locations

1. **(Hold up a workbook. Point to the farm.)** Everybody, what place do you see in the circle? **(Touch.)** *A farm.* Yes, a farm.

2. Some of the objects around the circle belong on a farm, and some do not. **(Point to each object, and ask:)** What is this? Would you find this object on a farm? **(Correct any wrong answers.)**

3. First you're going to cross out the objects that don't belong on a farm. The lion has already been crossed out for you. Cross out the other objects that do not belong on a farm. ✔

4. Now you're going to draw lines to show which objects belong on a farm. Draw the lines from the objects that belong on a farm to the picture of the farm. ✔

Same/Different

Activities involving **same** begin in lesson 112. Children follow a rule about objects that are the same. Here are the teacher directions and student material from lesson 113.

Same

1. Everybody, turn your workbook page over. Find the nail. ✔

2. Here's a rule for this picture: The objects that are made of metal should be connected with a blue line.
Connect the objects that are made of metal material. ✔

3. Here is another rule: Any animals that are doing the same thing should be connected with a brown line.
Connect any animals that are doing the same thing. ✔

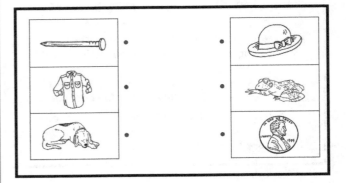

The children draw lines from objects that are made of the **same** material. Then they draw lines from characters who are doing the **same** thing.

In later variations the children engage in a number of activities involving **same**. They follow rules involving the **same** place, the **same** color, the **same** class, the **same** material, and the **same** actions.

Starting in lesson 127, variations appear that involve **same** and **different.** Children are given a rule about how things are the same and different. They connect the things that are the same and cross out the thing that is different. Here is the student material from lesson 127.

For the first two boxes, the children draw lines to connect the two objects that are in the same class. The children then cross out the object that is not in this class. In the last box, the children draw lines to connect the two animals that are doing the same thing. They cross out the box in which the animal is not doing the same thing.

Some, All, None

Activities involving **some, all,** and **none** begin in lesson 132. The children follow coloring rules that involve these concepts. Here are the teacher directions and student material from lesson 132.

Some, All, None

1. Find the eggs. ✔
   You're going to color the eggs.

   a. One picture shows some of the eggs in the basket. Those eggs should be green.
      Make a green mark on the picture that shows some of the eggs in the basket. ✔

   b. Here's the rule for the picture that shows all of the eggs in the basket: Those eggs should be purple.
      Make a purple mark on the picture that shows all of the eggs in the basket. ✔

   c. Here's the rule for the picture that shows none of the eggs in the basket: Those eggs should be yellow.
      Make a yellow mark in the picture that shows none of the eggs in the basket. ✔

2. Later you'll color the pictures.

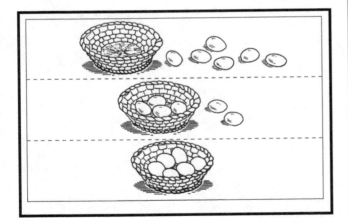

A later variation combines opposites and **some, all,** and **none.** Here are the teacher directions and student material from lesson 149.

WORKBOOK LESSON 149

Some, All, None

1. Find the dogs. ✔

   a. Here's a rule about the animals that are not in a boat: Some of the animals that are not in a boat should be blue. Some of the animals that are not in a boat should be red.
      Make marks to show that some of the animals that are not in a boat are blue and some are red. ✔

   b. Here's a rule about the boats: All of the boats should be black.
      Make a mark to show that all the boats should be black. ✔

   c. Here's a rule about all the animals that are the opposite of wet: All the animals that are the opposite of wet should have long whiskers.
      Make long whiskers on all the animals that are the opposite of wet. ✔

2. Later you'll fix this picture.

Notice that these directions require the children to use a variety of concepts that are taught in the program.

Materials

Activities that review the material the children are learning begin in lesson 132. Children apply coloring rules to identify objects made of the material they have learned. This example from lesson 132 shows a group of objects, most of which are made of wood.

The children follow the coloring rules: The things that are made of wood should be red. The things that are not made of wood should be some other color.

Stories and Poems

Twenty-three stories and six poems were written to accompany *Language for Learning.* Each story focuses on one or more of the concepts the children are learning in the daily lessons. The stories are important for a number of reasons, including the following:

1. Children are given examples of narratives that follow common story forms. For example, a character has a problem and overcomes that problem.
2. Children are familiarized with the sequence of events that occur in stories.
3. Children have to respond to questions and instructions that are presented as part of the story.
4. Children are given an opportunity to hear and practice role-playing parts of stories.
5. Teachers and children enjoy the stories.

The poems were written to be fun for the children to hear, learn, and recite.

Stories and poems are found at the end of each presentation book in the Storybook section. The following list gives the titles of the stories and poems, the concepts emphasized in each story, and the lesson number at which the story or poem is to be first read to the children. The schedule was designed so that the children hear a story about a set of concepts **after** they have been presented in the lessons.

Story or Poem	Concepts	Lesson to Begin Reading
Polly and the Lion	Identity Statements	21
My Cat, My Dog, My Frog	(Poem)	23
Dozy, Bring a Hamburger	Identity Statements	26
Oscar the Worm	Actions	33
Painting	(Poem)	35
Marvin the Eagle	Prepositions	38
Sarah the Toymaker	Parts	44
In a Tree	(Poem)	47
Melissa Hides the Bag of Popcorn	Prepositions	51
Curious Carla Gets into Trouble	Why	56
Dozy Brings the Shovels	Plurals	62
What We Saw	(Poem)	64
Curious Carla Makes Everybody Happy	Why	68
What Did I Do?	(Poem)	71
Dozy at the Zoo	Prepositions	74
Melissa Will Try	Verb Tense	81
Dozy Gets a Vehicle	Classification	86
My Dream	(Poem)	88
Melissa on the Ranch	Description	91
Denise Builds a House	Parts of a House	97
Doris Goes to the Store	Or	103
The Strongest Animal in the Jungle	Superlatives	106
My Balloon	(Poem)	109
Dozy Paints the House	Opposites	116
Dozy Goes Fishing	Before/After	121
Dozy Goes on a Hike	Some/All	128
Denise Fixes the Inside of the House	Absurdities	131
Dozy Delivers the Nails	Location	141
The Little Blue Bug	Rules	143
Miss Edna Does the Same Thing	Same/Different	145

Reading the Stories and Poems

The reference for which story or poem is to be read appears at the end of each lesson, starting in lesson 21. These directions indicate that you alternate among the stories, introducing new stories on some days and rereading stories on other days. Some days are "Children's Choice": The children pick the story they want to hear. The idea is that you will read the stories often enough for the children to become familiar with the story line and the vocabulary, just as children become familiar with stories read to them many times at home.

When you read a story, react to it in the way you expect the children to respond. Laugh when the story is funny; sound concerned when one of the characters seems headed for trouble. Make sure that the children respond to the questions that appear in the stories. You may want to add other questions as well.

Expanded Language Activities

The expanded language activities provide you with ideas that will give your children some additional experiences with the language concepts and skills of the program. A schedule and description of the expanded language activities appear at the beginning of each teacher's presentation book. The activities give the children the opportunity to use and apply what they are learning in a variety of contexts: stories, poems, games, and art projects.

The expanded language activities include

- songs, games, and other activities to help children learn names, colors, shapes, and actions.
- drawings and other activities that support concept learning, story narratives, and other sequencing activities.
- ideas for creating puzzles, posters, murals, calendars, and a variety of scrapbooks.
- suggestions for playing finger games, circle games, word games, board games, and logic games.

The expanded language activities are a supplement to the daily lessons and can be presented either at the end of the lesson or at another time during the day. The children will be able to do some of the activities independently, whereas others must be led by an adult. If you have two groups of children at about the same lesson in the program, they can be combined for expanded language activities. If you have an aide or volunteer helping out in your classroom, the expanded language activities can be a part of his or her assignment.

The expanded language activities are enjoyable—your children will have fun and at the same time learn a lot as they play games, create art projects, and role-play stories and poems. You are encouraged to develop other language activities that will provide children opportunities to apply the language concepts and skills they are learning to new situations and contexts.

Appendix

Appendix A—The Placement Test 149
   Placement Test Scoring Sheet 153

Appendix B—The Transition Lesson 154

Appendix C—The 15 Program Assessments 160
   Individual Score Sheets—Assessments 162
   Percent Correct Tables...165

Appendix D—The Management System...168
   Individual Profile Charts 171
   Group Summary Chart 173

Appendix E—Home Connection...174
   Family Letters 175

Appendix F—The Practice Lesson 179

Appendix A: The Placement Test

The Placement Test that begins on the next page is to be administered individually to each child before language instruction begins. All testing should be completed during the first week of school.

Before Giving the Test

The testing material consists of the Placement Test, the Picture Book, and the Placement Test Scoring Sheet. You will need a scoring sheet for each child in your class. (See page 153 for a scoring sheet that you can duplicate for each child.)

Familiarize yourself with the instructions, the Picture Book, and the scoring sheet before testing. Practice presenting the test items using these materials.

The test is divided into three parts. A child's score is based on the number of errors he or she makes.

- If a child makes more than three errors in Part 1, do not use Parts 2 or 3.
- If a child makes three or fewer errors in Part 1, continue testing the child in Part 2.
- If a child makes more than two errors in Part 2, stop testing; do not use Part 3.
- If a child makes two or fewer errors in Part 2, continue testing, and present all of the items in Part 3.

How to Give the Test

1. Allow three to five minutes per child for administering the placement test.
2. Sit at a low table with a child, preferably in a quiet corner of the room.
3. Score the child's response on his or her scoring sheet as you present the test. Circle 0 to indicate a correct response to a test item. Circle 1 to indicate an incorrect response.
4. Accept all reasonable answers, using the suggested answers as guidelines.
5. On statement repetition items (9 and 11 in Part 1, for example), circle a 1 each time you have to repeat the statement until the student produces a correct response. Repeat the statement no more than four times. (If the student repeats the statement the first time you say it, circle the zero.)
6. At the end of Part 1, total the 1s you have circled. Write the number of incorrect responses in the box.
7. Use the directions at the end of each part of the scoring sheet to determine if the student should be tested on the next part or if you should terminate the testing.
8. For administering Part 2, item 15, you will need a pencil with an eraser. For Part 3, items 1 through 4, you will need a big empty glass and a small glass full of water. For items 6 through 8 you will need a pencil.
9. When referring to the pictures in Parts 1 and 2, you may point to the pictures in the Picture Book or use the pictures in the test.

Determining the Starting Lesson

The directions at the bottom of the scoring sheet indicate the lesson at which each child should be placed in the program.

- Children who score six or more errors in Part 1 begin at lesson 1.
- Children who score four or five errors in Part 1 begin at Lesson 11.
- Children who score six or more errors in Part 2 begin at Lesson 21.
- Children who score between three and five errors in Part 2 and children who score eight or more errors in Part 3 begin at lesson 31. Start these children in the fast cycle of the program.
- Children who score seven or fewer errors in Part 3 begin at lesson 41 and go into the fast-cycle program.

Teaching the Transition Lesson

All children who do not begin the program with lesson 1 must be taught the transition lesson on the first day of language instruction. You will find the transition lesson in Appendix B of this guide.

Part 1

(You may use the Picture Book, or use the pictures in the test, for items 8 through 13.)

1. Show me your nose.
   (The child must point to his/her nose.)

2. Show me your head.
   (The child may point anywhere on his/her head.)

3. Show me your ear.
   (The child may point to one or both ears.)

4. Show me your hand.
   (The child may hold up one hand or both hands.)

5. Show me your chin.
   (The child must point to his/her chin.)

6. Show me your cheek.
   (The child may touch one cheek or both cheeks.)

7. Show me your shoulder.
   (The child may point to one shoulder or both shoulders.)

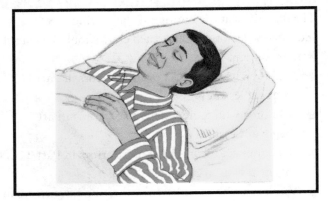

8. (Point to the man.)
   What is this man doing?
   (Accept *Sleeping, Going to sleep,* or *Lying down.* Don't accept *Sleep, Eyes shut,* or *Got to sleep.*)

9. My turn to say the whole thing.
   This man is sleeping. Say that.
   This (or that) *man is sleeping.*

10. (Point to the girl.)
    What is this girl doing?
    (Accept *Eating, Eating a cookie,* or an entire correct sentence. Don't accept *Eat* or *Eat a cookie.*)

11. My turn to say the whole thing.
    This girl is eating. Say that.
    This girl is eating or
    This girl is eating a cookie.

12. (Point to the cat.)
    What is this cat doing?
    (Accept *Climbing the tree, Going up the tree, Climbing on a tree, Climbing up there,* or *Climbing.*)

13. My turn to say the whole thing.
    This cat is climbing the tree. Say that.
    This cat is climbing the tree.

14. What's your whole name?
    (The child must give first and last name; middle name is optional.)

15. What's your first name?
    (The child must give first name only.)

End of Part 1

You may use the Picture Book (or use the pictures in the test) for items 1 through 7 and item 14. You will need a pencil with an eraser and a point for item 15.

1. (Point to the picture of the car.)
   Tell me what is **in front of** the car.
   (Accept *Ball* or *A ball.*)
2. Tell me what is **on** the car.
   A dog.
3. Tell me what is **in** the car.
   (Accept *A man* or *A boy.*)
4. Look at the dog. Is the dog sleeping?
   No.
5. My turn to say the whole thing.
   This dog is not sleeping. Say that.
   This dog is not sleeping.
6. Look at the dog. Is the dog climbing a tree?
   (Accept *No* or *No, he's on the car.*)
7. My turn to say the whole thing.
   This dog is not climbing a tree. Say that.
   This dog is not climbing a tree.
8. Show me your chest.
   (The child is to point to his/her chest.)
9. Show me your waist.
   (The child is to point to his/her waist.)
10. Put your hand on your head, and hold it there.
    Look at me. (Touch your own nose.)
    What am I doing?
    (Accept *Touching your nose* or *Putting your hand on your nose.*)
    Keep your hand on your head.

11. (The child should still be touching his/her head.)
    What are you doing?
    (Accept *Touching my head, Putting my hand on my head,* or an entire correct sentence.)
12. (The child must answer both parts correctly to score 0.)
    Hold your hand **over** your leg.
    (The child must hold his/her hand over leg.)
    Tell me where you are holding your hand.
    Over my leg.
13. (The child must answer both parts correctly to score 0.)
    Hold your hand **under** your leg.
    (The child must hold his/her hand under his/her leg.)
    Tell me where you are holding your hand.
    Under my leg.

14. (Point to the apple.)
    This is **an** apple. What is this?
    (Accept *An apple.* Don't accept *Apple* or *A apple.*)
15. (The child must answer all three parts correctly to score 0. Stop testing if the child misses one item.)
    a. (Point to the eraser of a pencil.)
       What's this part of a pencil called?
       (Accept *Eraser* or *An (the) eraser.*)
    b. (Point to the pencil point.)
       What is this part of a pencil called?
       (Accept *Point, A point,* or *Lead.*
       Don't accept *Drawer* or *Writer.*)
    c. (Point to the whole pencil.)
       What do you call the whole thing?
       (Accept *Pencil* or *A pencil.*)

End of Part 2

Part 3

(You will need a big glass that is empty and a small glass that is full for items 1 through 4. You will need a pencil for items 6 through 8.)

(Present a big glass and a small glass. The big glass should be empty, and the small glass full.)

1. Touch the **big** glass.
   (The child touches the big glass.) Put your hand down.

2. Touch the glass that is **empty**.
   (The child touches the empty glass.) Put your hand down.

3. Touch the glass that is **full**.
   (The child touches the full glass.) Put your hand down.

4. Touch the **small** glass.
   (The child touches the small glass.) Put your hand down.

5. My turn to say the days of the week: Sunday, Monday, Tuesday, Wednesday, Thursday, Friday, Saturday.
   (Do not repeat the days more than twice.)
   Say the days of the week. Start with Sunday.
   Sunday, Monday, Tuesday, Wednesday, Thursday, Friday, Saturday.

6. (The child must answer all three parts correctly to score 0.)
   (You place the pencil on the table.)
   Is the pencil **on** the table? *Yes.*
   (Hold the pencil over the table.)
   Is the pencil **on** the table? *No.*
   (Keep holding the pencil over the table.)
   Was the pencil on the table? *Yes.*

7. (Keep holding the pencil.)
   My turn to say the whole thing.
   The pencil was on the table. Say that.
   The pencil was on the table.

8. Where is the pencil?
   (Accept *In your hand, Over the table,* or *Off the table.*)

9. (The child must answer all four parts correctly to score 0.)
   Touch your ears.
   (The child must touch both ears.)
   Touch your leg.
   (The child must touch one leg.)
   Touch your ear.
   (The child must touch one ear.)
   Touch your legs.
   (The child must touch both legs.)

10. Put your hand in back of your head. **(The child may put one or both hands in back of his/her head or neck.)** Put your hand down.

11. Point to the floor, and point to the ceiling.
    (The child must point to the floor **and** to the ceiling.)

12. What do we call the white fluffy things in the sky?
    Clouds.

13. What do we call a person who fixes teeth?
    (Accept *A dentist* or *A doctor.*)

14. Name three kinds of food.
    (Accept all appropriate responses.)

15. Name three kinds of vehicles.
    (Accept all appropriate responses.)

End of Test

Placement Test Scoring Sheet

Student's Name _____ **Date** _____

PART 1			PART 2			PART 3		
Items	Correct Responses	Incorrect Responses	Items	Correct Responses	Incorrect Responses	Items	Correct Responses	Incorrect Responses
1	0	1	1	0	1	1	0	1
2	0	1	2	0	1	2	0	1
3	0	1	3	0	1	3	0	1
4	0	1	4	0	1	4	0	1
5	0	1	5	0	1 1 1 1	5	0	1 1
6	0	1	6	0	1	6	0	1
7	0	1	7	0	1 1 1 1	7	0	1 1 1 1
8	0	1	8	0	1	8	0	1
9	0	1 1 1 1	9	0	1	9	0	1
10	0	1	10	0	1	10	0	1
11	0	1 1 1 1	11	0	1	11	0	1
12	0	1	12	0	1	12	0	1
13	0	1 1 1 1	13	0	1	13	0	1
14	0	1	14	0	1	14	0	1
15	0	1	15	0	1	15	0	1

Total of All Incorrect Responses			Total of All Incorrect Responses			Total of All Incorrect Responses		
		Score			Score			Score

Student's Score	Starts at Lesson	Student's Score	Starts at Lesson	Student's Score	Starts at Lesson
6 or more	1	6 or more	21	8 or more	31
4 or 5	11	3 to 5	31	0 to 7	41
	(Circle the lesson)		(Circle the lesson)		(Circle the lesson)
0 to 3	Continue testing in part 2.	0 to 2	Continue testing in part 3.		
	(Check box) ☐		(Check box) ☐		

Copyright by © SRA/McGraw-Hill. Permission is granted to reproduce this page for classroom use.

Appendix B: The Transition Lesson

The transition lesson is intended to help groups of children who place at lessons 11, 21, 31, or 41 learn how to take part in a *Language for Learning* lesson. The transition lesson contains a set of exercises drawn from the first seventeen lessons of the program. It is to be taught to all groups that begin the program with lessons 11, 21, 31, or 41. It is not to be used with groups that start at lesson 1.

The transition lesson should be presented on the first day of instruction. The content of the lesson will be easy for the children, but by the end of the lesson they should know that

1. the touch signal and the hand-drop signal indicate when they are to respond.

2. the instruction Say the whole thing indicates that they are to make a complete statement.

3. a complete statement is not called for unless the teacher says, Say the whole thing.

On the second day of instruction, teach the lesson at which the group is to begin—for example, lesson 21, if that is where the group placed.

The children who are placed at lessons 21, 31, or 41 may have some difficulty with some of the content of the first few lessons. Make sure that their responses are firm on all the exercises even if it takes two periods to present a lesson.

The Transition Lesson

The transition lesson is for children who place beyond lesson 1.

EXERCISE 1 Actions—Following Directions and Body Parts

1. Get ready to do some actions. Watch my hand. Remember to wait for the signal.
a. Everybody, stand up. (Signal. Children are to stand up.)
b. Everybody, touch your nose. (Signal. Wait.)
c. Everybody, sit down. (Signal. Wait.)
d. Everybody, touch your hand. (Signal. Wait.)
e. Everybody, put your hand down. (Signal.)
f. (Repeat steps a through e until all children respond to your signal.)

2. Now let's talk more about those actions.
a. Everybody, stand up. (Signal.) What are you doing? (Signal.) *Standing up.*
b. Everybody, touch your nose. (Signal.) What are you doing? (Signal.) *Touching my nose.*
c. Everybody, sit down. (Signal.) What are you doing? (Signal.) *Sitting down.*
d. Everybody, touch your hand. (Signal.) What are you doing? (Signal.) *Touching my hand.* Everybody, put your hand down. (Signal.)

3. Let's do that again.
(Repeat part 2 until all children can perform the actions and say what they are doing.)

EXERCISE 2 Identity Statements

1. We're going to talk about a girl.
a. (Ask a girl in the group to stand up.) Everybody, what is this? (Signal.) *A girl.* Yes, a girl.
b. My turn. I can say the whole thing. This is a girl. Listen again. This is a girl.
c. Say the whole thing with me. (Signal. Respond with children.) *This is a girl.*
d. Again. (Signal. Respond with children.) *This is a girl.*
e. (Repeat step d until all children are making the statement with you.)
f. Your turn. All by yourselves. Say the whole thing. (Signal. Do not respond with children.) *This is a girl.*
g. (Repeat step f until all children can make the statement.)

2. We're going to talk about a boy.
a. (Ask a boy in the group to stand up.) Everybody, what is this? (Signal.) *A boy.* Yes, a boy.
b. My turn. I can say the whole thing. This is a boy. Listen again. This is a boy.
c. Say the whole thing with me. (Signal. Respond with children.) *This is a boy.*
d. Again. (Signal. Respond with children.) *This is a boy.*
e. (Repeat step d until all children are making the statement with you.)
f. Now it's your turn. All by yourselves. Say the whole thing. (Signal. Do not respond with children.) *This is a boy.*
g. (Repeat step f until all children can make the statement.)

Individual Turns
(Call on different children to make the statements.)

CORRECTIONS

EXERCISE 1
● **Error**
(Children don't say *Touching my nose.*)

Correction
1. Touching my nose. Say it with me. (Signal. Respond with children.) *Touching my nose.*
2. Again. (Signal. Respond with children.) *Touching my nose.*
3. All by yourselves. Say it. (Signal. Do not respond with children.) *Touching my nose.*
4. (Have children put their hands down.) *Touching my nose.*
5. (Repeat part 2b.)

In this exercise, children learn to identify objects and to follow the point and touch signals.

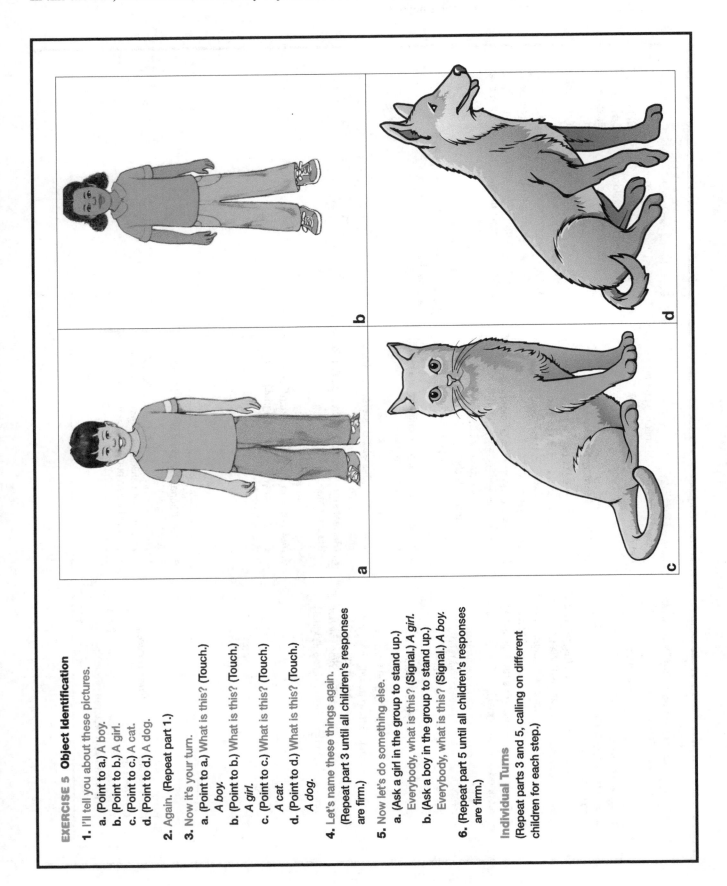

EXERCISE 5 Object Identification

1. I'll tell you about these pictures.
   a. (Point to a.) A boy.
   b. (Point to b.) A girl.
   c. (Point to c.) A cat.
   d. (Point to d.) A dog.

2. Again. (Repeat part 1.)

3. Now it's your turn.
   a. (Point to a.) What is this? (Touch.)
      A boy.
   b. (Point to b.) What is this? (Touch.)
      A girl.
   c. (Point to c.) What is this? (Touch.)
      A cat.
   d. (Point to d.) What is this? (Touch.)
      A dog.

4. Let's name these things again.
   (Repeat part 3 until all children's responses
   are firm.)

5. Now let's do something else.
   a. (Ask a girl in the group to stand up.)
      Everybody, what is this? (Signal.) *A girl.*
   b. (Ask a boy in the group to stand up.)
      Everybody, what is this? (Signal.) *A boy.*

6. (Repeat part 5 until all children's responses
   are firm.)

Individual Turns
(Repeat parts 3 and 5, calling on different
children for each step.)

In this exercise, you introduce the children to the complete statement.

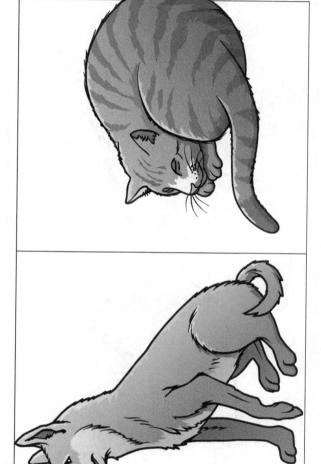

EXERCISE 7 Identity Statements

1. We're going to talk about a dog. When I touch it, you tell me about it.

 a. (Point to the dog.) Everybody, what is this? (Touch.) *A dog.*
 Yes, a dog.

 b. My turn. I can say the whole thing. This is a dog. Listen again. This is a dog. Say the whole thing with me. (Touch. Respond with children.) *This is a dog.*

 c. Again. (Touch. Respond with children.) *This is a dog.*
 (Repeat until all children can make the statement with you.)

 d. Your turn. All by yourselves. Say the whole thing. (Touch. Do not respond with children.) *This is a dog.*
 Again. (Touch. Do not respond with children.) *This is a dog.*

2. (Repeat part 1 until all children can make the statement.)

3. We're going to talk about a cat. When I touch it, you tell me about it.

 a. (Point to the cat.) Everybody, what is this? (Touch.) *A cat.*
 Yes, a cat.

 b. My turn. I can say the whole thing. This is a cat. Listen again. This is a cat. Say the whole thing with me. (Touch. Respond with children.) *This is a cat.*

 c. Again. (Touch. Respond with children.) *This is a cat.*
 (Repeat until all children are making the statement with you.)

 d. Your turn. All by yourselves. Say the whole thing. (Touch. Do not respond with children.) *This is a cat.*

 e. Again. (Touch. Do not respond with children.) *This is a cat.*

4. (Repeat part 3 until all children can make the statement.)

Individual Turns
(Call on different children to say the whole thing about each picture.)

In this exercise, the children identify objects and make complete statements in response to your instructions.

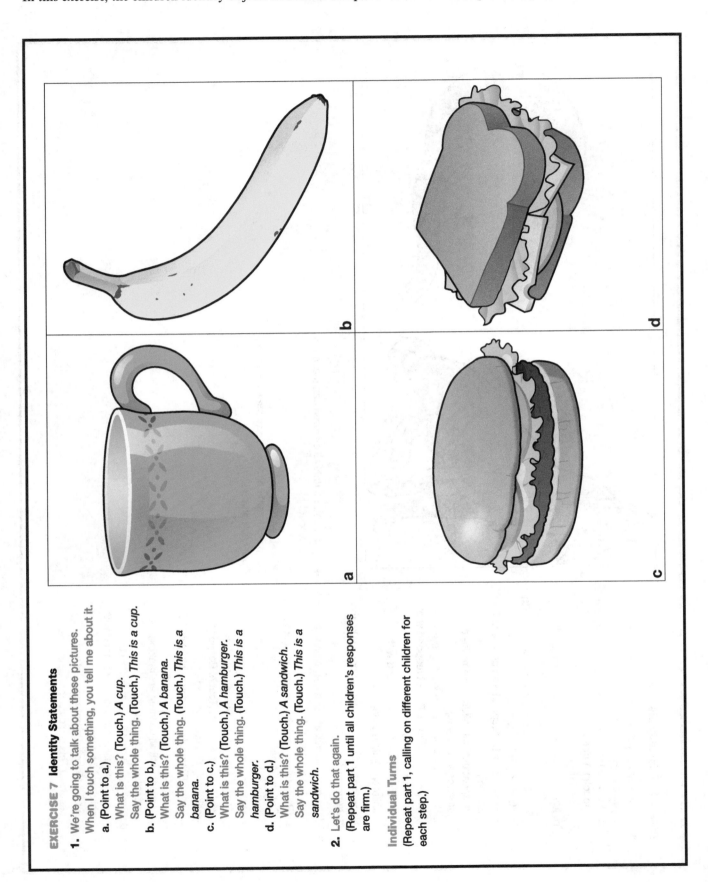

EXERCISE 7 Identity Statements

1. We're going to talk about these pictures.
When I touch something, you tell me about it.
a. (Point to a.)
What is this? (Touch.) *A cup.*
Say the whole thing. (Touch.) *This is a cup.*
b. (Point to b.)
What is this? (Touch.) *A banana.*
Say the whole thing. (Touch.) *This is a banana.*
c. (Point to c.)
What is this? (Touch.) *A hamburger.*
Say the whole thing. (Touch.) *This is a hamburger.*
d. (Point to d.)
What is this? (Touch.) *A sandwich.*
Say the whole thing. (Touch.) *This is a sandwich.*

2. Let's do that again.
(Repeat part 1 until all children's responses are firm.)

Individual Turns
(Repeat part 1, calling on different children for each step.)

In this exercise, the children learn to make an action statement about a picture.

EXERCISE 5 Action Statements—Pictures

1. We're going to talk about some actions.

a. (Point to the girl.) Everybody, what is this? (Touch.) *A girl.*

Say the whole thing. (Touch.) *This is a girl.*

b. Listen. What is this girl doing? (Touch.) *Standing.*

c. Let's say the whole thing about what this girl is doing. (Touch. Respond with children.) *This girl is standing.*

d. Again. (Touch.) *This girl is standing.*

e. All by yourselves. Say the whole thing about what this girl is doing. (Touch.) *This girl is standing.*

f. (Repeat steps a through e until all children's responses are firm.)

2. Now we'll talk about some more actions.

a. (Point to the dog.) Everybody, what is this? (Touch.) *A dog.*

Say the whole thing. (Touch.) *This is a dog.*

b. What is this dog doing? (Touch.) *Sitting.*

c. Say the whole thing about what this dog is doing. (Touch. Do not respond with children.) *This dog is sitting.*

d. Again. (Touch.) *This dog is sitting.*

e. (Repeat steps a through d until all children's responses are firm.)

3. Get ready to do some more.

a. (Point to the cat.) Everybody, what is this? (Touch.) *A cat.*

Say the whole thing. (Touch.) *This is a cat.*

b. What is the cat doing? (Touch.) *Standing.*

c. Say the whole thing about what this cat is doing. (Touch.) *This cat is standing.*

d. Again. (Touch.) *This cat is standing.*

e. (Repeat steps a through d until all children's responses are firm.)

4. Let's do those again.

a. (Point to the girl.) Everybody, what is this? (Touch.) *A girl.*

b. What is this girl doing? (Touch.) *Standing.*

c. Say the whole thing about what this girl is doing. (Touch.) *This girl is standing.*

5. (Repeat parts 2 and 3 until all children's responses are firm.)

Individual Turns

(Repeat the exercise, calling on different children for each step.)

Appendix C: The 15 Program Assessments

Language for Learning contains fifteen Program Assessments. A program assessment appears in the presentation books after every tenth lesson. The fifteen assessments are to be given at the ten-lesson intervals, beginning when the children complete lesson 10 and ending when they complete lesson 150. These assessments, to be administered individually, will provide you with information that will help you monitor the progress of the children as they move through the program. The assessments will also help you identify the children who need extra help.

Directions for Giving the Assessments

When Give the children in each of your groups an assessment at the end of each 10-lesson block. Assessment 1 is given when the children complete lesson 10, Assessment 6 when they complete lesson 60.

Time Requirements Most children require about five minutes to complete each of the first ten assessments. They may take a little more time on the later assessments. Remember that each item in each assessment is to be presented individually, and that the children must be given adequate time to respond.

Materials To give an assessment, you will need the assessment in the Presentation Book, an Individual Score Sheet for each student, the Picture Book, and a pencil. (The blackline masters for the Individual Score Sheets are in this appendix. There are separate score sheets for Assessments 1–5, 6–10, 11–15.) You will need several real objects for Assessments 5 and 6. (See the directions at the top of these assessments.)

The following typefaces are used in each assessment:

This blue typeface indicates what you say.

This bold typeface indicates words that you stress.

(This typeface, in parentheses, indicates what you do or what the child does.)

This italic typeface indicates the child's responses.

The Individual Score Sheets Each Individual Score Sheet lists an item number for each scorable response. Record the child's responses on the Individual Score Sheet by slashing through the numbers of any items the child does not respond to correctly.

The Picture Book For some of the items, you or the child will point to pictures in the Picture Book. Make sure the child can see the pictures and that you are pointing to the picture specified for the item you are giving. Remember to show only one page of the Picture Book at a time.

The Percent Correct Tables These tables will enable you to quickly calculate the percentage of assessment items each child gets correct. You will find a percent-correct table for each assessment in the program on pages 165–167 of this appendix.

Where Pick a fairly quiet place in your classroom. It is important that you are able to hear the child's responses.

How Identify the assessment number on the Individual Score Sheet and mark that column by highlighting it. Present each item exactly as written and listen carefully to the child's response. Move from item to item at a good pace.

Evaluating Student Responses Present each item as written. Give the child time to respond to your instructions and questions. The correct responses are specified in the assessment materials. If a child gives a response that is not specified, but is a reasonable response, accept the alternative response as correct. If the child does not respond after a 10-second interval, mark the item as incorrect, and move on to the next item.

Statement Production Items Statement production items are marked with quotes around item numbers ("5", "8", etc.). These items are difficult for some children. To receive credit, a child must produce the full statement. Do not give credit for a response that omits words or substitutes other words for those in the statement. However, if a student responds to an object identification item with a full statement (rather than first identifying the object and then making the full statement after you have said, "Say the whole thing"), count the answer as correct.

Tallying the Responses When the child completes the assessment, you tally the child's incorrect answers and write that number at the bottom of the Individual Score Sheet. Subtract that number from the total number of items in the assessment. You can calculate the percentage of items the child got correct by referring to the Percent Correct Tables found in this appendix.

Extra Help If a child gets 90 percent or more of the items correct, no extra help is necessary. If a child gets fewer than 90 percent of the items correct, he or she should be given extra help so as to be able to progress through the program. Groups that average below 80 percent on an assessment should be provided with extra help. Suggestions for Extra Help exercises in the Language for Learning program appear at the end of each assessment in the Differentiated Instruction charts. Work with individual children or small groups of children on these suggested exercises for a few days.

Readministering the Assessment Readminister only those items the child did not answer correctly. Record any errors on the same Individual Score Sheet, using a different color pencil. Refigure the percentage correct of the total number of items, and write the new score in the final box.

Name _____

Assessment 1		Assessment 2		Assessment 3		Assessment 4		Assessment 5	
A 1.	C 16.	A 1.	D 16.	A 1.	D 19.	A 1.	D 16.	A 1.	D 17.
2.	17.	2.	"17."	2.	20.	2.	17.	"2."	18.
3.	18.	B 3.	18.	B 3.	"21."	3.	18.	B 3.	19.
B 4.	"19."	4.	"19."	4.	22.	B 4.	"19."	4.	20.
5.	20.	5.	20.	5.	"23."	5.	E 20.	5.	21.
6.	"21."	6.	"21."	"6."	E 24.	"6."	21.	6.	"22."
7.	22.	7.	E 22.	7.	"25."	7.	22.	"7."	23.
8.	"23."	8.	"23."	"8."	26.	"8."	"23."	8.	24.
9.	24.	"9."	24.	9.	"27."	9.	24.	"9."	"25."
"10."	"25."	C 10.	"25."	"10."	28.	"10."	25.	C 10.	E "26."
11.		"11."		11.	29.	C "11."	26.	11.	"27."
12.		12.		"12."		"12."	"27."	12.	"28."
13.		"13."		C 13.		"13."		13.	"29."
14.		14.		14.		"14."		"14."	30.
"15."		"15."		15.		"15."		15.	
				16.				"16."	
				17.					
				18.					

# items passed / total # items			# items passed / total # items			# items passed / total # items			# items passed / total # items			# items passed / total # items		
		25			25			29			27			30
% correct			% correct			% correct			% correct			% correct		

Copyright © by SRA/McGraw-Hill. Permission is granted to reproduce this page for classroom use

Name _____

Assessment 6		Assessment 7		Assessment 8		Assessment 9		Assessment 10	
A 1.	**D** 13.	**A** "1."	**D** 13.	**A** 1.	**D** 17.	**A** 1.	**E** 17.	**A** 1.	**D** 18.
"2."	14.	"2."	14.	"2."	"18."	"2."	"18."	2.	19.
3.	15.	"3."	"15."	3.	19.	3.	19.	3.	"20."
4.	16.	"4."	16.	"4."	"20."	"4."	"20."	4.	**E** 21.
B 5.	17.	"5."	17.	5.	**E** 21.	5.	21.	5.	22.
6.	"18."	"6."	"18."	"6."	22.	6.	"22."	**B** 6.	23.
"7."	**E** "19."	**B** 7.	**E** 19.	**B** 7.	23.	7.	**F** 23.	7.	"24."
8.	20.	"8."	**F** 20.	8.	24.	**B** 8.	24.	8.	**F** 25.
"9."	21.	**C** 9.	21.	9.	**F** 25.	9.	25.	9.	26.
C 10.	22.	10.	22.	"10."	26.	**C** 10.	26.	10.	27.
11.	23.	11.	23.	**C** 11.	27.	11.	27.	11.	28.
12.	24.	"12."	24.	"12."	28.	12.	28.	**C** 12.	29.
	25.		25.	13.	"29."	"13."	29.	"13."	30.
	26.			"14."		"14."	30.	14.	31.
	"27."			15.		**D** 15.	31.	"15."	32.
				16.		16.	32.	16.	33.
							"33."	"17."	34.
									"35."

# items passed / total # items		# items passed / total # items		# items passed / total # items		# items passed / total # items		# items passed / total # items	
	27		25		29		33		35
% correct		% correct		% correct		% correct		% correct	

Copyright © by SRA/McGraw-Hill. Permission is granted to reproduce this page for classroom use.

LANGUAGE FOR LEARNING
INDIVIDUAL SCORE SHEET—ASSESSMENTS 11–15

Name _____

Assessment 11				Assessment 12				Assessment 13				Assessment 14				Assessment 15			
A	"1."	E	15.	A	1.	D	22.	A	1.	D	17.	A	1.	E	21.	A	1.	D	28.
B	2.		16.		"2."		23.		"2."		18.		"2."		22.		"2."		"29."
	3.		17.		3.		24.		"3."		19.		3.		23.		3.		30.
	4.	F	18.		"4."		25.		4.		20.		"4."		24.		"4."		"31."
	5.		19.		5.		26.		"5."		21.		5.		25.		5.		32.
	6.		20.		6.		27.	B	6.		22.		6.		26.		"6."		33.
	7.		21.	B	7.		28.		7.		23.		"7."		27.		7.		34.
C	8.		22.		8.	E	"29."		8.	E	24.	B	8.		28.		8.		35.
	9.		23.		9.		30.		9.		25.		9.		29.		"9."	E	36.
D	"10."	G	24.		10.		31.	C	10.		26.		10.		"30."		10.		37.
	"11."		"25."		11.		32.		"11."		27.		11.	F	31.		11.		38.
	"12."		26.		12.		33.		12.		28.	C	12.		32.		12.		39.
	"13."		27.		13.		34.		13.		"29."		13.	G	33.		13.		40.
	14.		28.	C	14.		35.		14.		30.	D	14.		"34."	B	14.	F	41.
			29.		15.		36.		15.	F	31.		15.		35.		"15."		"42."
			"30."		16.		"37."		16.		32.		16.		"36."		16.		"43."
					"17."						33.		17.				17.	G	44.
					18.						34.		18.				18.		45.
					"19."								19.				19.	H	46.
					20.								20.				20.		47.
					21.												21.		48.
																	22.		49.
																	23.		50.
																C	24.		
																	25.		
																	26.		
																	27.		

# items passed / total # items	30	# items passed / total # items	37	# items passed / total # items	34	# items passed / total # items	36	# items passed / total # items	50
% correct		% correct		% correct		% correct		% correct	

Copyright © by SRA/McGraw-Hill. Permission is granted to reproduce this page for classroom use.

Appendix C

PERCENT CORRECT TABLES

Assessment 1
A perfect score is 25 points.

%	Total Correct	%	Total Correct	%	Total Correct
100 = 25		76 = 19		52 = 13	
96 = 24		72 = 18		48 = 12	
92 = 23		68 = 17		44 = 11	
88 = 22		64 = 16		40 = 10	
84 = 21		60 = 15		36 = 9	
80 = 20		56 = 14		32 = 8	

Assessment 2
A perfect score is 25 points.

%	Total Correct	%	Total Correct	%	Total Correct
100 = 25		76 = 19		52 = 13	
97 = 24		72 = 18		48 = 12	
92 = 23		68 = 17		44 = 11	
88 = 22		64 = 16		40 = 10	
84 = 21		60 = 15		36 = 9	
80 = 20		56 = 14		32 = 8	

Assessment 3
A perfect score is 29 points.

%	Total Correct	%	Total Correct	%	Total Correct
100 = 29		79 = 23		59 = 17	
96 = 28		76 = 22		55 = 16	
93 = 27		72 = 21		52 = 15	
90 = 26		69 = 20		48 = 14	
86 = 25		66 = 19		45 = 13	
83 = 24		62 = 18		41 = 12	

Assessment 4
A perfect score is 27 points.

%	Total Correct	%	Total Correct	%	Total Correct
100 = 27		78 = 21		56 = 15	
96 = 26		74 = 20		52 = 14	
93 = 25		70 = 19		48 = 13	
89 = 24		67 = 18		44 = 12	
85 = 23		63 = 17		41 = 11	
81 = 22		59 = 16		37 = 10	

Assessment 5
A perfect score is 30 points.

%	Total Correct	%	Total Correct	%	Total Correct
100 = 30		80 = 24		60 = 18	
97 = 29		77 = 23		57 = 17	
93 = 28		73 = 22		53 = 16	
90 = 27		70 = 21		50 = 15	
87 = 26		67 = 20		47 = 14	
83 = 25		63 = 19		43 = 13	

Assessment 6
A perfect score is 27 points.

%	Total Correct	%	Total Correct	%	Total Correct
100 = 27		78 = 21		56 = 15	
96 = 26		74 = 20		52 = 14	
93 = 25		70 = 19		48 = 13	
89 = 24		67 = 18		44 = 12	
85 = 23		63 = 17		41 = 11	
81 = 22		59 = 16		37 = 10	

Assessment 7
A perfect score is 25 points.

%	Total Correct	%	Total Correct	%	Total Correct
100 = 25		76 = 19		52 = 13	
97 = 24		72 = 18		48 = 12	
92 = 23		68 = 17		44 = 11	
88 = 22		64 = 16		40 = 10	
84 = 21		60 = 15		36 = 9	
80 = 20		56 = 14		32 = 8	

Assessment 10
A perfect score is 35 points.

%	Total Correct	%	Total Correct	%	Total Correct
100 = 35		83 = 29		66 = 23	
97 = 34		80 = 28		63 = 22	
94 = 33		77 = 27		60 = 21	
91 = 32		74 = 26		57 = 20	
89 = 31		71 = 25		54 = 19	
86 = 30		69 = 24		51 = 18	

Assessment 8
A perfect score is 29 points.

%	Total Correct	%	Total Correct	%	Total Correct
100 = 29		79 = 23		59 = 17	
96 = 28		76 = 22		55 = 16	
93 = 27		72 = 21		52 = 15	
90 = 26		69 = 20		48 = 14	
86 = 25		66 = 19		45 = 13	
83 = 24		62 = 18		41 = 12	

Assessment 11
A perfect score is 30 points.

%	Total Correct	%	Total Correct	%	Total Correct
100 = 30		80 = 24		60 = 18	
97 = 29		77 = 23		57 = 17	
93 = 28		73 = 22		53 = 16	
90 = 27		70 = 21		50 = 15	
87 = 26		67 = 20		47 = 14	
83 = 25		63 = 19		43 = 13	

Assessment 9
A perfect score is 33 points.

%	Total Correct	%	Total Correct	%	Total Correct
100 = 33		82 = 27		64 = 21	
97 = 32		79 = 26		61 = 20	
94 = 31		76 = 25		58 = 19	
91 = 30		73 = 24		55 = 18	
88 = 29		70 = 23		52 = 17	
85 = 28		67 = 22		48 = 16	

Assessment 12
A perfect score is 37 points.

%	Total Correct	%	Total Correct	%	Total Correct
100 = 37		84 = 31		67 = 25	
97 = 36		81 = 30		65 = 24	
95 = 35		78 = 29		62 = 23	
92 = 34		76 = 28		59 = 22	
89 = 33		73 = 27		57 = 21	
86 = 32		70 = 26		54 = 20	

Assessment 13
A perfect score is 34 points.

%	Total Correct
100 = 34
97 = 33
94 = 32
91 = 31
88 = 30
85 = 29

%	Total Correct
82 = 28
79 = 27
76 = 26
74 = 25
71 = 24
68 = 23

%	Total Correct
65 = 22
62 = 21
59 = 20
56 = 19
53 = 18
50 = 17

Assessment 14
A perfect score is 36 points.

%	Total Correct
100 = 36
97 = 35
94 = 34
92 = 33
89 = 32
86 = 31

%	Total Correct
83 = 30
81 = 29
78 = 28
75 = 27
72 = 26
69 = 25

%	Total Correct
67 = 24
64 = 23
61 = 22
58 = 21
56 = 20
53 = 19

Assessment 15
A perfect score is 50 points.

%	Total Correct
100 = 50
98 = 49
96 = 48
94 = 47
92 = 46
90 = 45

%	Total Correct
88 = 44
86 = 43
84 = 42
82 = 41
80 = 40
78 = 39

%	Total Correct
76 = 38
74 = 37
72 = 36
70 = 35
68 = 34
66 = 33

Appendix D: The Management System

The testing and assessment materials and the management system will help you do the following:

- ensure that the children are properly placed in the program.
- group and re-group children for instruction.
- objectively monitor the achievements of the children as they progress through the program.
- dentify specific concepts the children need to work on.
- target exercises for the children who need extra help.
- maintain individual and group records.

Two charts developed for the *Language for Learning* Management System will provide you with valuable information about the progress of the children. They are the Individual Profile Charts and the Group Summary Chart. The data you recorded on the Individual Score Sheets when giving the program assessments will be used to complete the Individual Profile Charts and the Group Summary Charts.

Here is an example of how the management system works:

1. As you give assessment 3, you record the student responses on the Individual Score Sheet. (See figure 1 below.)

2. When you have given assessment 3 to all of the children in the group, you transfer the information from the Individual Score Sheets onto each student's Individual Profile Chart. (See figure 2 below.)

3. Finally, you use the Percent Correct Table for Assessment 3 to enter the percent correct score for each member of the group into the Group Summary Chart. (See figure 3 and figure 4.)

How to Use the Individual Profile Charts

The Individual Profile Charts will show (a) how well individual children understand and apply the concepts presented in the program and (b) each child's ability to produce statements. Thus, these charts can be used for diagnostic purposes and to help you determine the extra help some children may need. If you have students with special needs, you will find the Individual Profile Charts particularly helpful. Reproducible Individual Profile Charts are found in this appendix. The first chart is for assessments 1 through 8, and the second is for assessments 9 through 15.

To use an Individual Profile Chart, you first enter the date the assessment was completed and then the child's percent correct score from the Individual Score Sheet. Next, on the Individual Profile Chart, you circle the letters of the parts of the assessment in which the child missed one or more numbered items.

Look at the following example. As you can tell from his Individual Score Sheet shown in Figure 1, John got 79 percent of the items in Assessment 3 correct. He missed items 5 and 8 in Part B, item 14 in Part C, item 22 in Part D, and items 25 and 28 in Part E. His teacher circled B, C, D, and E on his Individual Profile Chart shown in Figure 2. She concluded that John needed further work with: (B) Identity Statements with Not, (C) Instructional Words—First/Next, (D) Actions—Pronouns, and (E) Actions—Pictures.

LANGUAGE FOR LEARNING
INDIVIDUAL SCORE SHEET—ASSESSMENTS 1–5

Name *John*

Assessment 1		Assessment 2		Assessment 3		Assessment 4		Assessment 5	
A 1.	C 16.	A 1.	D 16.	A 1.	D 19.	A 1.	D 16.	A 1.	D 17.
2.	17.	2.	"17."	2.	20.	2.	17.	"2."	18.
3.	18.	B 3.	18.	B 3.	"21."	3.	18.	B 3.	19.
B 4.	"19."	4.	"19."	4.	22.	B 4.	"19."	4.	20.
5.	20.	5.	20.	5.	"23."	5.	E 20.	5.	21.
6.	"21."	6.	"21."	"6."	E 24.	"6."	21.	6.	"22."
7.	22.	7.	E 22.	7.	"25."	7.	22.	"7."	23.
8.	"23."	8.	"23."	"8."	26.	"8."	"23."	8.	24.
9.	24.	"9."	24.	9.	"27."	9.	24.	"9."	"25."
"10."	"25."	C 10.	"25."	"10."	28.	"10."	25.	C 10.	E "26."
11.		"11."		11.	29.	C "11."	26.	11.	"27."
12.		12.		"12."		"12."	"27."	12.	"28."
13.		"13."		C 13.		"13."		13.	"29."
14.		14.		14.		"14."		"14."	30.
"15."		"15."		15.		"15."		15.	
				16.				"16."	
				17.					
				18.					
# items passed / total # items	25	# items passed / total # items	25	# items passed / total # items	23 / 29	# items passed / total # items	27	# items passed / total # items	30
% correct		% correct		% correct	79	% correct		% correct	

Copyright © by SRA/McGraw-Hill. Permission is granted to reproduce this page for classroom use

Figure 1

Another feature of the Individual Profile Chart is the statement production score at the bottom of the chart below the double line. Statement production items are enclosed in quotation marks on the Individual Score Sheet. (In Assessment 3 they appear in items 6, 8, 10, 12, 21, 23, 25, and 27.) You can calculate the percent correct of the statement production items by tallying the number of correct items with quotation marks around them. Enter this number at the top of the fraction that appears next to Statement Production # of " " Errors on the Individual Profile Chart. John's Individual Profile Chart reveals that he missed statement production items 8 and 25 and thus scored 75 percent on the statement production items in Assessment 3. His teacher knows that 90 percent is the goal and decides that he will benefit from some more practice with statement production exercises.

How to Use the Group Summary Chart The Group Summary Chart will give you a measure of how all your students are doing in the *Language for Learning* program. It will provide you with an objective and on-going picture of each group's progress through the program, and it can also be used to evaluate each group's overall performance. This information can

Assessment 3
A perfect score is 29 points.

%	Total Correct	%	Total Correct	%	Total Correct
100 = 29		79 = 23		59 = 17	
96 = 28		76 = 22		55 = 16	
93 = 27		72 = 21		52 = 15	
90 = 26		69 = 20		48 = 14	
86 = 25		66 = 19		45 = 13	
83 = 24		62 = 18		41 = 12	

Figure 3

assist you in determining if a group should move into the fast-cycle, if a group needs to be slowed down and given some additional help, or if only individual students need extra help. The reproducible Group Summary Chart (Figure 3) also appears in this appendix. You will need to reproduce one Group Summary Chart for each Language for Learning group in your classroom.

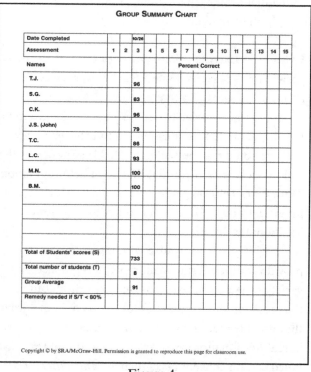

Figure 4

When all of the children in a group have completed an assessment, write the date the assessment was completed and the name of each child on the Group Summary Chart. Record each child's percent correct score ("% Correct" from the Individual Score Sheet) for the assessment you are summarizing.

INDIVIDUAL PROFILE CHART LESSONS 1–80

Name John

Date Completed			10/26					
Assessment	1	2	3	4	5	6	7	8
Lessons	1–10	11–20	21–30	31–40	41–50	51–60	61–70	71–80
Individual Score Sheet Percent Correct			79%					
Actions	B	E	(E)					B
Pronouns			(D)	B	B			
Tense						D	C	B
Information	A	A	A	A	A	A	E	
Part/Whole				C	E		A	E
Materials								
Occ./Loc.								A
Description of Objects								
Common Objects	C	C	(B)					
Plurals						C		D
Opposites				E	C			
Instructional Word/ Concepts			(C)					
Prepositions				D	D			
Before/After								
Same/Different								
Some/All/None								
Or								
Where/Who etc.								
If-Then Rules								
Classification						B	D	C
Problem-Solving Strategies								
Concept Application						E	F	F
Absurdities								
Statement Production # of " " errors	6	8	2 8	11	11	6	10	9
% Correct of " " Statement Production			75%					
Retest ISS % Correct			96%					

Figure 2

GROUP SUMMARY CHART

Date Completed			10/26												
Assessment	1	2	3	4	5	6	7	8	9	10	11	12	13	14	15
Names			Percent Correct												
T.J.			96												
S.G.			83												
C.K.			96												
J.S. (John)			79												
T.C.			86												
L.C.			93												
M.N.			100												
B.M.			100												
Total of Students' scores (S)			733												
Total number of students (T)			8												
Group Average			91												
Remedy needed if S/T < 80%															

Copyright © by SRA/McGraw-Hill. Permission is granted to reproduce this page for classroom use.

The Group Summary Chart shows that this group had three children who scored below 90 percent. John (J.S.), S.G., and T.C. required extra help.

Next you will calculate the group average. To calculate the group average, divide the total of the students' scores (S) by the total number of children in the group (T). The group example in Figure 4 averaged 91 percent and does not need to do extra help exercises as a group. If the group average is 80 percent or above, continue with the program, but do extra help exercises with individual children as needed—for example, S.G., J.S., and T.C. If the group average is less than 80 percent, take the entire group through the extra help exercises. When you have completed these exercises, you may wish to readminister the assessment to the children who have scored less than 90 percent. For example, John is retested after receiving extra help. This time he gets 28 out of 29 items correct and scores 96 percent on the retest. This is recorded in the bottom row of the Individual Profile Chart (Retest ISS % Correct). (See sample chart in figure 2.)

Extra Help Exercises John got 79 percent of the items correct on Assessment 3. His teacher was concerned about his progress. So that he could get a general review, she might have transferred him to the group in her classroom that is at lesson 25. But she also knew that she could use the Differentiated Instruction at the end of each assessment that lists extra help suggestions. These extra help suggestions specify exercises in the program to be used with students who need some additional instruction.

If children have trouble with the statement items, provide additional statement repetition practice on the variety of statement patterns that are introduced in the program. Have children practice them in the order they are introduced, and encourage them to use them in real-life situations in the classroom. If children have failed certain concept tasks such as *same/different* or *some, all, none,* give them extra help on those concepts. If children encounter difficulties with **both** the concepts and the statement patterns, follow the guidelines discussed in the *Language for Learning* Teacher's Guide, pages 12–15, in the section Teaching Children Whose First Language Is Not English. These guidelines can be useful for all children who need extra help, not just those whose first language is not English.

Readministering the Assessment You may want to readminister the assessment to those children who were given extra help. Use the same Individual Score Sheet. Readminister only those items that the child had not answered correctly. Using a different colored pencil, make a small check mark next to the items the child responds to correctly. Record any additional errors on the same Individual Score Sheet in that color. Refigure the percent correct, and write the new score in the final box. Transfer this updated information from the Individual Score Sheet to the Individual Profile Chart by erasing the circles from any concepts that were circled. However, draw a circle around items that were missed a second time.

Reporting Student Progress A growing number of school districts are looking at student performance to evaluate programs. If your district is interested in documenting the instructional effect of *Language for Learning,* consider the following ideas:

1. Use Assessment 15 as a summative evaluation and measure of student progress. Consider this measure as the posttest and the Placement Test as the pretest.
2. For a standardized measure of the impact of Language for Learning on the achievement of pre-school children, consider the Brigance Screen for pre-kindergarten children.
3. Some school districts using the Language for Learning program recommend using the listening subtest of the Iowa Test of Basic Skills.

INDIVIDUAL PROFILE CHART LESSONS 1–80

Name _____

Date Completed								
Assessment	1	2	3	4	5	6	7	8
Lessons	1–10	11–20	21–30	31–40	41–50	51–60	61–70	71–80
Individual Score Sheet Percent Correct								
Actions	B	E	E				B	
Pronouns			D	B	B			
Tense						D	C	B
Information	A	A	A	A	A	A	E	
Part/Whole				C	E		A	E
Materials								
Occ./Loc.								A
Description of Objects								
Common Objects	C	C	B					
Plurals						C		D
Opposites				E	C			
Instructional Word/ Concepts			C					
Prepositions				D	D			
Before/After								
Same/Different								
Some/All/None								
Or								
Where/Who etc.								
If-Then Rules								
Classification						B	D	C
Problem-Solving Strategies								
Concept Application						E	F	F
Absurdities								
Statement Production # of " " errors	6	8	8	11	11	6	10	9
% Correct of " " Statement Production								
Retest ISS % Correct								

Copyright © by SRA/McGraw-Hill. Permission is granted to reproduce this page for classroom use.

INDIVIDUAL PROFILE CHART LESSONS 81–150

Name _____

Date Completed							
Assessment	9	10	11	12	13	14	15
Lessons	81–90	91–100	101–110	111–120	121–130	131–140	Final
Individual Score Sheet Percent Correct							
Actions							
Pronouns							
Tense	C	C	B				
Information	A		A	A	A	A	A
Part/Whole		B	D				
Materials	B	A			C	A	C
Occ./Loc.		A			C	A	
Description of Objects							
Common Objects							
Plurals							
Opposites	D		E		B		D
Instructional Word/ Concepts						C	
Prepositions							
Before/After				D			
Same/Different		E	C		F	B	G
Some/All/None		D		B			
Or						E	B
Where/Who etc.					D	D	H
If-Then Rules						G	F
Classification	E		F	C	E		
Problem-Solving Strategies							
Concept Application	F	F	G	E			
Absurdities						F	E
Statement Production # of " " errors	8	6	7	6	5	6	9
% Correct of " " Statement Production							
Retest ISS % Correct							

Copyright © by SRA/McGraw-Hill. Permission is granted to reproduce this page for classroom use.

GROUP SUMMARY CHART

Date Completed															
Assessment	1	2	3	4	5	6	7	8	9	10	11	12	13	14	15
Names						Percent Correct									
Total of Students' scores (S)															
Total number of students (T)															
Group Average															
Remedy needed if S/T < 80%															

Copyright © by SRA/McGraw-Hill. Permission is granted to reproduce this page for classroom use.

Appendix E: Home Connection

FAMILY LETTERS

Two family letters are provided as blackline masters. The letters provide parents and caregivers with information about some of the content of *Language for Learning*.

The first letter provides a brief introduction to the *Language for Learning* program and offers some suggestions for home activities. It should be sent to families during the first week of the program. The second letter should be sent home at the end of the school year.

Family Letter

To the family of _____

Your child is beginning a program called *Language for Learning*. This program helps develop the listening, speaking, and thinking skills that will help your child do well in school. Your child will learn to listen carefully, speak clearly, and follow directions accurately.

Here are some things you can do at home:

1. Go over each part of the workbook pages your child brings home. The activities on these pages illustrate some of the language concepts your child is working on. After each activity on the workbook pages you will find home-connection suggestions. For example,

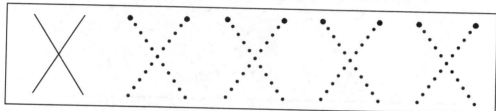

Touch a cross-out mark. Ask, "What is this?"

Use these directions with your child to review the daily lessons.

If your child has colored the workbook page, ask your child to identify each color on the page. Then ask what the pictures show.

Praise your child for answering your questions. But remember that there may be some things your child has not yet learned. Don't scold your child for not knowing something. Instead, tell your child the answer, and ask the question again.

2. Keep the workbook pages in a box or drawer, and go over them with your child every week or so. Praise your child for good answers.

3. Ask your child about school. Here are some good questions:

    What's the name of your school?

    What's your teacher's name?

    Who are some of the children in your class?

    Who are your new friends in school?

    What did you do today that you liked best?

The most important thing you can do is to let your child know that the work in *Language for Learning* is very important because it gives him or her practice with the language of school learning.

If you have any questions about what your child is learning or if your child is having problems, please call me at school. I'll be happy to talk to you.

Thank you,

_____

1
Carta familiar

Para la familia de _____

Su niño comienza un programa importante llamado *Language for Learning.* Este programa ayuda a desarrollar las destrezas orales y de pensamiento que necesitan los niños para hacer un buen trabajo en la escuela. Su niño aprenderá a escuchar cuidadosamente, decir bien las cosas y seguir instrucciones.

A continuación hay algunas cosas que Ud. puede hacer en casa:

1. Repase cada parte del cuaderno que su niño lleva a casa. Las actividades en estas hojas ilustran algunos conceptos de la lenguage en las que está trabajando su niño. Despues de cada actividad en el cuaderno encontrara sugerencias para casa. Por ejemplo:

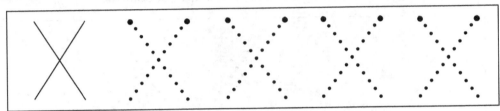

Touch a cross-out mark. Ask, "What is this?"

Se puede usar estas instrucciones para repasar las lecciones diarias con su niño.

Si una parte de la hoja de trabajo está coloreada, pida a su niño que identifique cada color en la página. Pregunte lo que muestran las ilustraciones.

Elogie a su niño por contestar las preguntas, pero recuerde que quizás hay algunas cosas que su niño aún no ha aprendido. No regañe a su niño si no sabe algo. En su lugar, dígale la respuesta y elogie a su niño por contestar las preguntas.

2. Mantenga las hojas de trabajo en una caja o una gaveta y obsérvelas con su niño cada semana. Haga preguntas. Elogie a su niño por las respuestas correctas.

3. Pregúntele a su niño sobre la escuela. A continuación hay unas preguntas adecuadas:

      ¿ Cuál es el nombre de tu escuela?

      ¿ Cuál es el nombre de tu maestro/a?

      ¿ Quienes son algunos de los niños de tu clase?

      ¿ Quienes son tus amigos nuevos en la escuela?

      ¿ Qué te gustó más de lo que hiciste hoy?

      ¿ Qué almorzaste (o qué bocadillo comiste) hoy?

4. La cosa más importante que Ud. puede hacer es decirle a su hijo que el trabajo en *Language for Learning* es muy importante. Éste le muestra a los niños lo que es el aprendizaje en la escuela y les da la práctica con el lenguaje del aprendizaje escolar.

Si tiene alguna pregunta acerca de lo que su niño está aprendiendo o si su niño tiene problemas, por favor llámeme a la escuela. Me encantará hablar con Ud.

              Gracias,

              _____

2
Family Letter

To the family of _____

Your child has finished the *Language for Learning* program. We have worked on listening, speaking, following directions, and thinking. I hope you have noticed some of the things that we have worked on in school. Your child knows many things about language that will make school much easier. What your child has learned will help in reading, writing, math, and other subjects.

Thank you for helping your child take the first big step in school learning.

Thank you,

_____

2

Carta familiar

Para la familia de _____

Su niño acaba de terminar el programa *Language for Learning.* Hemos trabajado en muchas destrezas como escuchar, hablar, como seguir instrucciones, y pensar. Estoy seguro de que Ud. ha notado muchas de las cosas en las que hemos trabajado en la escuela. Su niño muchas cosas sobre lenguage que harán más fácil el trabajo escolar. Lo que su niño ha aprendido ayudará en lectura, escritura, matemáticas y otras materias.

Gracias por ayudar a su niño a dar el primer paso en el aprendizaje escolar.

Gracias,

_____

Appendix F: The Practice Lesson

This practice lesson is a reproduction of lesson 44 from Presentation Book A.

LESSON 44

★ EXERCISE 1 Actions — Pronouns

1. I'm going to ask two children to do an action.

a. (Ask two children to stand up.) Everybody, what are they doing? (Signal.) *Standing up.* Say the whole thing about what they are doing. (Signal.) *They are standing up.*

b. (Ask the two children to sit down.) Everybody, what are they doing? (Signal.) *Sitting down.* Say the whole thing about what they are doing. (Signal.) *They are sitting down.*

c. (Repeat steps a and b until all children's responses are firm.)

2. Now we're all going to do that.

a. Everybody, let's all stand up. (Signal. Stand up with children.)

b. Everybody, what are you doing? (Signal.) *Standing up.* Say the whole thing. (Signal.) *I am standing up.*

c. What are we doing? (Signal.) *Standing up.* Say the whole thing. (Signal.) *We are standing up.*

d. What am I doing? (Signal.) *Standing up.* Say the whole thing. (Signal.) *You are standing up.*

3. (Point to a boy.) Look at him.

a. What is he doing? (Signal.) *Standing up.*

b. Say the whole thing. (Signal.) *He is standing up.*

4. (Point to a girl.) Look at her.

a. What is she doing? (Signal.) *Standing up.*

b. Say the whole thing. (Signal.) *She is standing up.*

5. (Point to two children.) Look at them.

a. What are they doing? (Signal.) *Standing up.*

b. Say the whole thing. (Signal.) *They are standing up.*

c. (Repeat steps a and b until all children's responses are firm.)

★ EXERCISE 2 Information — Days of the Week

1. Let's do the days of the week.

a. Everybody, how many days are there in a week? (Signal.) *Seven.* Say the whole thing. (Signal.) *There are seven days in a week.*

b. Again. (Signal.) *There are seven days in a week.* (Repeat step b until all children's responses are firm.)

c. Get ready to say all the days of the week. (Signal. Do not respond with children.) *Sunday, Monday, Tuesday, Wednesday, Thursday, Friday, Saturday.*

2. (Repeat part 1 until all children's responses are firm.)

Individual Turns

(Repeat the exercise, calling on different children for each step.)

★ EXERCISE 3 Concept Application

1. We're going to figure out which frog will jump. Only one frog will jump.

a. Listen to the rule. The big frog will jump. Listen again. The big frog will jump. Everybody, say the rule about the big frog. (Signal.) *The big frog will jump.*

b. Again. (Signal.) *The big frog will jump.* (Repeat step b until all children can say the rule.) Remember that rule. (Turn the page quickly.)

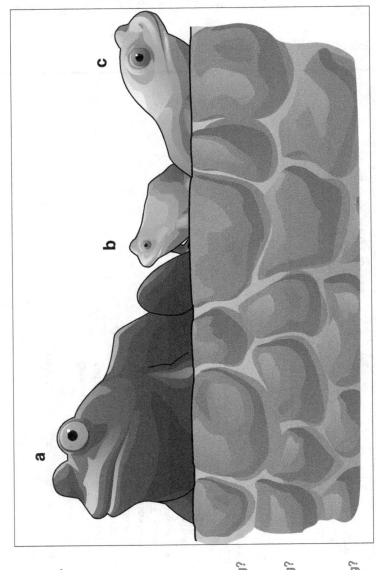

EXERCISE 3 Concept Application (cont.)

2. Remember, only one of these frogs will jump. Which frog will jump? (Signal.) *The big frog.* Yes, the big frog.

a. (Point to a.) Is this frog big? (Touch.) *Yes.*
So will this frog jump? (Touch.) *Yes.*

b. (Point to b.) Is this frog big? (Touch.) *No.*
So will this frog jump? (Touch.) *No.*

c. (Point to c.) Is this frog big? (Touch.) *No.*
So will this frog jump? (Touch.) *No.*

3. We're going to talk more about the frogs.

a. (Point to a.) Is this frog big? (Touch.) *Yes.*
So, what else do you know about this frog?
(Touch.) *This frog will jump.*

b. (Point to b.) Is this frog big? (Touch.) *No.*
So, what else do you know about this frog?
(Touch.) *This frog will not jump.*
Right, this frog will not jump.

c. (Point to c.) Is this frog big? (Touch.) *No.*
So, what else do you know about this frog?
(Touch.) *This frog will not jump.*
Right, this frog will not jump.

4. (Call on a child.) Show me the frog that will jump. (The child should point to the big frog.)
Let's see if you are right.
(Turn the page quickly.)

EXERCISE 3 **Concept Application (cont.)**

5. (Do not point to the picture.)
- Tell me which frog is jumping. (Signal.) *The big frog.*
- Say the whole thing about what the big frog is doing. (Signal.) *The big frog is jumping.*

6. Listen.

a. (Point to a.) Is this frog jumping? (Touch.) *Yes.*

b. (Point to b.) Is this frog jumping? (Touch.) *No.*

c. (Point to c.) Is this frog jumping? (Touch.) *No.*

7. Listen again.
- (Point to b.) What is this frog doing? (Touch.) *Swimming.* Say the whole thing. (Touch.) *This frog is swimming.*
- (Point to c.) What is this frog doing? (Touch.) *Sitting.* Say the whole thing. (Touch.) *This frog is sitting.*

8. Let's talk about frogs. (Call on different children.)
- What would you do if a frog jumped on you?
- Would you like to go swimming with the frog?
- Do you like frogs? (Praise all acceptable responses.)

Individual Turns

(Repeat parts 5 through 7, calling on different children for each question.)

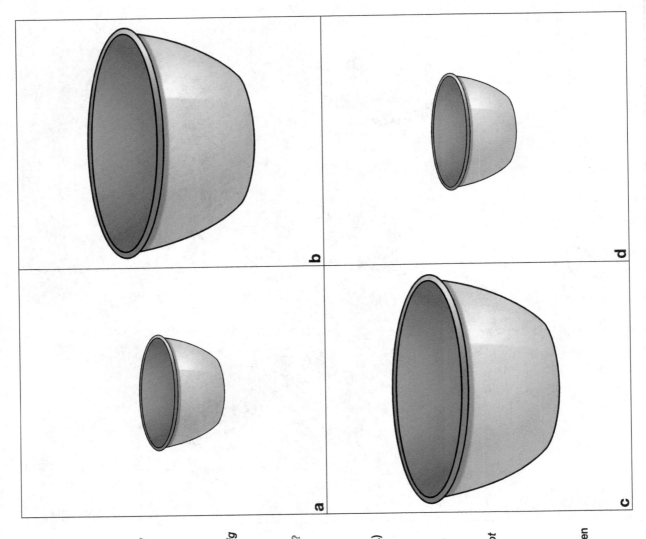

a

b

c

d

EXERCISE 4 Opposites — Big/Small

1. Some of these bowls are big. Some of these bowls are small.

 a. (Touch a.) Is this bowl big? (Signal.) *No.* This bowl is small. What is this bowl? (Touch.) *Small.*

 b. (Touch b.) Is this bowl big? (Signal.) *Yes.*

2. I'll point to each bowl. Say big if it is big. Say small if it is small.

 • What are you going to say if it is big? (Touch.) *Big.* What are you going to say if it is small? (Touch.) *Small.*

 • (Point to each bowl. Children are to say *big* or *small*.) (Repeat until all children's responses are firm.)

3. (Point to each bowl, and ask:) Is this bowl big? (Children are to answer *yes* or *no*.)

4. (Point to a.) Is this bowl big? (Touch.) *No.* So, this bowl is small. Say the whole thing about this bowl. (Touch.) *This bowl is small.*

5. (Point to c.) Is this bowl big? (Touch.) *Yes.* Say the whole thing. (Touch.) *This bowl is big.*

6. (Point to d.) Is this bowl big? (Touch.) *No.* Say the whole thing. (Touch.) *This bowl is not big.*

7. (Repeat parts 4 through 6 until all children's responses are firm.)

Individual Turns
(Repeat the exercise, calling on different children for each step.)

EXERCISE 5 Part/Whole – Wagon

1. You're going to learn the parts of a wagon.
   a. (Circle the top wagon with your finger.)
      Everybody, what is this? (Touch.) *A wagon.*
      Say the whole thing. (Touch.) *This is a
      wagon.*
   b. (Point to the bottom wagon.) Here's a
      wagon that is in parts. I'll name the parts.
      (Point to the body.) This is a body.
      (Point to the wheels.) These are wheels.
      (Point to the frame.) This is a frame.
      (Point to the handle.) This is a handle.

2. Let's see if you can name the parts.
   a. (Point to the body of the bottom wagon.)
      What is this part called? (Pause. Touch.)
      A body.
      (Point to the wheels.) What are these parts
      called? (Pause. Touch.) *Wheels.*
      (Point to the frame.) What is this part
      called? (Pause. Touch.) *A frame.*
      (Point to the handle.) What is this part
      called? (Pause. Touch.) *A handle.*
   b. (Circle the wagon with your finger.) Body,
      wheels, frame, and handles are parts of . . .
      (touch) *a wagon.*
   c. (Repeat steps a and b until all children's
      responses are firm.)

3. Listen.
   a. (Point to the body of the top wagon.)
      A wagon has . . . (touch) *a body.*
      (Point to the wheels.) A wagon has . . .
      (touch) *wheels.*
      (Point to the frame.) A wagon has . . .
      (touch) *a frame.*
      (Point to the handle.) A wagon has . . .
      (touch) *a handle.*
   b. (Circle the wagon.) And what's the whole
      object called? (Touch.) *A wagon.*

   c. (Repeat steps a and b until all children's
      responses are firm.)

Individual Turns
(Repeat parts 2 and 3, calling on different
children for each step.)

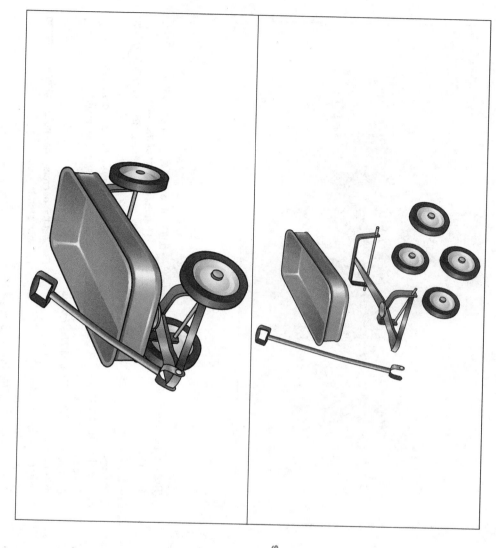

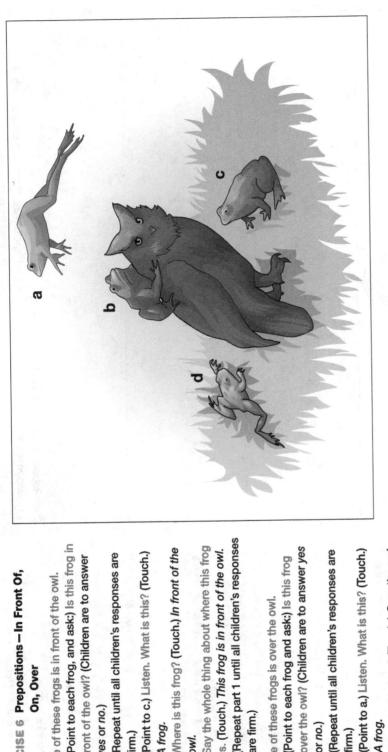

EXERCISE 6 Prepositions—In Front Of, On, Over

1. One of these frogs is in front of the owl.

- (Point to each frog, and ask:) Is this frog in front of the owl? (Children are to answer *yes or no.*)

  (Repeat until all children's responses are firm.)

- (Point to c.) Listen. What is this? (Touch.) *A frog.*

  Where is this frog? (Touch.) *In front of the owl.*

  Say the whole thing about where this frog is. (Touch.) *This frog is in front of the owl.*

  (Repeat part 1 until all children's responses are firm.)

2. One of these frogs is over the owl.

- (Point to each frog and ask:) Is this frog over the owl? (Children are to answer yes or no.)

  (Repeat until all children's responses are firm.)

- (Point to a.) Listen. What is this? (Touch.) *A frog.*

  Where is this frog? (Touch.) *Over the owl.*

  Say the whole thing about where this frog is. (Touch.) *This frog is over the owl.*

  (Repeat part 2 until all children's responses are firm.)

3. One of these frogs is on the owl.

- (Point to each frog and ask:) Is this frog on the owl? (Children are to answer yes or no.)

  (Repeat until all children's responses are firm.)

- (Point to b.) Listen. What is this? (Touch.) *A frog.*

  Where is this frog? (Touch.) *On the owl.*

  Say the whole thing about where this frog is. (Touch.) *This frog is on the owl.*

  (Repeat part 3 until all children's responses are firm.)

4. Let's talk about the owl and the frogs one more time.

  a. (Point to a.) Everybody, where is this frog? (Touch.) *Over the owl.*

  Say the whole thing. (Touch.) *This frog is over the owl.*

  b. (Point to b.) Everybody, where is this frog? (Touch.) *On the owl.*

  Say the whole thing. (Touch.) *This frog is on the owl.*

  c. (Point to c.) Everybody, where is this frog? (Touch.) *In front of the owl.*

  Say the whole thing. (Touch.) *This frog is in front of the owl.*

  d. (Repeat steps a through c until all children's responses are firm.)

Individual Turns

(Repeat the exercise, calling on different children for each step.)

EXERCISE 7 Review

[Note: Do not point to the picture.]

1. Look at these girls. One of these girls is wearing a hat. One of these girls is wearing shoes.

a. What is the big girl wearing? (Signal.)
A hat.
What is the little girl wearing? (Signal.)
Shoes.

b. My turn. Which girl is big? The girl wearing a hat.
Your turn. Which girl is big? (Signal.)
The girl wearing a hat.
Yes, the girl wearing a hat.

c. My turn to say the whole thing about the girl wearing a hat. The girl wearing a hat is big.
Your turn. Say the whole thing about the girl wearing a hat. (Signal.) ***The girl wearing a hat is big.***

2. Let's talk some more about these girls.

a. My turn. Which girl is small? The girl wearing shoes.
Your turn. Which girl is small? (Signal.) ***The girl wearing shoes.***
Yes, the girl wearing shoes.

b. My turn to say the whole thing about the girl wearing shoes. The girl wearing shoes is small.
Your turn. Say the whole thing about the girl wearing shoes. (Signal.) ***The girl wearing shoes is small.***

3. Listen.

a. Your turn. Say the whole thing about the girl wearing a hat. (Signal.) ***The girl wearing a hat is big.***

b. Your turn to say the whole thing about the girl wearing shoes. (Signal.) ***The girl wearing shoes is small.***

Individual Turns
(Repeat part 3, calling on different children for each step.)

(Repeat part 3 until all children's responses are firm.)

WORKBOOK
LESSON 44

[Note: Each child will need crayons.]

Pair Relations

(Pass out crayons to each child.)

1. Find a bug. ✔
   You're going to tell me about the boxes.
   a. Here's the rule about the boxes: Each box should have a bug and a rug.
      What should each box have? (Signal.) *A bug and a rug.*
   b. Touch the first box. ✔
      Everybody, tell me what that box has. Get ready. (Signal.) *A bug and a bottle.*
      Does that box have a bug and a rug? (Signal.) *No.*
   c. Touch the next box. ✔
      Everybody, tell me what that box has. Get ready. (Signal.) *A bug and a rug.*
      Does that box have a bug and a rug? (Signal.) *Yes.*
   d. Touch the next box. ✔
      Everybody, tell me what that box has. Get ready. (Signal.) *A snake and a cake.*
      Does that box have a bug and a rug? (Signal.) *No.*
   e. Touch the last box. ✔
      Everybody, tell me what that box has. Get ready. (Signal.) *A bug and a rug.*
      Does that box have a bug and a rug? (Signal.) *Yes.*

2. Get ready to cross out and circle boxes.
   a. Here's the circling rule: Circle each box that has a bug and a rug.
      Do it. ✔
   b. Here's the cross-out rule: Cross out each box that does not have a bug and a rug.
      Do it. ✔

Coloring

1. Touch a table. ✔
   a. Here's a coloring rule for this picture: Make the balls red.
      Everybody, say that rule. (Signal.) *Make the balls red.*
      Everybody, make a little red mark on every ball. ✔
   b. Here's the next coloring rule: Make the shoes yellow.
      Everybody, say that rule. (Signal.) *Make the shoes yellow.*
      Everybody, make a little yellow mark on every shoe. ✔
   c. Here's the last coloring rule: Make the tables blue.
      Everybody, say that rule. (Signal.) *Make the tables blue.*
      Everybody, make a little blue mark on every table. ✔

2. Later you'll color the objects.

Completion

1. Everybody, turn your workbook page over. ✔
   a. (Hold up a workbook. Touch the bottle.)
      Touch this picture on your workbook. ✔
      This picture should show a bottle, but some of the bottle is missing.
   b. (Touch the dots.) I am going to follow these dots and draw in the missing line. Watch. (Trace the dotted segment.)
   c. Your turn. Follow the dots and draw in the missing line. ✔

2. Later you'll color the bottle.

Temporal First, Next

1. Find the hands. ✔
   The pictures show what you do first and what you do next.
   a. You are going to tell me what to do.
      Everybody, touch the ball. Get ready. (Tap.) ✔
      Move to the first mark. Get ready. (Tap.)
      Tell me what to do. (Signal.) *Clap.*
   b. Everybody, move to the next mark. Get ready. (Tap.)
      Tell me what to do. (Signal.) *Touch your nose.*
   c. See if you can do those things without looking at the book.
      Everybody, show me what you do first. (Signal. Children respond.)
      Show me what you do next. (Signal. Children respond.)

Read "Sarah the Toymaker" in Storybook 1, page 35.

The front section of this Presentation Book contains Expanded Language Activities for this lesson.

Lesson 44

Name _____

"Touch a box you circled." "What's in the box?" "Touch another box you circled." "What's in that box?"

Touch each object in the picture. Ask, "What is it?" "What color is it?"

Copyright ©SRA/McGraw-Hill

Side 1 _____

Appendix F

187

Lesson 44   Name _____

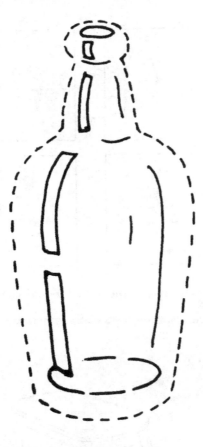

"Show me the line you drew." Touch the picture. Ask, "What is it?"

"Show me what you do first." "Show me what you do next."

Copyright ©SRA/McGraw-Hill

Side 2 _____

Appendix F